Praise for This Book

*"Rabbi Weinsberg draws on his own medical ordeal
to bring guidance and comfort to others."*
—Rabbi Harold Kushner, author of *When Bad Things Happen to Good People*

*"This humane book successfully wrestles
with the concerns of those confronted by prostate cancer."*
—Dr. Robert Butler, M.D., President and CEO,
International Longevity Center
Pulitzer Prize-winning author of *Why Survive? Being Old in America*
Author of *The New Love and Sex After Sixty* and *The Longevity Revolution*

*"Understanding that sickness does not have to end intimacy is
vital for every marriage. Rabbi Weinsberg helps readers resolve
this important issue to create a lifetime of love and fulfillment."*
—John Gray, author of *Men Are from Mars, Women Are from Venus,*
and frequent guest on national media including *Oprah,*
Larry King Live, Phil Donahue and *Redbook*

"Experience the joys of sex again ... brilliant, inspiring, and gutsy."
—Dr. Ellen Kreidman, breast cancer survivor, psychologist, and expert in
relationship and marriage enrichment on *Oprah, The View,* the *Today Show,*
Montel Williams, CNN, and featured in the *New York Times*
(*www.LightHisFire.com* and *www.LightHerFire.com*)

*"... helped me overcome the pain and stress
of my prostate cancer surgery."*
—Rev. Dr. Richard Byrne, prostate cancer survivor
and Director of Pastoral Ministries, Brooksby/Erickson Village

*"I applaud the author for recognizing that wives,
in their own way, get prostate cancer too."*
—Leah Cohen, wife of a prostate cancer survivor
and editor of *Living with Prostate Cancer Blog*
(*www.prostatecancerblog.net*)

CONQUER PROSTATE CANCER

How Medicine, Faith, Love and Sex Can Renew Your Life

Rabbi Ed Weinsberg
with Dr. Robert Carey

Foreword by
Dr. Vipul Patel

Health Success Media

For information about this title or to order other books and/or electronic media, contact the publisher:

Health Success Media, LLC
PO Box 21092
Bradenton, Florida 34204

www.HealthSuccessMedia.com and
www.ConquerProstateCancer.com or *www.ConquerProstateCancerNow.com*

1-866-878-5986

Library of Congress Control Number: 2008934218

ISBN: 978-0-9820121-0-9

Printed in the United States of America

Book and Cover design by: 1106 Design, LLC, Phoenix, Arizona

Publisher's Cataloging-In-Publication Data

Weinsberg, Ed.
   Conquer prostate cancer : how medicine, faith love
and sex can renew your life/ by Ed Weinsberg ; with
Robert Carey.
   p. cm.
   Includes bibliographical references and index.
   LCCN 2008934218
   ISBN-13: 978-0-9820121-0-9
   ISBN-10: 0-9820121-0-1

   1. Prostate—Cancer—Popular works.   2. Prostate—
Cancer—Treatment—Popular works.   I. Carey, Robert,
1963– II. Title.

RC280.P7W45 2008   616.88′463
                           QBI08-600224

Disclaimer

This book suggests effective ways to overcome prostate cancer and its treatment side effects, but the primary author, Rabbi Ed Weinsberg, does not purport to give medical advice. Physicians cited in this book, including contributing author, Dr. Robert Carey, and medical advisor, Dr. David Kauder, are quoted only for educational purposes. Before making any medical decisions, you should see your doctor or another qualified medical professional.

Due to the personal, sexually explicit nature of this book, all patients' names are reported anonymously. In addition three of the author's health caregivers were assigned pseudonyms to protect their privacy: oncological urologist, Dr. Jonathan Jones; oncological radiologist, Dr. Warren Goldman; and sex therapist, Dr. Rhonda Levine, working out of "St. Petersburg Hospital" in Florida.

All other names, character depictions, places, statistics and details, in addition to personal backgrounds, experiences and opinions are reported as factually and accurately as possible.

Dedication

"You have shouldered your unique burdens better than most,
with me among them!"
—Rabbi Ed

Yvonne R. Weinsberg

This book is dedicated to my wife, Yvonne, for her mostly unwavering patience as I wrote this book at home. I am extremely grateful to her for constantly reminding me that, despite my diseased and "missing" prostate, removed by robotic surgery, I am still a complete person who can continue offering much to my family and others.

Yvonne's ongoing support was instrumental in encouraging me to complete this project. I cannot thank her enough for allowing me to reveal intimate aspects of our life together before and after prostate cancer surgery. She agreed to this so others could better comprehend the impact of prostate cancer and its treatment side effects, and how to contend with them.

Yvonne's previous thirty-plus years as a congregational rabbi's wife by itself entitles her to an honored placed in the "*Eyshet Hayil* Women's Hall of Fame." Beyond that her capacity to endure ongoing personal pain and stress due to fibromyalgia, chronic fatigue and major back problems is a source of inspiration to me. I salute her and women everywhere, who seem to deal with pain better than most men. In my mind you are all members of the stronger sex.

In Tribute to
Prostate Cancer Support and Education Organizations

The American Cancer Society Man to Man Program
Patient Support Groups

Malecare International
Education and Support Network

Us TOO International Prostate Cancer
Education and Support Network

Vital Options International
Cancer Communications, Support and Advocacy

The Wellness Community's
Prostate Cancer Support Services

ZERO—The Project to End Prostate Cancer
(Previously known as The National Prostate Cancer Coalition)
Patient Screening Services

We also wish to express our gratitude to The Prostate Cancer Foundation and The Prostate Cancer Research Institute for their educational endeavors and for raising funds for medical research.

In addition, kudos go to the BrownByrd Prostate Cancer Foundation established by African-American actor and social activist, Kevin Byrd. Kudos also to Gilda's Club Worldwide, for the emotional, social and fiscal support they provide to all people with cancer,—men, women and children.

A portion of this book's proceeds will be donated to a few of these organizations for their ongoing efforts in behalf of prostate cancer patients, survivors, and those who love them.

Acknowledgements

"Good fortune almost always shows up in the form of another."
—Anonymous

"I divide the world into three classes:
the few who make things happen, the many who watch things happen,
and the vast majority who have no idea what has happened."
—Nicholas M. Butler, 19th–20th Century Educator
President, Teachers College and Columbia University

I would like to acknowledge a number of people, who have "shown up" and made things happen for me, particularly with reference to this book.

First and foremost I thank my wife, Yvonne, for being a constant partner on my life's journey. She was the first to read the initial draft of the manuscript as I got it ready for publication. Her vivid recall of various health providers' comments, along with her recollection of actual sequences of events, helped me make order out of chaos. Then too, her correspondence with various friends, reflected in italicized citations in various chapters of this book, added a woman's perspective to the uniquely male form of cancer I endured.

My hearty thanks go to the urologists who took me under their wings during my bout with prostate cancer. I refer especially to my robotics prostate cancer surgeon, Dr. Robert Carey, who graciously provided some extremely valuable segments for this book and reviewed the book for medical accuracy. Another urologist I'd like to thank for helping me thoroughly review the book's content for accurate medical terms and facts is this book's medical advisor, Dr. David Kauder, my friend and former urologist in Boston's North

Shore area, where I lived for twenty-one years. I hasten to add that I take full responsibility for any errors or omissions on my part.

I'm grateful to Dr. Winston Barzell for referring me to Dr. Carey at the Urology Treatment Center in Sarasota, Florida, where they and their other colleagues practice medicine. In January 2007, four months after my family and I arrived in Sarasota, Dr. Jonathan Jones determined I had prostate cancer, but that February it was Dr. Barzell who re-assessed my condition and treatment options. The professionalism and technical excellence of these doctors were matched by their abiding concern for me and all their patients.

I would also like to acknowledge Sarasota Memorial Hospital's staff, including nurses and orderlies, whose cheerful countenance and attention to detail (some of which was not too pretty) never ceased to amaze me. Their mission to reduce pain as much as possible, while avoiding drug dependence, is of critical importance.

My gratitude is extended as well to Lynne Klippel, whose "Book School" teleconference series encouraged me to write this, my first book. Similarly I am indebted to book and internet marketing experts John Kremer, Kathleen Gage and Jason Oman for generously giving me their time and thought.

Becoming a book author followed in the wake of my thirty years of writing newspaper and journal articles of Jewish and global interest. That's apart from several years of articulating my concerns in panel discussions on the radio and television as well as on a t.v. interview show I hosted for two years on public access television. Through the printed word and audio-visually I've tried to make my mark in a way that will enhance my legacy to humanity long after I'm gone.

I'd like to convey my admiration for various individuals whose actions and thoughts inspired me and expanded my horizons over the years: Dr. Arnold Band, former Professor of Hebrew and Comparative Literature, taught me critical thinking skills when I was still an undergraduate student at UCLA. Prof. Elliot Avedon and later, Prof. Ruth Bennett, furthered my interest in the process of aging when I was a doctoral student at Teachers College, Columbia University.

More recently I acknowledge how the following individuals have influenced my views: Dr. Herbert Benson, M.D., who has written books on the "Relaxation Response" that have played a pivotal role in bringing the mind-body connection to the forefront of people's consciousness. Peggy Huddleston, a psychotherapist, has created visualization techniques that have made preparation for surgery surprisingly easy. Dr. Harvey Zarren, M.D., a specialist in alternative medicine and a cardiologist with a "heart," has led enlightening spirituality groups I helped facilitate for five years at my former synagogue. And Tony Robbins, has excelled as a self-help, mind-body motivational speaker and mentor to thousands like me.

A special thanks to renowned sex therapist, author and radio and TV personality, Dr. Ruth Westheimer. I last spoke with her in September 2007, a year before this book's publication and a few years after she addressed a large audience at my previous synagogue. Her open-minded, principled approach to consensual sexual relations between adults of all ages, has profoundly influenced my own thinking as reflected in these pages.

I am grateful to various individuals and organizations for material cited or portrayed in this book, as evidenced by the numerous end notes for each chapter. I also wish to express my gratitude to individuals who generously helped fund this project, including John Rimer, of Swampscott, Massachusetts and Palm Beach, Florida.

I'm indebted to the many individuals who helped me proofread, edit, design, publish and promote this book, including my marketing consultant, Dana Smith, who helped me keep my eyes on the ball; former publisher and book marketing strategist, Jan King, who read the entire manuscript and encouraged its publication; my precise, thorough editor, Kim Pearson; Christine Frank, for her comprehensive indexing; Michele DeFilippo and the staff of 1106 Design for creating the powerful cover of this book and its interior design. Furthermore I am grateful to those who provided the book's illustrations and photographs: Intuitive Surgical's development specialist, Nora DeStefano, for photographs and illustrations that depict the da Vinci robotic device; and photographers Dr. Donna Carey, David Dessauer, Herb Goldberg, Tariq Hakky, Fred Mailloux, Herbert Payne and Roger Surprenant for their photographs of my family and me. These individuals and others have demonstrated that nobody can write a book all by himself.

Last, but not least, I offer my thanks to my daughter Elana Weinsberg, who along with my son Daniel, his wife Deb and my precious granddaughter, Cayla, helped keep up my morale when I was ill. More than that, Elana served as my publisher under the imprint of Health Success Media.

Contents

Illustrations and Photographs

PRELUDE:

CONQUER PROSTATE CANCER

Foreword

Preface

Introduction

Foreword
The Patient as Healthcare Educator
—Dr. Vipul Patel, M.D.

The diagnosis of prostate cancer is a seminal event in the life of any male who is unfortunate enough to be afflicted by the disease. However, now more than ever before, there is greater optimism regarding treatment options and outcomes. Indeed, today the majority of men diagnosed with prostate cancer are "diagnosed early" at a treatable stage and can expect long term survival treatment benefits.

Earlier diagnosis has been the result of improved screening using serum PSA testing routinely in the United States. As the screening of males for prostate cancer has evolved, so have various treatment modalities of which robotic assisted radical prostatectomy is the most recent.

Conquer Prostate Cancer provides great insight into the benefits of robotic surgery as well as the "myths" and sometimes negativism surrounding it. Robotic-assisted surgery now accounts for over 70% of all men treated surgically for prostate cancer. Its benefits have gone far beyond those of just a minimally invasive nature, leading to less blood loss, less pain and shorter recovery.

The outcomes of the "trifecta" of cancer control, earlier recovery of sexual function and continence, are quite encouraging and are improving continually. As a surgeon and a patient advocate, I have seen first-hand the benefits of robotic surgery for prostate cancer in the over 2000 men I have treated using this state of the art technology. Robotic surgery will now serve as the new benchmark by which to measure all new treatments for prostate cancer. Today, thanks in part to earlier diagnosis, improved surgical technique and robotic technology, a man's chance of beating prostate cancer and still keeping his quality of life are better than ever.

In this book Rabbi Ed Weinsberg openly reveals his quest for "answers" to these issues. A prostate cancer patient and then a survivor, he has now become a healthcare educator. He explores not only robotic surgery but other treatment options, along with ways to reduce related pain and stress. He also conveys in very personal terms how to contend with urological and sexual dysfunction. In doing so he provides delightful and candid insights into one man's journey, while sharing what other men like him have gone through.

His account of the obstacles in his path and others', and his moments of enlightenment are revealing and heartening. His thoughtful and sometimes humorous approach in coming to terms with his and others' trials, tribulations and triumphs are a great resource for both patients and healthcare providers alike. Indeed Rabbi Ed's sensitive portrayals from diagnosis through viable survival offer hope to other men and their families who have confronted or will face this disease.

This book serves as a testament to the evolution of prostate cancer treatment. It also confirms how modern day prostate cancer patients have made great progress in understanding how best to proceed under very trying circumstances.

In writing this book as a highly informed patient, Rabbi Ed provides a superb addition to medical literature. So too has his contributing author, my colleague Dr. Robert Carey, who has dedicated his career and his practice to the synthesis of robotic technology and prostate surgery. These professional skills, combined with Dr. Carey's insistence on assuring his patients' quality of life, are representative of the talents and concerns the surgeons of tomorrow must possess.

Conquer Prostate Cancer is a rallying cry for everyone who has been touched directly or indirectly by prostate cancer. It provides a sobering yet encouraging look at the very real implications of this disease and underscores the courage and determination needed to overcome adverse treatment effects. In their quest to prevail, Rabbi Weinsberg and Dr. Carey represent us all.

—Dr. Vipul Patel, M.D.
July 2008

Dr. Vipul Patel, M.D. is an Associate Professor of Urology at the University of Central Florida. He also serves as Director, Global Robotic Institute, Florida Hospital, and Director, Urologic Oncology, Florida Hospital Cancer Institute in Celebration, Florida.

Preface
A Robotic Prostate Cancer Patient Speaks Out,
Up Close and Personal

During the final week of January 2007, I learned I had early stage, localized prostate cancer. A few weeks later I met Dr. Robert Carey, a urological surgeon and robotics specialist.

Dr. Carey promptly scheduled me for robotic surgery that April. Little did I know then that I would write a book about the medical, social and spiritual implications of my experience. Nor did I initially have an inkling that Dr. Carey would become my book's contributing author while Dr. David Kauder, my former Massachusetts urologist, would serve as this book's medical advisor. I'm doubly fortunate that my friendships with both men blossomed as the book evolved.

I have written this book not just as a prostate cancer survivor, but as a gerontologist and rabbi. However, this book does not espouse any one religious outlook. In fact it's concerned with prostate cancer patients and families who come from different faith backgrounds and maintain varying spiritual views. This universal approach reflects my emphasis on interfaith relationships throughout my rabbinical career.

The prostate cancer survivors I interviewed opted for various treatment modalities, including robotic or open surgery (radical prostatectomy); radiotherapy—whether external beam or "seeding" (brachytherapy); or alternative approaches such as "watchful waiting," cryoablation, or High Intensity Focused Ultrasound (HIFU). I and my wife, and these cancer survivors and their wives, contended with two leading side effects of most prostate cancer treatments: impotence and incontinence—both temporary and permanent. Apart from medicine and faith, love and sex have a lot to do with recovering from prostate cancer and its adverse treatment outcomes.

What you'll read here is far from clinical, since I get "up close and personal." I've revealed many personal concerns, including the stress and physical pain many patients like me have endured. I've included numerous intimate details about my life in the year following my robotic surgery and personal details various survivors shared with me. For that reason I've kept the identities of others anonymous and assigned them pseudonyms. For the sake of preserving privacy, three of my healthcare providers also have pseudonyms: my first urologist, "Dr. Jonathan Jones," the urologist who initially confirmed I had prostate cancer; "Dr. Warren Goldman," an oncological radiologist; and sex therapist, "Dr. Rhonda Levine," all associated with "St. Petersburg Hospital."

For a while I debated using a pen name myself, thinking anonymity would help me be more open in reporting my quest for renewed love and sex. However, after considerable thought I opted to use my real name as a credible eyewitness to the events, thoughts, and feelings other prostate patients and I have confronted.

Most people refer to me as "Rabbi Edgar Weinsberg," but I've also been called "Rabbi Ed," and I'm fine with that. After all, Dr. Phil of television fame uses the short form of his first name without adding his family name, probably to accentuate his accessibility and unique personality. Since I value these traits, I am comfortable doing the same.

This book is intended for various audiences. If you've recently been diagnosed with prostate cancer, after reading this you'll know a lot more about it, not just as a medical problem but as a social disease. Those who seek treatment for this illness will learn more about your options from a patient's point of view, and you'll find out how to relax before surgery or whatever approach you decide on. You'll also be prepared for what will come after your treatment ends and will be able to determine how best to renew your life as you recover. If you're a prostate cancer survivor, reading these chapters may help you better understand what you went through, or may still have to face.

If you're a man who has not had prostate difficulties, whether benign or malignant, you'll learn what others like you have done to offset such concerns when they got older. Perhaps you'll be encouraged to make better lifestyle decisions involving nutrition, exercise, and annual screening to lessen the impact of prostate cancer should it occur.

If you're a woman, you're probably aware that prostate cancer is not only a man's disease. It has tremendous implications for you as a spouse or significant other, or as a daughter or granddaughter. And if your relative with this illness is a younger man, perhaps in his forties or fifties, and you're his mom, his problem will be yours as well. For this reason I have also set aside a special column, "For Women Only," at my blog, *www.ConquerProstateCancerNow.com.*

I've written this book for the benefit of doctors too, especially urologists, oncologists, internists, or family doctors. The vast majority of physicians are technically capable and are decent, caring folks. Some are one or the other. If you're a doctor this book will remind you it's vital to be both. More importantly it will help you see your profession and that of other healthcare providers from your patients' point-of-view.

As far as physicians are concerned, I've aimed to accomplish something akin to one of my former congregants, Dr. H., a wonderful doctor who eventually died of cancer. I knew her well, largely because at one time she was the pediatrician of hundreds of youngsters where I used to live in Boston's North Shore area. My son and daughter were also her patients.

Toward the end of her life, while suffering from another form of cancer, Dr. H. made it her business to serve as a volunteer lecturer at her alma mater, Harvard Medical School in Cambridge, Massachusetts. Her primary objective and mission was to let her younger colleagues and medical students fully absorb what it's like for a doctor to be on the receiving end of cancer treatment. By offering her personal example and telling it like it is, she had a huge impact on the way those doctors practiced medicine.

With this book I aspire to do the same. I plan to tell it like it is as long as I can, since I've survived to tell the tale.

Pain is part of being alive, and we need to learn that.
Pain does not last forever, nor is it necessarily unbeatable,
And we need to be taught that.

—Rabbi Harold Kushner,
popular speaker and author of numerous books,
including *When Bad Things Happen to Good People*

Introduction
What You Can Do When the Going Gets Tough

"If I'm only for myself, what am I?"
—Hillel, 1st Century Rabbinic Sage

"I always wondered why somebody doesn't do something about that.
Then I realized I was somebody."
—Lily Tomlin, 20th–21st Century actress

Can Prostate Cancer be Conquered?

On April 12, 2007, robotic-assisted surgery eradicated my cancerous prostate and reconstructed part of my bladder. A number of days later my surgeon removed the catheter he had inserted at the beginning of the operation. Then, after reviewing the post-op biopsy reports, he declared me cancer-free. My wife gulped and whispered to me, "You are now a cancer survivor."

Even before the doctor gave me a clean bill of health, I knew I had to share my experience and what I learned from other prostate cancer patients. I began writing this book just a week after my surgery. Sitting in front of my home computer on an office chair while my "bottom" was still raw was a bit daunting. But I felt compelled to record what I went through before and during the surgery, and in the first year after the operation.

Sharing my experiences was sufficient reason for beginning to write this book, but a more comprehensive goal led me to complete it. I knew I had to write about localized prostate cancer since it accounts for three-fourths of newly diagnosed prostate cancers each year and because it threatens so many men who don't realize it has become increasingly treatable. Also more people need to hear a patient's perspective on how to deal with prostate cancer. I wanted to provide the latest information about recent developments concerning robotic and other medical treatments. Equally important I felt it was important to convey ways men and their families can cope effectively when this disease strikes.

Although prostate cancer is widespread, there is cause for optimism. After considerable research I became increasingly aware of new developments in biotechnology and the availability of coping strategies. Rather than dwelling on the negative, I want to confirm that these considerations mean we are well on our way toward conquering prostate cancer.

Medical researchers, physicians, patients, and their supporters have become part of a large team determined to conquer prostate cancer and treatment side effects, such as impotence and incontinence. From 1904, when the first radical prostatectomy (surgical prostate removal) was developed, until the early 1980s, ninety percent of men were diagnosed when it was too late. Their cancer was so advanced they couldn't be cured by surgery or radiation. Now at least 75% of American men diagnosed with prostate cancer are diagnosed early, due to better screening, when their cancer is localized and can be cured with little likelihood of recurrence.[1a]

Those with more advanced, aggressive cancers can utilize treatments that provide more effective palliative care. For this and other reasons, over the past thirty years the death rate of prostate cancer has been cut by a third. Dr. Patrick Walsh of Johns Hopkins Medical Center, and one of the leading urologists in the world, has recently corroborated these figures in a brief televised overview.[1b]

One of the most important advances in prostate surgery first occurred in 1981. At that time Dr. Patrick Walsh redesigned open surgery after German pathologist, Dr. Pieter Donker, had located the nerve bundles adjacent to the prostate. Dr. Walsh's new procedure made it possible for doctors to keep at least half of their surgical patients potent, and enable many of the others to experience reduced erectile dysfunction. Earlier, virtually 100% remained impotent. Similarly, until a quarter century ago, 25 percent of men remained incontinent after prostate treatment, whether surgery or radiation. Now that figure is about five percent for both sets of procedures.[2]

Dr. Walsh has cited even more optimistic findings. In his experience 95 percent of men with prostate cancer will retain potency after open prostate surgery—at times "with a little help from Viagra;"[3] and 98 percent will remain continent. Here Dr. Walsh referred specifically to men age 60 who have no other disease. In any case, medical developments over the past quarter century have resulted in a vastly improved quality of life.

Prostate Specific Antigen (PSA) blood tests, first used in the early 1980s, detect the level of a protein in the blood, indicating the possible presence of prostate cancer. Current experimental biomarkers with much greater accuracy may soon replace these PSA tests. For now the PSA score suffices as a relatively accurate measure to assess if there is a need for follow-up. If so, a biopsy, followed by a bone scan and a pelvic CAT scan, if warranted, can determine if a man has cancer and if it is localized or not.

Surgical refinements and radiotherapy advances have raised remission and cure rates and decreased fatalities. This applies to standard surgery and to robotic surgery, although the latter's outcomes have been studied only during the eight years it has been available. It also applies to various radiation methods such as radioactive "seeding" and external beam radiotherapy. These approaches have now achieved high cure rates for men with early, localized cancer. More advanced methods in the future may yield even better results. In general terms such methods result in nearly 100% survival of localized prostate cancer patients for five years after their initial treatment. This stands in sharp contrast to a 32 percent survival rate in the first five years for patients with metastasized cancer, who often undergo chemotherapy and palliative hormone treatment.

> *Robotic surgery represents further progress for prostate cancer patients*

Treatment options that have been available and studied for longer periods result in an average survival rate of close to 91 percent of patients after ten years, and an average of 76 percent after fifteen years.[4] In addition cancer control is relatively high for all these treatment modalities. In most cases patients remain cancer-free after treatment, and recurrence is limited.

In other specific areas robotic surgery, compared to open surgery, represents further progress for prostate cancer patients. Robotics allows for a lower risk of blood loss, except for about two percent of patients requiring transfusion, as opposed to a higher proportion of patients who opt for open surgery. But others maintain that in the hands of experienced surgeons, transfusion required during traditional open surgery is equally limited and low-risk.[5] Robotic surgery requires shorter hospital stays; usually one day as opposed to two to three days. Recovery time is shorter, due to the less invasive nature of robotic surgery. By the same token, patients experience less pain and can stop pain medication sooner.[6] These medical developments have made it possible for doctors to determine appropriate treatments and help patients renew their lives.

Preliminary research findings with laboratory mice at the University of Southern California indicate that once human protocols are developed, we may even develop a vaccine to prevent prostate cancer. Some feel this could happen within five years.[7] And recently a Rutgers University researcher noted it may soon be possible to stop localized prostate cancer from reaching a more aggressive stage, with a treatment that combines Lipitor and Celebrex.[8]

In the meantime there are various tools to help prostate patients recover from treatment side-effects like incontinence or impotence. For incontinence, Kegel exercises can strengthen pelvic floor muscles. Patients who remain incontinent after prostate surgery can be fitted with an artificial sphincter during additional surgery. For impotence, several pills have been developed such as Viagra (sildendafil), Cialis (tadalafil), and Levitra (vardenafil). Other helpful devices to enhance sexual relationships include vacuum erection pumps, MUSE pellets (Alprostadil intraurethral suppositories), intracavernosal injections, and penile implants.

In addition to this, biofeedback, mind-body techniques and faith perspectives have enabled patients to begin conquering prostate cancer physically, emotionally and spiritually. People have become increasingly proactive in learning more on their own about prostate cancer treatment options and how best to cope if this disease occurs. Home computer access has provided access to information about prostate cancer and its treatment, although this is often outdated and biased by commercial or research interests.

Many patients also are eager to work with their physicians so the medical staff is not the sole source of healing. Such patients recognize their own responsibility and ability to help conquer prostate cancer by augmenting their treatment plan with relaxation techniques, healthier diets, life style changes, and weight loss programs. Complementary therapies like acupuncture or high quality, herbal supplements under medical supervision can help patients renew their lives. These and other approaches described in this book can eliminate or at least reduce the pain and stress caused by prostate cancer and its side-effects.

Of course, the war with prostate cancer is far from over. It's still true that one of six men will get prostate cancer in his lifetime. And as the number of Americans age 65 and above increases, we still risk seeing an increase in prostate cancer incidents and deaths until preventative methods are put in place.

Although things are far from perfect, it appears that collectively we are on our way toward conquering and destroying prostate cancer and its negative treatment side effects. In this and subsequent chapters I will amplify how you can harness these technologies and techniques to renew your life. While I will emphasize robotic surgery, I will make reference to other treatment modalities. But first let's take a more global look at the extent of prostate cancer as it now exists.

Just the Facts—Medical Statistics

In February 2008, ten months after I began writing, I held the initial complete draft of this book in my hands. By that time I was even more determined to share my experiences and newly acquired knowledge. What reinforced my resolve was that I just became aware of the latest prostate cancer statistics in the U.S.A. and around the world.

> *Other than skin cancer, prostate cancer is the leading cancer among men*

Every year prostate cancer strikes an estimated 670,000 men worldwide and causes 221,000 deaths. New patients diagnosed annually include nearly 200,000 Americans and 300,000 Europeans. In Canada nearly 25,000 men are diagnosed with prostate cancer annually, and over 4,000 men die from this disease. Another 35,000 men are newly diagnosed yearly in the United Kingdom alone, with 5,000 annual deaths. Each year in Australia 18,700 men are newly diagnosed and 3,000 die due to this disease.[9] In France 10,000 men a year succumb to prostate cancer. The number of new prostate patients is even greater in Northern Europe and Scandinavia than in heavily populated countries like India and China.

Other than skin cancer, prostate cancer is the leading cancer among men in many nations, including the U.S. For men it is the second leading cancer (after lung cancer) that results in death. This cancer and various treatments to eliminate it can not only threaten men's health and longevity, but the quality of their lives.

For instance after conventional treatments involving surgery or radiotherapy, many patients tend to have sexual problems and are unable to produce seminal fluid. An estimated 50–70% of men treated by surgery or radiation will become incapable of spontaneous erections.[10] Tens of thousands of men each year end up suffering from a degree of temporary impotence for as little as one month to two years, and others permanently. Impotence, whether temporary or permanent—now more politely called "erectile dysfunction" (ED)—can be offset medically, but remains an ongoing problem for many men with prostate cancer. In addition most surgical and radiotherapy patients (approximately 95%) will return to continence within the year, though external beam radiation therapy patients may be confronted by additional bladder or rectal problems as well as secondary malignancies.[11] In the process of their illness and treatment side effects such as short-term or long-term impotence or incontinence, patients will experience pain or stress. Under such circumstances how can they go about renewing their lives? This book provides some answers.

The good news, noted earlier, is that of American men annually diagnosed with prostate cancer no more than an estimated ten to twenty-five percent have advanced, metastatic cancer. While some 28,000 men die annually of prostate cancer, there are now two million American prostate cancer survivors who have conquered this disease, mostly because they were patients with localized cancer when first treated. This book primarily addresses these patients and survivors, as well as their families and caregivers, but will also benefit those whose cancers may have metastasized.

Of particular interest to me is that every year one-third of newly diagnosed American prostate cancer patients—some 66,500 men—are Baby Boomers, referring to those born after World War Two between 1946 and 1964. Demographers indicate that currently there are 78 million Baby Boomers, the largest age groups in America, representing thirty percent of all U.S. residents. It's expected that by the year 2030 one out of three Americans will be age 65 or over, and nearly half of them will be men.[12]

At the time I read or calculated these statistics in February 2008, I had just turned 64. I suddenly realized I stood midway between the older and younger age groups of prostate patients and survivors. In that sense I was in the vanguard of the Baby Boomer generation. It troubled me that many more prostate cases will emerge as men in this age group rapidly increase in number. But nearly 70,000 Baby Boomer men, aged 44 to 63, already have prostate cancer. These observations compelled me to dispel the myth that prostate cancer is only an "old man's disease." I believe this realization will help a growing portion of the population get ready for the inevitable. On the other hand perhaps these statistics may encourage people to support efforts that will lead to a better prostate cancer cure rate or an even more concerted effort to prevent this disease.[13]

Screening at a Younger Age

There are many practical implications for the fact that nearly 70,000 American Baby Boomer men are diagnosed with prostate cancer every year. One implication is that we should lower the age suggested for men's annual Protein Specific Antigen (PSA) tests. PSA tests check the level of a protein in the blood—the first indication that a man might have prostate cancer.

For years the American Urological Association and the American Cancer Society have advised that all men start PSA testing by the time they reach age fifty. Others suggest that men get a baseline PSA reading at age 40, to see if it is 0.6 or less. If the PSA is higher, a biopsy might be in order; if all is well, a man should consider repeating the PSA at age 45 and annually starting at age 50.[14] In my view testing from the age of 40 or at least 45 could save lives. It should be a priority for men with close family members who have had prostate cancer.

> *We should lower the age suggested for men's annual Protein Specific Antigen (PSA) tests*

Scientists have recently changed other norms of PSA testing. For instance, it wasn't that long ago that a PSA score of 4 ng/ml (4 nanograms per milliliter) or above was thought to be the upper limit of normal where cancer could be present. An upper limit of 2.5 ng/ml has now been suggested by some researchers.

Relative velocity, or upward movement of a man's PSA score by as little as 0.4, is another reason for a urologist to take notice. This is the case even if a man's PSA is first a low 1.6, but then goes up to 2.0 or more. If this occurs a patient needs additional testing to check whether cancer is present. It could be that it's not cancer, since other factors like an infection or an enlarged or swollen prostate, known as Benign Prostate Hyperplasia (BPH), can also cause a PSA elevation.

Some doctors and others maintain the PSA has very little value. They feel that all too often it measures false positives or negatives, which obfuscate whether a man is likely to have developed prostate cancer. Medical scientists have continued to develop more precise markers. One of the most promising markers is called early PSA Marker-2, currently in trials that might conclude by mid-2009.[15] Another new test called the PCA-3, still not clinically available, may determine the presence of cancer cells in a man's urine specimen after prostate massage. This test requires a doctor to first prod the patient's prostate digitally through the rectum. This can be accomplished at the time of the DRE, an annual digital rectal exam that tests if there's a hard area or nodule, indicating a possible tumor. Yet another experimental test, which may be more accurate than the PSA reading, examines as many as five biomarkers found in a man's blood stream at the cellular level in his RNA (ribonucleic acid). Whether these or some other experimental tests eventually take the place of PSA testing remains to be seen.

Once a PSA is found to be abnormal or a nodule is palpated on the digital exam, a doctor usually administers a TRUS-a transrectal ultrasound for a guided biopsy. In my case Dr. Jones elected to do the ultrasound first. Within a week or two of the ultrasound the doctor determined he would perform a biopsy, taking sample tissues from six to twelve prostate cores or segments. The biopsy allows the pathologist to diagnose the presence of cancer of the prostate. It also allows the pathologist to evaluate the grade (aggressiveness) of the cancer.

Even when a PSA test followed by a biopsy confirms a man's prostate is not malignant, that's not necessarily the end of a man's problems. A staggering number of American men, some fifteen million in their fifties or older, have another but far less dangerous condition—benign prostate enlargement or hyperplasia (BPH). These men are generally treated with prescription drugs or surgery. Like prostate cancer, BPH can affect a man's urinary stream and potency.

While a benign prostate condition is not generally followed by a malignancy, this occurs often enough—as it did in my case. There's a world of difference between having a benign enlargement or a malignant prostate, but I'll briefly point out some similarities. In my personal experience, a benign or malignant prostate that has become swollen has a vice-like grip on the base of the urethra that restricts the flow of urine and seminal fluid. It can cause frequent runs to the bathroom, day and night, and result in Erectile Dysfunction (a.k.a. impotence). This is what I endured for some three months before my cancer was diagnosed.

Far from being an exception to the rule, I was one of twenty-five percent of American men, including men in their early forties to early sixties, who will eventually live with some sort of urological problem, whether or not cancer is diagnosed.[16]

Why Me? Why Not Me?—
How to Avoid Cancer or Its Recurrence

Whenever ill people ask, "Why me?" I'm tempted to answer, "Why not you?" So many things can and will go wrong in our daily lives. To me it's amazing more people don't suffer from a catastrophic illness, let alone a generally controllable disease like prostate cancer. We should not be dumfounded when a serious illness comes our way. Instead we should feel lucky that we did not have to contend with such an illness sooner.

Rather than ask, "Why me?" a more practical question may be, "How does prostate cancer occur and could it have been prevented?" For those of us whose prostate has been treated, there's a related question: are there ways to avoid a recurrence of prostate cancer, in the event that some cancer cells remain in the body after treatment? To answer these questions we need to briefly discuss what we mean by cancer and examine where the prostate is and how it functions.

At its simplest, cancer in the prostate or any other part of the body refers to the unending, out-of-control duplication of damaged cells that can result in tremendous pain and stress. Such constant duplication occurs along with the annual replacement of some ninety-nine per cent of healthy human cells throughout our bodies. What is not understood is why during our lifetime cancer cells of any kind, including the prostate, will erupt in one in three Americans, even though two-thirds will be spared this disease.

More specifically, nobody understands why a DNA enzyme embedded in each prostate cell does not always work to protect us against damaged cells by either repairing or destroying them. That is one of life's great mysteries. As such, as long as cancer is not altered biologically, it cannot be prevented. Instead it requires the best efforts of physicians to eradicate it through a variety of methods devised by medical researchers.[17]

An anatomical illustration will help us clarify the prostate's location and function before we explore factors associated with prostate cancer:

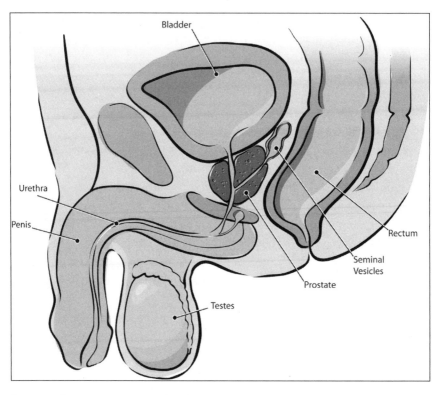

Anatomy of a prostate. © 2008 Intuitive Surgical, reproduced with permission

The prostate gland, a key part of the male reproductive system, is linked closely with the urinary system. It is a small gland that secretes about a third of the liquid portion of semen, the milky fluid that transports sperm through the penis during ejaculation. (The remaining semen is produced by the testes and seminal vesicles. The vesicles are eliminated with the prostate during most procedures to eradicate cancer.) The prostate is located just beneath the bladder, where urine is stored, and in front of the rectum. It encircles, like a donut, a section of the urethra. The urethra is the tube that carries urine from the bladder out through the penis. During ejaculation, semen is secreted by the prostate through small pores of the urethra's walls.[18]

When you get down to it, nobody knows what triggers prostate cancer and nearly 200 other types of cancer. However, a number of factors are associated with this disease. This includes what we eat and do, our genetics and environment, and the way we age.

Poor nutrition may be a factor in causing prostate and other cancers. If a person follows an appropriate diet, this can help prevent various forms of cancer in general, although there are no guarantees. According to one source, "Eating selenium-rich foods, such as Brazil nuts and tuna, or taking a selenium supplement, may help reduce the risk of prostate cancer."[19] I hasten to add that recent studies indicate selenium can raise blood sugar levels, so diabetics like me need to monitor our intake of selenium.

Other studies show that foods rich in antioxidants like lycopene may help prevent prostate cancer. Such foods include tomato, grapefruit, guava, ketchup and watermelon. Additional foods promoted to prevent prostate cancer include soy, tofu, broccoli, salmon, lentils, shrimp, and almonds.[20] Importantly, scientists point out that no high level randomized, controlled trials support claims that lycopene, selenium, soy, or Vitamin E can prevent cancer.

Another more hopeful study has indicated that broccoli and cauliflower can reduce incidents of more advanced prostate cancer;[21] A flavonoid known as Quercetin may also combat or help prevent prostate and other cancers. Foods containing Quercetin include onions, apples, raspberries, red wine and grapes, citrus fruits, broccoli and cherries, as well as black and green tea. Quercetin may also have anti-inflammatory properties that can relieve an inflamed prostate. Vitamin E from nuts and seeds and drinking lots of clear fluids is also recommended to help flush the bladder.[22]

Cancer also may be associated with eating unsafe food, including milk from cows that were injected with hormones. The problem, as underscored by Dr. Samuel Epstein, is that such food products are associated with a higher proportion of cancer in the population. By the same token many beauty products are carcinogenic, even though there are suitable products to replace them.[23]

Losing weight and exercising might not prevent prostate cancer but can influence the outcome of a patient who has developed this disease. As such the National Cancer Institute, in its online report of March 3, 2007, reported that, "The impact of excess weight on prostate cancer has been studied extensively without consistent findings." Still, it was concluded that "… obese men are more likely to die from prostate cancer than men of normal weight, though no more likely to actually develop the disease." This conclusion was based on the follow-up of a 1995–96 study of nearly 300,000 men, ages 50 and over.[24]

In asking why men develop prostate cancer, we should not overlook the role of genetics. Recently four genetic markers have been identified that can predict whether a man will get prostate cancer. The practical applications will not be available for humans for at least a couple of years, but scientists feel optimistic that greater accuracy will be attained.

It is known that due to genetic factors individuals whose fathers or brothers have had prostate cancer are more likely to get it themselves. In addition, black people around the world have a higher incidence of prostate cancer than other races. For example, in the United States, African-American men are sixty percent more likely than Caucasians to have prostate cancer. This has been attributed to a genetic variant for blacks at the 8q24 region of chromosome 8.[25] While genetics helps explain how prostate cancer may be more widespread among black men, it's been noted that these differences may also be due to "…environmental and social influences (such as access to health care), which affect the development and progression of the disease. Differences in screening practices have also had a substantial influence on prostate cancer incidence, by permitting prostate cancer to be diagnosed in some patients before symptoms develop or before abnormalities on physical examination are detectable."[26]

Toxic environmental substances also cause prostate and other cancers. Anyone who has seen the movie *Erin Brokovitch* starring Julia Roberts, knows how Pacific Gas and Electric (PG&E) was successfully sued by legal representatives of a rural community, due to toxic waste matter that got into their systems. A similar saga occurred in Woburn, Massachusetts, 25 minutes from my former home on Boston's North Shore. A parallel challenge to toxic waste was mounted in Salem, Massachusetts by one of my former congregants, Laurie Ehrlich, before becoming a Massachusetts State Representative. She became a leader who struggled to get a major utilities firm to stop emitting black ash and to comply with clean air standards.

Age is a major risk factor associated with prostate cancer. According to the National Cancer Institute, "Prostate cancer is rarely seen in men younger than 40 years; the incidence rises rapidly with each decade thereafter. For example, the probability of being diagnosed with prostate cancer is 1 in

19,299 for men younger than 40 years, 1 in 45 for men aged 40 through 59 years, and 1 in 7 for men aged 60 through 79 years, with an overall lifetime risk of developing prostate cancer of 1 in 6."[27]

The scary thing about prostate cancer is that no man is immune from this disease, regardless of age or economic class. It's equally apparent that we cannot say with any precision what causes or prevents it. However, apart from treatment modalities, common sense and science have the power to lessen its impact on our lives. Through it all, one factor remains certain: this is a uniquely male illness, although women too have an important stake in this disease, given their roles as mothers, wives, sisters, daughters and friends of men. Perhaps together we shall prevail!

When a Small Prostate Becomes a Big Problem

What makes the prostate so important? How could this small, walnut-sized gland located just beneath the skin between the rectum and scrotum, wreak such havoc? On an individual level, it's important because this organ, wrapped around the base of the urethra, produces seminal fluid along with the testes and seminal vesicles; as such it's essential for ordinary urinary functioning and for normal sexual activity. On a universal level, the prostate is important because it affects virtually every man alive. In turn it has an impact on their companions, spouses and families—for better or for worse.

I am glad to say that for me, as of now, after being prodded and scanned and having my blood drawn from my arm numerous times, and ultimately having my prostate robotically removed, my prostate cancer, not to mention my BPH (benign enlarged prostate) and prostatitis, are things of the past! So are my severe bladder difficulties which, after years of being impinged upon, invaded, or "pushed around" by my prostate, have now been quickly resolved through robotic surgery. For this reason—from the perspective of a rabbi, gerontologist, teacher and consultant—I'm convinced that others can learn from what I went through. After all, in the words of Jewish tradition, "Who is truly wise? One who learns from everyone."

Apart from worrying about the possible metastasis of prostate cancer, there is an equally insidious concern men share about this disease. I refer to the realistic fear that prostate surgery, or other forms of treatment, may lower a man's testosterone, weaken his libido, make it impossible to ejaculate during moments of sexual intimacy, and potentially cause incontinence. This is true especially with regard to radiation treatments and standard surgical options. Most surgical options remove the cancerous prostate, generally with the surrounding seminal vesicles and, in advanced cases, with the lymph nodes and nerves.

It's true that surgery, robotic or open, can save a man's life. However, both types of surgery and many other treatment options are problematic: they are generally accompanied by impotence for as many as fifty percent of patients (some claim up to seventy-five percent), and incontinence of at least five percent of patients (some say less.) (This was personally reported to me by Dr. Jeffrey Jones, one of my urologists, in January 2007, and was later confirmed by Dr. David Kauder. A similar statistic is found in cancer literature cited in this book.) As used here "incontinence" ranges from an occasional urinary "dribble" to a constant urinary stream that requires ongoing use of a catheter.

However, to avoid or lessen the likelihood of these daunting outcomes, scientists have now developed robotic surgery, apart from other procedures mentioned in this book. Robotic surgery is technically called "robotic-assisted laparoscopic radical prostatectomy," or total removal of the prostate through minimally invasive surgery using a robotic device. It is one of the more innovative approaches currently available for eliminating prostate cancer.

Why is this good news? According to some—but not all—physicians, it offers many prostate patients a potential means for avoiding impotence and incontinence, given its precision and nerve-sparing approach.[28] Most doctors and medical scientists claim this may be true to some extent, but robotic surgery's superiority over open surgery must stand the test of time.

As the long-term effectiveness of robotic surgery, with time, is subjected to further evidence-based scientific analysis, skeptical physicians will be more accepting of this treatment. One skeptic is Dr. Peter Albertsen, a professor of surgery at the University of Connecticut Health Center. In his view the robotic approach is insignificant compared to standard prostatectomy in the hands of an experienced surgeon. World-famous Dr. Patrick Walsh of Johns Hopkins Medical Center recently has concurred with this sentiment.[29]

Various urologists point out that robotics is more expensive; the patient is in surgery as long as those who go through standard surgery; and continence, potency, and cancer-cure rates are more dependent on the individual surgeon than on the surgical technique. It's often asserted that robotic surgery only

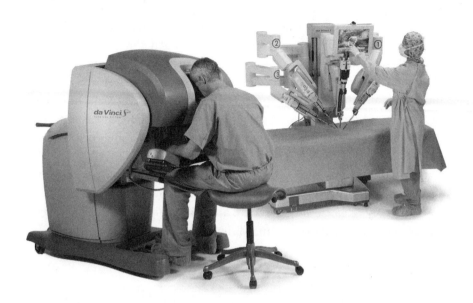

Using the da Vinci surgical System, a surgeon operates while seated at a console viewing a High Definition 3-D image of the surgical field.
©Intuitive Surgical 2008, reproduced with permission.

offers slightly greater advantages than open surgery. Both types of prostate surgery have spurred debate among many physicians, as noted in this book (see Chapter 17).

Despite these objections, what makes the robotic approach worthwhile? According to its advocates, robotic technology allows for minimal surgical invasion of the body and less likelihood of blood loss or need for transfusions. It makes for a quicker recovery once surgery is over, followed by an earlier hospital release—often within a day, compared to a two-day average for open-surgery patients. It has yet to be verified whether robotic surgery makes nerve-sparing more likely than open surgery, thus increasing the chances for a return to sexual potency. Robotic or standard surgeries are equally advantageous in restoring most men to continence (about 95%, although 99% for experienced surgeons) within a year of either type of prostate surgery.[30]

Robotic surgery has other advantages from the physician's point of view. Rather than standing and straining his back, robotic surgery allows a surgeon to sit more comfortably at a console and work with greater visual acuity, while directing four robotic arms, each the size of a pencil. One robotic arm can manipulate a high-definition two-pronged "stereo-like" camera with greatly increased 3-D magnification; another arm works as a retractor; and the third and fourth arms replicate the surgeon's exact hand movements, as he cuts more precisely than he could "free-hand." According to robotic doctors this technique enables them to make minimal cuts into the abdomen, remove the prostate and do bodily repairs within a sub-millimeter. All this, as the surgeon simply moves his fingers and wrists attached to straps located near the console screen in order to guide the robot's movement.[31]

Apart from robotic surgery, there are a host of other options prostate cancer patients can choose from. Many of them are "high-tech," such as Intensity Modulated Radiation Therapy (IMRT). This form of radiation and others involve the use of computerized graphs with such precision that tissue around the prostate is not affected. In my mind, though, robotic surgery is the most "cutting edge"—pardon the pun! All of these options have their place, and for that reason I will discuss them in greater detail when presenting patient profiles. However, there are so many alternative treatments to consider that I, like most patients, was initially overwhelmed and confused before finally deciding what to do after I learned I had prostate cancer. My consternation ended only when I learned more about robotic surgery and decided it was for me.

> *I, like most patients, was initially overwhelmed and confused*

I admit that this book leans heavily toward the option of robotic surgery. At the same time it aims to help any man with prostate cancer consider which treatment is best for him. Before making their final decision men should decide these matters by consulting their physicians and their loved ones. After all, prostate cancer personally affects loved ones as they relate to and care for the men in their lives. That's why it's important to make an informed effort to assess which treatment option appeals most to you and meets your needs. This may include both objective and subjective perceptions. For instance, when looking into different options you need to consider which approach might cause you the least pain and stress abut sexual or urinary dysfunctions. When it comes to such highly personal matters, what may work for one person may not necessarily work for another. Such is the nature of life.

Regardless of the approach one chooses, remember that it has become increasingly possible to conquer prostate cancer. The five sections of this book discuss ways to do so: 1) by taking action; 2) by taking certain steps before and after surgery; 3) through sustaining sexual relationships and maintaining faith; 4) by connecting with others; and 5) by listening to and really hearing what other prostate patients and doctors have to say.

Coping with Prostate Cancer in Body, Mind and Spirit

This book aims to help others conquer prostate cancer in body, mind and spirit—quite a lofty goal. Fortunately I could devote a lot of my free time to writing about this, because seven months before I was diagnosed, I had ended my thirty-year career as the spiritual leader of several synagogues.

My work as a rabbi was interspersed by three additional years as a Coordinator of Educational Gerontology and Lecturer in Judaic Studies at Beit Berl College. Located in Kvar Sava, Israel, north of Tel Aviv, this college is one of Israel's largest public school teacher training centers. Teaching there gave me many opportunities to help shape the minds of teachers and students alike about the aging process and problems of the elderly.

Engaging in both congregational and classroom work has enhanced my ability to articulate events in my life, including how to contend with cancer of the prostate. I am a rabbi with a doctoral degree in gerontology, but when all is said and done, I am simply a teacher.

A month before my prostate cancer operation, my wife wrote me a personal e-mail during National Educators' Week. It was the first time I recall her telling me how my passion for teaching has had a personal impact on her.

> *Dear Ed,*
>
> *....You have been my teacher and mentor every day since we met before our marriage nearly 35 years ago. You have encouraged me to explore my world within me and around me and have given me the courage to "fly." Most importantly you have given me the courage to be a teacher too. For that and more, I love you.*
>
> *—Yvonne*

At first, when I got her note, I thought Yvonne was exaggerating. Then I realized this was her way of reassuring me of her abiding affection during this vulnerable period of our lives.

My personal drive to teach has led me to reach out to countless prostate and other cancer patients and those who love them. My aim is to help people cope more effectively in body, mind and spirit with one of humanity's most feared and least understood dilemmas. It's precisely because of the fear cancer evokes, that I've done my best to inject my upbeat and at times off-beat sense of humor in this book.

While this book is primarily educational, it is intensely personal. It's so personal that at times it may be a bit too revealing. On occasion, it might even be a source of embarrassment to you, not to mention my wife and me. Nonetheless, I have recorded our experiences here for the sake of authenticity and credibility. I hope the intimate details I share will resonate with you. In revealing matters that others would consider taboo, I hope to benefit you or others you know who have prostate cancer. Even if you are a cancer survivor or have no current health issue, I trust my thoughts will broaden your perspectives about prostate cancer or help prepare you to deal with it if it ever comes your way.

> *I hope the intimate details I share will resonate with you*

While I believe scientific research will eventually help prevent this and other forms of cancer, I'm equally convinced we have to confront realities as they are. It's my hope that the resources and procedures highlighted here will help pave the way.

In my opinion two of the leading tools for coping with prostate cancer are medicine and faith. You can begin to control your physical, and in turn, emotional and spiritual states, by choosing robotic-assisted surgery or some other curative treatment option. What you also need is a positive outlook that elicits faith in yourself, in your doctor, and in God or whatever Higher Power you revere.

Medicine and faith are significant but not sufficient if you're isolated from others. You must be buttressed by support from family and friends or a support group. Equally important, most people require physical intimacy to validate their very being. All this and more will be explored when considering your treatment options.

Educating yourself on how to cope with the emotional and physical turmoil that comes with prostate cancer is equally important. All of us need to reflect on different ways to deal with the stress or pain of such an illness and its treatment outcomes, whatever adverse outcomes we experience. In referring to "pain," I mean subjective or objective aching that spans the gamut from mild physical soreness to extreme agony, often measurable in heightened brain wave activity. The pain that may occur for a few days after standard prostate surgery is a case in point. Another type of pain is caused by certain radiation treatment that may lead to rectal burning or bleeding.

The term "stress" suggests elevated anxiety in its various forms. These range from momentary emotional distress to abiding depression and anxiety about anticipated trauma, and even post-traumatic stress disorder. As such, stress can be subjective or objective. It's often accompanied by physical symptoms such as elevated blood pressure, a faster pulse rate, or hyperventilation. Stress occurs when a patient is first diagnosed. A patient and his wife are easily stressed when they first learn about the cancer and then try to figure out which treatment will best serve their needs. Stress also accompanies impotence and incontinence, two of the main side effects of virtually all prostate cancer procedures. Stress is "in the air" during discussions about cancer, and when a patient has cancer that nobody deals with directly—the proverbial "elephant in the room." Such stress can be great or little, long-lasting or brief.

By now you can tell I didn't write this book simply to vent or spill my guts about my prostate cancer problems and cure in a tell-all manner. Rather I've written this account because I care about those of you who have faced or will be confronted by prostate cancer, whether you or someone close to you. I hope you'll learn from my experiences and those of others. I particularly hope to convey methods for reducing pain and stress and ways for you to get through prostate cancer or any turmoil in your life. Perhaps you in turn will share your experiences and insights with others in person or at *www. ConquerProstateCancerNow.com.*

This book is not some form of "show and tell"! Rather it is a practical, and in part, spiritual guide for those who have to ponder the best course of action they or their loved ones might wish to take when confronted by prostate cancer.

Part I:
CONQUER PROSTATE CANCER BY TAKING ACTION

1

How to Confront the "Big C" Calmly

"Misfortune may become fortune through patience."
—Solomon Ibn Gabirol, 11th Century rabbi and poet

"If it's true that adversity builds character, your character's been getting quite a workout lately!"
—Message on a get-well greeting card received after my prostate cancer surgery

A Life-Altering Event

At the end of January 2007, the unthinkable happened. Four months after my wife and I moved from Boston to Sarasota, I arranged for my semiannual urological checkup and met my new urologist, Dr. Jonathan Jones of St. Petersburg Hospital, about half an hour north of our new home. First he conducted the usual DRE—the digital rectal exam, palpating with a gloved hand for any tumors or bumpy, hardened prostate tissue. Following that he sent me to a lab next door to determine my Protein Specific Antigen (PSA) level—a standard blood test that might indicate whether my prostate should be biopsied for possible cancer. As it turned out my PSA level was 6.6 ng/ml (nanograms per milliliter of blood), with a free fraction of 20%. This was nearly three times the current acceptable standard PSA score of 2.5 and a lot more than 4.0, which other urologists see as the proper standard.

I felt fine until Dr. Jones insisted I had to take an ultrasound test as a preliminary way to rule out cancer. Four days after the ultrasound his nurse called saying that I would have to see the doctor again, based on the test results. In response I asked what the ultrasound procedure demonstrated, and she said rather bluntly, "It indicates you'll need a biopsy, since twenty percent of people with your ultrasound findings tend to have cancer." Not the most sensitive comment, but at least she gave it to me straight![1]

I realized then I was about to undergo a life-altering event. When I got to see Dr. Jones again, two weeks later, I was relatively comfortable with him. After all he had been highly recommended by two of my neighbors, and besides he had a low-key personality. Still I was a bit surprised that he had already mapped out a plan of action for me. A few minutes after ushering my wife and me into one of the patients' rooms, he did an eight-point biopsy on my prostrate.

I don't quite recall what he said, but in my mind it's as if he declared "You're under arrest—assume the position." Probably he actually said, "Stand up and lean forward with both of your hands on the table. We are going to take some prostate tissue samples by entering you from the rear with eight long needle probes. It might pinch a little and there might be some minor bleeding, but this is an absolute necessity for the sake of your health."

At the doctor's bidding, I "assumed the position" and hunched over, standing rigidly as he gently scraped some tissues from my prostate. While he did so, I had a sense of déjà vu, because this reminded me of my earlier prostate biopsy two years' earlier. At that time no cancer was detected. In fact, my former urologist and this book's medical advisor, Dr. David Kauder, simply remarked that, at 6'2", I was just a big man with a big prostate! He diagnosed me with having BPH (benign prostate hyperplasia), referring to an oversized benign prostate as large as 60 cubic centimeters (cc's), as opposed to 20 to 49 cc's, which is the norm for most men; but he indicated I had nothing even remotely fatal.

That was then, not now. A week after the new biopsy, the report came in and Dr. Jones' suspicions were confirmed. He told me he found cancer in twenty percent of a biopsy core taken from the left side of my prostate, and he added that I probably had the cancer for at least a year or two and possibly as long as ten years. It's not that he was any more competent than the previous doc. The fact is that finding cancer of the prostate is literally like finding a needle in a haystack! That's because the biopsies are "random" biopsies.[1] The previous attempt to find cancer did not pan out and was a "miss." This second attempt was an unfortunate "hit."

I was a bit surprised but not stunned. Actually I was relieved that something definitive was finally determined. My wife Yvonne, on the other hand, was in shock. That night we hugged as she cried on my shoulder. Like many other cancer patients, I found myself consoling her, although I was the one in trouble! Sobbing, she recalled that over the thirty-four years of our married life I had visited and counseled many former congregants with cancer. "But," she exclaimed," in all those years I never even contemplated that 'the big C' would invade our own household."

Is Prostate Cancer Inevitable?

One reason I accepted my newly discovered cancer was not just my inherent optimism or faith, but simply that I've been student of aging since 1970, when I enrolled in a doctoral program in gerontology at Columbia University. At that time my fellow students and I used to joke that prostate cancer is inevitable—if a man lives long enough. We added there is only one category of people that prostate cancer won't affect: women!

I was relieved. But my wife was in shock.

Recognizing this well in advance of my own prostate cancer helped soften the blow. I simply saw myself as one of millions of men, past, present and future, who have faced or will have to face this type of cancer. But now, in contrast to my doctoral student years, there was a crucial difference: I recognized that prostate cancer may be unique to men, but **it's a woman's problem too.** This was evident in my wife's anxiety over my condition, especially when she first learned about it. Like many women married to prostate cancer patients, she was even more stressed than I over this disruption in our lives.[2]

Dr. Jones reported my biopsy findings to me during the first week of February 2007. By then I was ready for my marching orders, and he did not disappoint me. He immediately scheduled me for a full bone scan as well as a pelvic CAT scan at St. Petersburg Hospital, to rule out any possibility of metastasis—the spreading of cancer elsewhere in my body.

A few days after my day-long hospital tests, my wife and I returned to the doctor. Sitting us down in one of his examination rooms, he assured us that the biopsy and extra tests strongly suggested that that I had early prostate cancer with a Gleason score of six and no metastasis. A Gleason total score of 2–4 indicates low grade or non-aggressive cancer; 5–7 is considered intermediate grade; and 8 or higher is regarded as high-grade or aggressive, but still localized within the prostate.[3] In layman's terms the primary and secondary cancer sites were slightly blurred under the microscope, compared to healthy prostate cells. While clearly contained within the prostate (hence "localized") this was at worst an "intermediate grade" cancer.

What You Can Do: Treatment Options

I asked Dr. Jones to lay out the treatment possibilities for me in my wife's presence. We both needed to learn what we could to make an informed decision. In asking what we could do, our ultimate goal was as to keep me alive for the long-haul. My wife agreed. This is what she wrote to her friends:

> *We sought expert opinions, and later on second opinions, and we very carefully evaluated all of Ed's options and their potential ramifications for all of us—especially him and me. This was not an easy, or always rational process. After hearing the treatment options we were frightened, frustrated, cried a lot, hugged a lot, and felt we had been granted another chance to re-evaluate what was most important to us: our family with him in it!*
>
> *—Yvonne*

Later on I read various books that offered a more systematic overview of the pros and cons of various treatment options for prostate cancer.[4] In delving further into this I ultimately wrote up a schematic diagram detailing the pluses and minuses of selected treatment options, now posted at *ConquerProstateCancer.com*. However, at that point Dr. Jones was our primary resource, so we asked him to describe my options in detail.

"The first is watchful waiting," he responded, and went on to explain. "If you were ten to twenty years older, say 72 or 82, you might consider waiting and seeing if your prostate cancer should be treated. In your case we caught it early and it has not metastasized. In fact early-stage prostate cancers tend to grow quite slowly, so frankly, if you were much older, you might die before the cancer has a chance to spread. I mean you'd die with cancer but not because of it. However, at not quite 63 you are a vibrant, relatively healthy individual. I know you have diabetes, neuropathy and related depression, so I would not advise you to go down the road of doing nothing about the cancer, even if it's monitored every few months. You don't want to take the chance that the cancer might spread in the years ahead."

I had already read the literature in his office waiting room describing the six main options he was about to explain. Nonetheless I asked him to highlight the pros and cons of each. He did so after a brief preamble indicating that there was a statistical likelihood of surviving for fifteen years or more after major options like standard surgery or radiation. This conclusion was based on survival rate studies of such prostate cancer treatments in several countries.

First the doctor described the option of standard surgery, or radical prostatectomy. This, he said, involves completely cutting out the prostate and adjacent seminal vesicles. The upside of this procedure is that the cancer would be completely removed with the prostate, and the PSA level would drop to zero. The downside of this procedure is that there is at least a five percent chance of incontinence and a fifty percent chance of permanent impotence. These adverse outcomes would occur particularly if the nerves bundles on either side of the prostate were accidentally severed during surgery.

As the doctor spoke I cringed. I recalled that my mother, then aged ninety-three, ultimately had to place my late stepfather in a nursing home twenty years earlier due to his incontinence. She simply could no longer stand cleaning up after him whenever he continually wet his pants. I sure did not want to put my wife in that position or end up in a nursing home! Secondly my enlarged benign prostate and prostatitis, along with my other ailments and my medications, had led to occasional impotence over the past few months. Still, I was hardly ready to become a permanent part of the "ED generation," even though years earlier I had earned an Ed.D. (Education Doctorate) and my nickname is Ed! ED, or Erectile Dysfunction, I thought, is something you see on television advertisements for Viagra or Levitra or Cialis. It was not something I wanted in my own personal life.

After expressing my reservations aloud, the doctor said, "Look! There are other options; but in deciding between cancer and sex, don't decide on sex."

Easy for him to say.

"So what's the next option?" I asked. "Well, there's always robotic laparo-scopic radical prostatectomy," he answered. "But that's a fairly new surgical procedure practiced in places as near as Tampa, where I could send you." For some reason his tone was dismissive and he did not mention a location closer to my house, right in Sarasota. It was only later on that I found out that at least one urologist performed robotic surgery at Sarasota Memorial Hospital, a mere twenty minutes south of my house.

Continuing, Dr. Jones said, "We don't have enough information to deter-mine how long prostate patients who choose this option might survive, since it's only been available for the past six years. It may be that its negative outcomes are comparable to regular radical prostatectomy. That includes things I did not mention yet, such as pain from stitches after surgery ends. As in standard, open surgery, you'd also have to wear a catheter for one to three weeks as your urinary functions readjust, before the catheter can be removed."

"Well," I thought out loud, "I guess we can discount that procedure as well."

Next Dr. Jones told me about two types of radiation. First was seeding, which involved injecting 90 to 120 "seeds" of radioactive titanium fragments, each about $\frac{1}{5}$ inch high, injected through the perineum, the area between a man's scrotum and rectum. These radioactive "seeds" are evenly distributed throughout a patient's prostate after giving him general anesthesia, so he will sleep during this 45 minute procedure. Seeding, known as "brachytherapy," would be followed up by a form of external beam radiation known as IGRT (image guided radiation therapy). This two-part procedure would eradicate the prostate cancer and the prostate itself without surgery.

Later I learned from Dr. Carey that many doctors view seeding more as a "brachytherapy boost," as opposed to being effective in and by itself. Besides, seeding would have been inappropriate for me, since my pros-tate was extremely enlarged and intruded into my bladder. At that time, though, it's what Dr. Jones said to me in a follow-up visit that led me to conclude that seeding was not for me. In his words, "For the next two months, after seeding, you'd need to stay at least a foot away from any adults, including your wife, and you should not even stand in the same room as any infant."

"Papa Ed" and Cayla at a family wedding some time after robotic surgery. There's no need to distance yourself for two months after surgery from those closest to you, for their protection, the way there is there is after radioactive "seeding".

Photo credit: Fred Mailloux, Moments In Time Photography

Here too, I cringed. Suddenly an enormous sense of isolation overcame me. How could I not at least hold my wife's hand as is our practice while falling asleep; and how could I not allow her to nestle against my side as our lips touched? Worse yet, for two months was I to be deprived of my greatest joy—holding and beholding our beautiful first grandchild, Cayla? Cayla was then seven-months old. She lived with her parents, our son Dan and his wife Deb, within half an hour of our house. Such separation seemed inhuman and was something I absolutely abhorred.

By contrast external radiation sounded far more acceptable. As the doctor explained, I would be sent to the same radiation oncologist, Dr. Warren Goldman. After assessing me, that physician would use a high-tech projection device to map out my prostate, while radiating one section at a time for twenty minutes a day, five days a week, for just over eight weeks. The external beam approach would not be invasive at all, and I would experience no discomfort during the procedure. Afterwards there would be no side effects other than occasional fatigue, with the unlikely exception of bladder or rectal irritation. By the same token, the small daily amounts of radiation would not endanger anyone nearby. What's more, for at least the next fifteen years it would prevent the recurrence of cancer as effectively as internal radioactive "seeding" or surgery, as demonstrated by previous long-term studies.

Needless to say, my instant and "conclusive" decision was to go the route of external radiation, also known as external beam radiation therapy or, in its high-tech version as "IMRT—Intensive Modulated Radiation Therapy." Traveling to the doctor's office for forty-three daily treatments, lasting twenty minutes each, would be time-consuming, but I wasn't worried, since I no longer worked as an active pulpit rabbi.

External radiation seemed reasonable, until I read an article by Dr. Jay Ciezki, of the Cleveland Clinic department of radiation oncology. He recently reported in *Coping with Cancer Magazine* that those who have surgery (a prostatectomy) for prostate cancer that's found early live longer than those who have seed implants (brachytherapy) followed by external radiation beam treatment.[5] Besides, as I later found out, the odds of becoming incontinent and impotent over time are evidently just as high using IMRT, although impotence may develop within a couple of years of such treatment.

Dr. Kauder, this book's medical advisor, added more specific insights when I consulted with him during a long-distance phone call. He told me the downside of radiation of any kind, is that in the long run there is a ten percent chance of incontinence and a thirty to fifty percent chance of permanent impotence, if not more. Beyond that, radiation can potentially cause a burning sensation of delicate body tissue, as well as rectal bleeding and diarrhea. These were hardly outcomes I wanted.

Going back to my conversation with Dr. Jones: the next option he briefly described was hormonal injection. He made special reference to Lupron, which is an agonist that would cause a spiking of my testosterone level followed by a steep testosterone decline. The objective of injecting Lupron was to reduce my testosterone level and slow down prostate cancer growth. It also could reduce the size of my prostate so it could benefit from potential radiation, such as brachytherapy or radioactive seeding. This hormonal treatment was also advisable before external radiation beaming, if I were to go that route, since my chances for survival would improve.

What he did not tell me is that Lupron is not advisable if a patient ultimately decides not to have radiotherapy, but instead to have his prostate removed surgically with a radical prostatectomy. Had I known at that point, when I still hadn't really decided what way to go, I would have absolutely refused the Lupron injection at that juncture, especially if I had fully understood and absorbed the doctor's next comment.

Dr. Jones informed me that Lupron is also known as an LHRH inhibitor, a luteneizing hormonal releasing hormone. In plain English this means that Lupron is a hormone that suppresses another hormone, namely testosterone. He added that by itself, without follow-up radiation, this kind of hormone could not guarantee that I or anyone would become cancer-free. In addition, he explained, it had undesirable side effects for many men, causing mood-swings and hot flashes, and in some cases an increase in breast tissue and bone loss. The thought of losing my

> *Don't let your doctor do anything until you have made up your mind what you want to do.*

male identity in the process of alleviating cancer was hardly appealing, to say the least, but at that point I didn't grasp the full implications of his comments. By the time I decided on surgery instead of radiation, he had already directed his nurse to inject me with Lupron. What a mistake that would prove to be. More about this later.

I urge other prostate patients or their life companions not to make the mistake I made. When exploring treatment options don't let your doctor do anything until you have made up your mind what you want to do. Under such circumstances don't comply too readily with your doctor's directives.

At any rate the final option Dr. Jones brought to my attention was cryotherapy or what some urologists call cryosurgery, also known as cryoablation. This involves freezing and removing the cancerous tissue to destroy only the cancerous part of the prostate rather than the entire prostate. As the doctor explained, this procedure was rarely used, since it might have an adverse effect on the organs adjacent to the prostate. So I quickly discounted that approach—even though it was minimally invasive and might help me avoid impotence and incontinence. Besides, why would anyone allow their nether parts to freeze to death? It simply made no sense to me.

The urologist did not mention three experimental therapies: gene therapy, proton therapy, and high intensity focused ultrasound (HIFU). Proton therapy is available at five locations in the United States and has been praised for directing radiation at the prostate and other cancerous areas of the body without touching or damaging surrounding tissue or bone. While its outcomes have not yet been scientifically compared to more standard treatments, it has gained broad acceptance in such places as Massachusetts General Hospital.[6]

HIFU is a non-invasive procedure currently available in 180 centers around the world, including Canada, Mexico, and Europe. Some 15,000 patients have been treated as of April 2008. However, to date it had not been granted approval by the FDA in the United States. Its medical staff hopes to complete HIFU's third and final year of protocol testing in the U.S. this year (2008). Its practitioners and many (but not all) HIFU patients speak glowingly of this procedure. However evidence-based medicine had not yet proved it any more effective or beneficial than conventional approaches. Despite a lot of anecdotal discussion, it has simply not been demonstrated that HIFU results in better cancer control and pain-control or enhances the prostate patient's longevity or quality of life more than other methods.[7]

Dr. Jones did not refer to chemotherapy, since that is strictly for patients whose cancer is aggressive and has metastasized. I had heard that chemotherapy and other advanced treatments can be relatively effective for men with advanced prostate cancer, but thankfully I was not at that stage.

To his credit, Dr. Jones insisted that it was entirely up to me and my wife to decide which type of procedure suited me best. He adequately explained the pros and cons of the more conventional approaches of open surgery and radiotherapy—whether seeding (brachytherapy) or external beam therapy. He also told me to carefully consider my options. He graciously added that I could also choose an approach that would not involve his surgical skills or collaborative work with a radiologist. He even added that if I decided on another physician, that would be fine with him.

More specifically he stated that in his eyes the patient came first. I was quite impressed by that, even though I realized that might have been a case of a "soft sell." As it happens, at that point my wife and I were still confused by the long menu of treatment choices, but we had already began to lean strongly in favor of working with him and possibly with the radiological oncologist of his choice. Little did we know then that was not what we'd end up doing. I'll elaborate later in this book and at *www.ConquerProstateCancer.com*. But let me tell you what happened first.

Initially we responded that non-invasive radiotherapy of some sort might be worth considering. Dr. Jones then made arrangements for us to see oncological radiologist, Dr. Warren Goldman. The two doctors often served as partners when a patient chose a course of internal or external radiation.

My wife and I were impressed by Dr. Goldman's congeniality and the precise technique he outlined. He explained that, were I to choose internal radiation, the approach also known as brachytherapy or "seeding," Dr. Jones would implant about 100 tiny titanium "seeds" in my prostate, which Dr. Goldman would systematically radiate to destroy the entire prostate. If I were to opt for external beam radiation, as was at first our likely choice, Dr. Goldman would take the lead, while Dr. Jones would serve as a medical consultant. This interchange led me to believe that maybe, just maybe, I could still conquer this cancer while preserving my "vital assets." But when I returned to Dr. Jones, I still had questions. Weeks later, in retrospect, my wife and I realized Dr. Jones had concluded by then that we had firmly decided on our course of action, which we had not.

As noted earlier, even before I first saw Dr. Jones, I suffered from occasional impotence and a lowered libido. This was due to medical conditions such as prostatitis, an enlarged benign prostate (BPH), and diabetes. My libido had also been diminished because Yvonne herself had to contend with severe, ongoing pain and I didn't want to impose my sexual advances on her. She suffered from severe spinal stenosis, fibromyalgia and chronic fatigue. Consequently, after reviewing my options for prostate cancer treatment, I nervously asked the doctor if he knew of a sex therapist. What my wife and I needed to know is how we could function more effectively in bed, despite our current maladies, even before finalizing which procedure was most suitable to eradicate the prostate cancer.

Dr. Jones indicated that a sex therapist's guidance was a long shot. He voiced his doubts that it would make any difference for us. Instead he stressed that, apart from the prostate cancer, my impotence might be caused by any or all of the medical factors I've described. He referred especially to my neuropathy, secondary to diabetes, with accompanying depression, and he added that my medications themselves might have diminished my sex drive.

After further thought—maybe it was that pleading look on my face—Dr. Jones referred us to a noted sexologist at St. Petersburg Hospital, Dr. Rhonda Levine. She was an experienced clinician, whose views on sex education and practices have appeared in local St. Petersburg newspapers and television. "She might be of help," opined the urologist. "After all," he added, "While a man has an orgasm in his pelvic area, sex starts in the mind."

2

Cancer or Not,
Where Sex Really Starts

*"It has been my philosophy of life that
difficulties vanish when faced boldly."*
—Isaac Asimov, 20th Century biochemist and prolific author,
whose science-fiction included stories that portray robots

Our Sex Therapy Sessions and How They May Help You

Dr. Rhonda Levine, the sex therapist, met with us three times. Each session lasted two hours and cost three hundred dollars, but my wife and I gratefully shelled out this fee at our own expense. We had no choice in the matter since our health plans did not cover issues like intimate relations. What health insurance company anywhere would deign to pay for wholesome conversations that might lead to less stressful and more fulfilling sex?

When we met Dr. Levine, the first thing that struck me was that she fit the stereotypical image of what a female sex therapist should be. She was a tall, sultry blonde, wearing a low-cut silk blouse matched by a colorful long skirt. She greeted us at the door in a professional yet lighthearted manner calculated to put us at ease.

Dr. Levine was not just a sex therapist but a registered psychotherapist. For that reason, I told her at the outset that we were not coming to her in order to rehash our life histories. We had done enough of that during many prior years of individual and couple's therapy.

In past sessions we had covered the impact of our respective parents' divorces, being uprooted from our homes, adjusting to the untimely deaths of our fathers and other close relatives. Other sessions had dealt with anxieties that come with being a professional social worker and teacher like my wife, or a teacher, rabbi and community leader, like me. We acknowledged there had been various sources of stress in our lives. However, our sole purpose now was limited to one goal: we wanted short term therapy to discuss our intimate relationship and, more specifically, my sexual functioning and low libido.

On that note, the therapist asked us to describe the problems we experienced in the past twelve months. Softly I mentioned my difficulties in getting and sustaining erections, both before and since I was diagnosed with prostate cancer. Then I explained that even when I got hard and became intimate with my wife, she could achieve an orgasm whereas I could not. I added that for the past couple of months I had been unable to produce any semen at all. In plain English, as much as I loved my wife, I just could not come to a climax.

As a rabbi it wasn't that easy to be so explicit with another woman, even in my wife's presence. However, given the therapist's professional standing, I didn't get all stressed out over my admission. I myself had heard such confessions (and matters far more outrageous) when counseling congregants in past years, so I figured this sex therapist too had probably heard it all.

Dr. Levine's response was objective and somewhat predictable. She indicated that whether they had cancer or not, one out of three men experienced ED (Erectile Dysfunction) at several points in their lives. She added that even with ED and some form of localized cancer treatment, men could have orgasms, first in their minds and then in their pelvic areas. Why? Because an orgasm really begins in the mind! It was almost as if she and my urologist, Dr. Jones, had discussed our personal issues earlier and were taking their cues from the same script.

During our sessions Dr. Levine asked question after question about personal "stuff" between my wife and me. She asked how we touched, how we kissed, how we aroused each other, and how often we did so. She even asked if we kissed while we made love. She also asked if our sexual relations had been good previously, before and since I learned about having an enlarged, benign but intrusive prostate and then cancer, and whether our love-making left us both very satisfied.

We responded that we had always enjoyed pleasurable relations and were mutually satisfied, except during those inevitable moments of day-to-day tensions. We concurred as well that ever since I retired as a rabbi half a year earlier, we had less intercourse but enjoyed greater intimacy, be it kissing, hugging, or just holding hands. In part, we explained, infrequent sex was the result of our highly stressful transition in moving to Florida after a couple of decades in the Boston area. We informed her that our level of intimacy also became more limited due to issues we had discussed earlier with Dr. Jones: my oversized prostate, my prostatitis, neuropathy and diabetes, along with various medications that lowered my libido. Nor did it help that my wife experienced increasing pain due to ongoing fibromyalgia and spinal stenosis.

My wife confessed that during our infrequent moments of sexual intimacy she felt guilty, since I helped her achieve an orgasm but she could not reciprocate. In fact, she stated that at times she felt so guilty she did not want to engage in sexual relations with me at all. Putting a positive spin on this, the sex therapist gushed, "How wonderful that a woman your age (then sixty-one) has always been so sexy!"

I agreed! I commented that I got great pleasure in "pleasuring" my responsive wife, to borrow a phrase from the famous sex therapist, Dr. Ruth Westheimer. I first heard Dr. Ruth use this phrase at a lecture in my Boston area synagogue a few years ago. But her view actually has a basis in highly regarded religious texts included in the Jewish marriage contract. At any rate I've long seen this as one of my more enjoyable conjugal duties. I would hope that many husbands agree, regardless of their faith background.

In the course of our thirty-six years together, Yvonne told me more than once how important it was not just to hop in bed together at the end of the day. She often felt the sting of my preoccupation with my rabbinic occupation, and more recently my preoccupation with writing this book! Accordingly she did her best to insist that we ought to greet each other during the day with a few words, a smile, a kiss and a hug and go to bed the same way.

While she had often told me this when we were alone, saying all this in front of the therapist made it clear to me not just intellectually but viscerally. Such actions are of great importance as a prelude to greater intimacy.

To reinforce this, Dr. Levine affirmed that being affectionate from day to day, in every way, whether clothed or not, was the best kind of foreplay. It led to the kind of physical intimacy both of us craved.

After both the first and second sex therapy sessions, Dr. Levine came up with some "homework." She directed my wife and me to start "dating" the way we had thirty-four years earlier, before we were married. Her specific directions were that in the week between the first and second session we were to decide in advance when to be emotionally and physically intimate, but with absolutely no attempt to have intercourse. Apparently she figured that couples like us, married for two or three decades or more, tend to put off the special moments that made them a twosome in the first place.

> *Being affectionate from day to day, in every way ... is the best kind of foreplay.*

After leaving Dr. Levine's office, my wife and I commented to each other how her assignment to put our intimate relations "on the clock" seemed contrived. While our first "date" was physically and emotionally satisfying, it was difficult to schedule having a second round of physical intimacy until the night before our next meeting with her. We felt like high school students who have to cram in order to finish a homework paper the night before it's due. As a result our second date was not all that pleasurable.

At our second session with Dr. Levine, one of the subjects that came up was jointly watching videos and movies with explicit or implied sexual content. A few years earlier, while surfing on some TV channels, my wife and I happened to watch a fifteen minute HBO re-run of a series called *Real Sex*. Picture this: an attractive African-American poet reads her passionate poem celebrating the vagina, reminiscent of *The Vagina Chronicles*. Simultaneously another woman, as shapely as she is naked, slowly enters a bath at stage-center. As we told the therapist, minutes after this scene ended, we turned off the television to have real sex ourselves! Dr. Levine asked if watching more sexy films might "turn us on" and help heighten our sexual intimacy.

Our response was both yes and no. We remembered a humorous cinematic spoof on contemporary sexual mores many years ago, featuring some twenty-something young lovelies. That kind of film had also prompted us to become quite amorous. On the other hand, in our earliest years together, we watched one of the first X-rated films to be shown in a standard movie theater. The controversial porn movie, called *Deep Throat*, was hardly a political thriller, although its title was later applied by the *Washington Post* to an anonymous "whistle-blower" who divulged the White House's notorious illegal activities during the Nixon era.

Deep Throat attracted a sellout crowd, including us, shortly after we got married in September 1972. After watching the film's opening scene, depicting oral sex between total strangers, we both got thoroughly disgusted, stood up and promptly left the theater. Mind you, it was not the idea of oral sex that turned us off; rather, it was the pornographic depiction of a woman being impersonally exploited by a manipulative man she had just met, that prompted us to exit the movie house even faster than we had entered. This movie, which reportedly grossed more income than any film prior to its release, succeeded only in "grossing us out"!

Switching subjects, the sex therapist asked if I had ever used Viagra before becoming intimate with my wife. I answered that I never had. She suggested I make an appointment with a well-known local urologist, Dr. Winston Barzell, with whom she was acquainted. In referring me to Dr. Barzell she not only thought I might ask him to prescribe Viagra, but that I would do well to see him in order to get a second opinion about my prostate cancer options. As I will explain in the next chapter, that referral would lead to a physical and life-altering decision.

After meeting with our sex therapist, it became clear to me that despite my previous qualms, I was going to become a bona fide part of the ED generation after all. A week later I saw Dr. Barzell and his associate, Dr. Robert Carey, who eventually would write two segments of this book. I obtained a Viagra prescription and purchased a few pills at a local pharmacy. When I got home, I asked my wife if I should take one Viagra that evening. Her answer was "Yes!" At ten dollars a pill, we didn't want to waste the opportunity for intimacy. That night we pleasured each other for half an hour in a way that I had never experienced before.

When we saw the sex therapist at a third session two weeks later, she asked, "So, how was it?" Knowing my wife has severe reservations about discussing such intimate details, I responded briefly but accurately. I simply declared that, "We just had the best sex we have ever had in nearly three and a half decades of being married." Without missing a beat, the sex therapist said, "Then I guess our sessions are over!"

And indeed they were! As a result, what started out as a stressful, psychologically painful subject ended up as a pain-free experience, to say the least. Our three sessions had enormous consequences for me and my wife, in terms of a new understanding of sexual interaction in the framework of marriage.

When Hormone Therapy Can "Stress You Out": Chemical Castration and Irritable Male Syndrome

Prior to my first sex therapy session with Dr. Levine, I got a call from the office of Dr. Jones, my initial urologist. Like many medical experts, he felt strongly that it was vital for me to begin hormone therapy. Had I known then that hormonal therapy is useful only before radiation and is not to be initiated before surgery, I would have registered a loud "No!"

I realized later that this was not only due to adhesions that could make surgery more difficult. I should have said, "No!" to Lupron because of the prolonged physical and emotional stress it would cause me and my family later on. At that point, I was simply an uninformed, indecisive patient who didn't know any better.[1]

It was about a month before I met Dr. Carey that I yielded to Dr. Jones' request for my first and only hormone injection. His nurse administered the Lupron after Dr. Jones told me again that this might lead to some uncomfortable side effects, including hot flashes and possible breast enlargement. But like many patients I was prone to follow the lead of medical experts, so I went along. I hasten to add that I did not follow Dr. Jones' lead blindly, since at that moment I was persuaded it made sense.

While receiving the shot, I asked the nurse what effect the hormone would really have on me. Her brief, but courteous response was that, "The hormone Lupron is a form of chemical castration." Dr. Jones had mentioned that this hormone would suppress testosterone produced by the testes, which in turn would retard my cancer; but it's one thing to hear a general explanation and another to realize he was talking about my gonads! By contrast the nurse's words hit home and made me shudder; but I laughed it off. What a mistake that was! Over the next year, due to the hormone injection, I would continue to regret that I did not research male hormone therapy in advance more thoroughly. Again I simply had no idea what havoc it would wreak on my body, my emotions, and my relationship with my family.

It took only two weeks for me to feel its effects. What followed were numerous daily hot flashes of the kind menopausal women experience. I had been told that the Lupron was to be administered again eighty-three days later. Trust me, I did not let that happen, not only because I would hear Dr. Carey's concerns that this was inappropriate before surgery, but because of the emotional roller-coaster I rode.

Lisa Marshall of the Scripps Howard news service wrote a relevant article called, "Hormones Got You Down? It's Not Just a Female Thing."[2] She writes about author and psychotherapist Jed Diamond, who tells us that if men are stressed or grumpy they may be suffering from "Irritable Male Syndrome."

As Ms. Marshall points out, "The term 'IMS' has hardly become a house-hold word" since the publication of Jed Diamond's book, *The Irritable Male Syndrome,* in September 2004.[3] Diamond's premise is that "irritability and anger are rampant especially among men in their late teens and early twenties and those forty to fifty." He asserts this because while all men's testosterone levels vary daily, alternately surging and dipping, he feels that the testosterone levels of those over forty are particularly prone to dipping downward.

This supposition regarding the dipping of testosterone from age forty onwards is actually one that most medical experts subscribe to. Among many studies, the Massachusetts Male Aging Study on impotence (conducted by the New England Research Institute of Watertown, MA, between 1987–1989) has demonstrated the gradual decline in testosterone and sexual function of men over forty. It is a linear curve although there continues to be the normal daily variations. It may therefore be true, as Diamond asserts, that "Those hormonal shifts [contribute] to both teenage angst and the prover-bial 'midlife crisis.'"

Diamond goes on to suggest that many women need synthetic hormone replacement therapy to replace the natural hormones they have lost due to menopause. Most men, though, who experience a drop in testosterone, could benefit from exercise, controlling their stress levels, eating properly, and getting counseling to offset some very real hormonal changes.

I don't know about most men, but there's no doubt in my mind that the hormone therapy I was given to suppress my level of testosterone really "did me in." Whatever shred of sexual prowess I had managed to rekindle in three

41

sessions of sex therapy totally dissipated in less than a month after beginning the hormone treatment. During the weeks before and after my prostate cancer surgery I suddenly became ornery, argumentative and downright depressed with accompanying mood swings.

> *Hormone therapy really did me in.*

To be sure, in the first two weeks after Lupron was administered, I recall joking with my wife, asking, "What hot flashes? What moodiness?" But those were words I quickly learned to regret. Soon after that I had all those symptoms and more. Before long, I got IMS "in spades," and nothing could stop it. It finally got to a point in the second month where virtually every hour, day and night, brought with it another hot flash. My wife and daughter can attest to the fact that I was no longer my usual, unflappable self, nor was I a pleasure to be around. They knew it, and I knew it. What's worse is that it took another ten weeks for these symptoms to decrease in frequency, to the point that my hot flashes came and went only about four times a day.

While immersed in IMS, I phoned my friendly former urologist, Dr. David Kauder. After suffering through several weeks of mood swings I asked him, "How long is this going to last?"

He answered, "The majority of men don't have as severe a reaction to hormone therapy as you. I would say that at most a third of men on this hormone suffer to the extent that you have. A third have some discomfort. And a third have virtually no discomfort at all. For example one of my prostate cancer patients to whom I administered the Lupron hormone is a police officer, who tells me he's had no reaction at all except for some loss of sleep. You, on the other hand, seem to be extremely irritable. You'd best count on your extreme response to siphon off no earlier than June, six months after you received your initial injection." After I heard that comment, my loud groan on the phone was probably heard around the world.

I became living proof of IMS. The stress-reducing impact of short-term sex therapy, and the profound intimacy the therapy helped reignite between Yvonne and me were gone. Sexual intimacy at any level was the last thing on my mind for the next half year and longer. The only good news about this entire experience was that I gained a visceral understanding about women who get hot flashes because of PMS or menopause. I really know now what they are going through, perhaps more than most men will ever know! Women everywhere: I empathize with you one hundred percent!

I am no stranger to stress, as some brief autobiographical comments at the outset of this chapter suggest. However, without a doubt, the hormonal treatment administered at Dr. Jones' office in late January raised my stress level to an all-time high.

Should you or your loved ones ever be confronted by prostate cancer, I urge you to exercise caution if a hormone like Lupron is offered as part of your treatment. On a more positive note, hormones work well in preparation for potential radiotherapy. They also offer palliative care if a man has an aggressive prostate cancer. However in my case Lupron was not required and doubled the anxiety of trying to decide which procedure would suit me best. This is apart from hormone therapy's causing adhesions that make surgical dissection more difficult, as I found out later on.

The one thing that did not concern me was rumors that Lupron hormone therapy might increase the possibility of heart attack. When addressing this with Dr. Kauder I learned that this applies only to men age 65 and over who are on long-term therapy, not for those like me who had short term therapy.[4]

In short order I realized that psychotherapy, counseling or stress-reduction techniques had limited value for someone with IMS and extreme hormonal side-effects. Some practitioners of yoga may be able to diminish the impact of hot flashes, but I wasn't into yoga.

Eventually I learned there have been some biochemical efforts to reduce the impact of hormonal side-effects. One approach is to use the anti-depressant Paroxetine, according to Dr. Charles Loprinzi, M.D., at the Mayo Clinic Division of Medical Oncology. Other Mayo Clinic researchers found that low doses of another drug reduce excessive hot flashes in men, namely, the anti-epileptic seizure drug, Gabapentin, which is also used to treat shingles and nerve disorders.[5]

Later I reviewed these medications with my surgeon, Dr. Carey. He mentioned that another hormone, Megace (megesterol) has been successfully used to treat breast cancer. He noted that Megace is sometimes used, although unreliably, to treat the hot flashes that beset me in the preceding months.[6]

Dr. Kauder concurred. He believes there really is no consistently effective therapy for hot flashes. He agreed that Megace remains one of the more effective therapies for long-term patients. But according to him this synthetic estrogen would not help the return of testosterone as it would still suppress it, further exacerbating my hot flashes. To borrow from the Bible, I guess there really was to be "no balm in Gilead"—at least not for me.

For all too many men, it appears that you just have to literally "sweat it out," until the hormone runs its natural course and at long last comes to an end. If I knew then what I know now, I would personally have "cancelled the order." Until making a final decision about which treatment is best, if you're told you need a hormone shot, think twice and ask a lot of questions first.

Stress-Free, Fun Alternatives for Enhancing Sexual Intimacy

Whether prostate cancer patients use hormones or not, what can they do to arouse their passions and keep their libido intact? This is a pertinent question for many men, both before and after mid-life. This is particularly relevant when prostate cancer patients face procedures like surgery, which can result in intermittent or permanent impotence or erectile dysfunction. Many men equate the loss of their sexual responsiveness with the loss of their "manhood." To offset such concerns it is worth reviewing some literature that can help.

Even if a man experiences erectile dysfunction he need not lose his capacity for sexual play. This is emphasized by Dr. Ruth Westheimer in a brief list of sex play suggestions. For instance if a man cannot sustain an erection, he or his partner can still perform a strip tease, caress each other with silk garments, engage in mutual masturbation, or play a board game calculated to arouse their sexual passions.[7]

Some alternatives that can elicit sexual arousal are offered by nationally known sex educator, Dr. Laura Berman. Dr. Berman is an extremely qualified individual, who earned a Master's degree in Clinical Social Work from New York University, as did my wife. In addition Laura Berman holds a Doctorate in Health Education and Therapy from the same university, with a specialty in human sexuality.

Dr. Berman writes a regular online newsletter, "Dr. Laura Berman's Passion Files," which makes for constructive reading (*www.drlauraberman.com*). Her material is not geared specifically to people with cancer; in fact it's intended for healthy women. Still it has many applications for men or women with cancer. For instance one of her articles is called "Get in Touch With Your

Senses".[8] In that article she advocates the importance of touch both during sex and at other times for mutual pleasure and personal rejuvenation. She also advocates the use of word games to spice up a relationship. One example is reading a popular novel out loud with a companion and substituting words that will create sexual attraction between lovers. In addition, Dr. Berman has a legitimate on-line sex-toy store, which some will find useful in heightening their relationships. All this is in the context of her work as a sex educator and therapist and as the founder of the Berman Center in Chicago, Illinois, which focuses on women's sexual health. I point this out only by way of reviewing a few of Dr. Berman's contributions, not because I endorse everything she says or offers. However, I applaud her efforts to bring couples together in a healthy, loving manner, without shame or embarrassment. My only cautionary note for couples who seek deeper satisfaction in their relationship, is that they first reach some agreement as to what is appropriate or not for both of them, before going to the next level.

Other perspectives specifically for prostate cancer patients have been presented by Ralph and Barbara Alterowitz. After experiencing prostate cancer as a couple, they wrote a book advocating that happiness is not only an erection. They offer different case examples and medically approved approaches for enhancing sexual intimacy.[9]

Virginia and Keith Laken offer a highly personal account following his prostate cancer treatment. Their thoughts are recorded in a book called *Making Love Again*. According to their book, the Lakens were both stressed out over Keith's experiences with his prostate cancer surgery—and make no mistake, prostate cancer is a family affair. For them oral sex led to Keith's first post-op orgasm and became a turning point in restoring his confidence that he was still "a man." Their nightly oral forays literally allowed him to resolve his high degree of stress and his fear that he would forever lose his manhood. Oral sex became an acceptable alternative for expressing their mutual love, accompanied by endearing caresses and ultimately intercourse. These physical behaviors were essential in helping bind this loving couple further in matrimony. Along the way they garnered some key insights, noted in my report at *www.ConquerProstateCancer.com*. They wrote their account in the same spirit as I have written this book. Like me they hoped their experiences would be a source of guidance for those who have walked in their shoes.

The way the Lakens chose to counter the effects of prostate cancer treatments may be inspiring to some, although embarrassing to others. For that matter, some of the thoughts I've conveyed in this book may produce similar responses. Still, I trust you'll remember that for the most part rabbis and their spouses have the same desires as anybody else!

Lest I be misunderstood, all the literature I've reviewed while preparing to write this book aims to help couples maintain or strengthen their strong connections. Whether stated or not, the objective of thoughtful, informed professionals and cancer survivors like myself, is to promote ever-increasing sexual intimacy in the framework of marriage. I might add, however reluctantly, that such discussion may also apply to those who are not officially married but enjoy a committed relationship. It can be argued that the drive for physical intimacy is also healthy for unmarried couples, when both individuals respect each other and wish to express their mutual affection. I refer to two adults who strongly wish to get to know each other at every level for the long-term. Others would probably not hesitate to add that this applies even for those who choose to get acquainted for a limited duration.

As I elaborate later in this book, the goal of sex is not necessarily procreative, but recreative. Human sexuality can provide physical bonding that recreates (that is, "re-creates") a couple's physical ties to enhance their sense of oneness. This simultaneously helps them achieve a large measure of personal and mutual fulfillment. This is what my rabbinic colleague, Irwin Kula, has called "sacred sex."[10] It is a view shared by several Christian pastors, including Rev. Paul Wirth of the Relevant Church in nearby Tampa, Florida, who in 2008 issued a 30-day challenge (posted at *www.30daysexchallenge. com*) to his married congregants and other married couples, to have sexual relations daily, for the sake of growing closer as couples. This outlook, while sparking national attention in the United States, is a far cry from the debasing, promiscuous sexuality played out in all too many real life situations and depicted in films like *Deep Throat*.

In summary, while sex really begins in the mind, it must be expressed physically in order to foster intimacy. To think otherwise is to imperil your physical and emotional health, causing needless pain and stress. Acting on your innate sexuality during your earlier or later adult years is the best way to go, as long as you retain and build on your sense of dignity and mutual enjoyment.

3

When Burning Your Bridges Makes Sense

"The die is now cast!"
—Julius Caesar, 1st Century B.C. Roman leader
before crossing the Rubicon River bridge

"We can't cross a bridge until we come to it;
but I always like to lay down a pontoon ahead of time."
—Bernard M. Baruch, 20th Century statesman

Patients: How to Decide Which Treatment Will Work Best for You

Dr. Levine wished me success in working with my new urologists, Drs. Barzell and Carey. As an intuitive therapist, it was her sense that those physicians would help me make a final decision as to which procedure would be most suitable for dealing with my prostate cancer. She was right, but I discovered this only when I stopped hesitating and finally took action.

I felt like Julius Caesar must have felt, as he hesitated before he decided to cross the Rubicon River to invade Italy and confront his enemies in Rome. The Roman senate warned him not to cross the river. Fearing civil war due to Caesar's popularity and power, they directed him to immediately step down from his command.

According to the Roman historian Suetonius, Caesar nonetheless crossed the river and resolved not to turn back. Instead he literally "burned his bridge behind him," declaring "the die is now cast!" I felt a bit like Caesar when I finally decided which option was most appropriate for handling my prostate cancer. It was at that point that I irretrievably crossed my own Rubicon.[1]

> *I irretrievably crossed my own Rubicon.*

The option I finally chose was the biggest mouthful of all: "robot-assisted laparoscopic radical prostatectomy." Recounting how I chose this treatment option from which there would be no retreat will perhaps lead others to carefully consider this procedure for themselves or those they love. However as I outline some of my thinking in this chapter, it's important to acknowledge this operation has minuses as well as pluses like all medical procedures.

I was thoroughly impressed by this high-tech, cutting-edge tool and what it could do for me. It has other applications as well, as it works for women's hysterectomies, for patients with mitral heart valve problems, and for individuals with other illnesses. The road to my decision was paved with serendipity or coincidence. Those who have a spiritual inclination might even say a Higher Power guided me along that path. On the other hand I made full use of my highly-honed skills in networking with others, from Dr. Jones to Dr. Levine to Dr. Barzell to Dr. Carey. These factors, along with Dr. Carey's gentle powers of persuasion, made all the difference.

Before meeting Dr. Carey, I spent some time with Dr. Barzell. One of the first things I learned about Dr. Barzell was that he was born in Israel. His first name, "Winston," is a quintessential British name, as any admirer of Sir Winston Churchill can attest; but his surname, "Barzell," is the Hebrew word for "iron." Having previously lived in Israel myself, I felt an affinity with Dr. Barzell before I even met him. More importantly I found out he was one of Sarasota's senior urological "statesmen." Both for personal and professional reasons, then, he was clearly the doctor I wanted to consult for a solid second opinion.

My wife Yvonne insisted on coming with me to my initial meeting with Dr. Barzell at the beginning of February 2007, shortly before my 63rd birthday. I was grateful since she served as my second set of ears. When we were admitted to Dr. Barzell's office, he wasn't there, so we began to look at an oversized book on his desk. That book just "happened" to be open to a lengthy article on prostate cancer treatment he had published a few years earlier. His article offered sound medical descriptions of prostate cancer and treatment modalities, written in a clear, down-to-earth manner. Given what we read, we already liked him, even though we had to wait another twenty minutes until he finally walked into his office.

Dr. Barzell spent over an hour with us, examining me and reviewing my case history. He also looked through the records forwarded to him by the receptionist of my former St. Petersburg urologist, Dr. Jones.

After due deliberation, Dr. Barzell concurred with Dr. Jones that "watchful waiting" was not for me, since I was a relatively young and healthy 63 year-old man, unlike many of his other patients. He added that brachytherapy or "seeding," the common form of internal radiation, was also not in my best interests. My wife and I found this refreshing, since we had learned that as a pioneer in his field, Dr. Barzell holds a few radiation "seeding" patents.

He thought I might have another thirty years ahead of me, if I followed in my mother's footsteps, as she was then 93 years old. I surmised that he also felt a heavy dose of radiation could cure my prostate cancer, but it might eventually result in secondary cancer. Dr. Barzell did not even make any reference to standard surgery, although he has expertise in that as well. I suspect that he felt it was not the best approach for me, since it is more invasive than the robotic surgery he then advised me to consider.

An hour after we met Dr. Barzell, he introduced us to his associate, Dr. Robert Carey. Dr. Carey was then the only doctor in that medical practice and in the Sarasota region who performed urological robotic surgery. My wife and I spent yet another hour as he gave us a detailed preview of the robotic approach. Here again I want to stress how important it was that I had my wife with me. No patient should take it upon himself to make such an important decision without having a spouse or friend present.

Dr. Carey confirmed that robotics for urological surgery is relatively new, since it was first FDA approved in 2001. However, he told us that in the past eight months alone he had done some seventy robotic surgeries at Sarasota Memorial Hospital nearby. Previously he had done hundreds more during four years of medical practice in Miami.

He informed us that a year earlier (2006) a newer version of the robotic device was developed with four, rather than three arms. Three or four steel arms notwithstanding, it seemed a bit eerie to think I would not be touched by human hands if I utilized his services. But then he told me that robotic surgery came with ten times magnification. That meant that while directing the robotic levers to which his hands and fingers would be strapped, and looking at a console screen nearby, he would see my insides ten times better than surgeons could with their own eyes, and at least two times greater than surgeons wearing standard loupes,—special surgical glasses with four times magnification. We were convinced that the robotic device was very precise.

This meant it was unlikely the nerves on either side of my prostate would be severed. Nerve-sparing meant I would most likely not be doomed to permanent total impotence. I knew my odds of some degree of post-surgical impotence were still 50-50, as in standard surgery. All the same, I felt reassured.

Nearly a year after my surgery, my friend Dr. David Kauder told me that increased magnification in robotic surgery has not translated into proven increased patient potency in peer-reviewed papers. Be that as it may, the notion that my robotic surgeon would see everything inside of me "larger than life" was still impressive. Even more impressive when I realized the camera positioned in my body would see things in three-dimension (3-D), and images would appear on the surgical console screen in high definition.

Since the robotic surgery would be laparoscopic, the only cutting needed would be five miniscule openings in my lower abdomen and another small one on my left side for blood drainage. Just contrast this to standard surgery's knife cut on a man's lower abdomen (at least 4" to 7" long) or, alternatively, though rarely, an incision through the perineum,—the area between his rectum and scrotum. The net result of the robotic surgery would be less invasive cutting, recovering a few days earlier, and fewer days of pain or discomfort compared to standard open surgery. And since robotics would assure the entire removal of my early, localized prostate cancer,—with a follow-up biopsy to reconfirm the one done before the operation, I figured, "Who could ask for anything more?"

It was clear, of course, that having robotic surgery (no less than open surgery or radiation) meant I would no longer have a prostate or the attached seminal vesicles. This meant that once the surgery was over, I would no longer produce semen and could only have a dry orgasm. But I felt this was

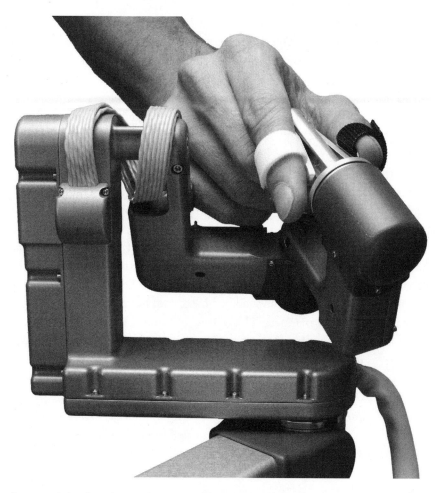

A surgeon's hand motions at the console allow for scaled-down micro-movements of the da Vinci robotic instruments inside the patient.
© Intuitive Surgical 2008, reproduced with permission

the best way to eradicate and remove my cancer. That, and knowing that Dr. Carey would be completely in command of the robotic procedure, led me to believe I had made the right decision.

Even though the da Vinci robotic system had been FDA-approved only six years before Dr. Carey and I first met in 2007, I was reassured when I learned about the large number of robotic machines and surgeons already "in the field." This was hardly experimental surgery. For all its high-tech newness in 2007, there were already 602 robotic systems available worldwide, and close to 150 more produced per year. In 2008, a year after my surgery, the number went up to 800 robotic machines used annually for at least half of prostate surgeries in the United States and elsewhere.[2] I felt I was in good company with thousands of other prostate cancer patients who, like me, ended up choosing robotic surgery to address their problems.[3]

So much for the technical side of the robotic procedure. What also convinced me this was the right decision was Dr. Carey himself. He was a humble yet witty gentleman, sincerely interested in the well-being of his patients. He clearly felt that the unit of care was not just me, his patient, but my wife and our family as well. In Yiddish we might say he was a "real Mentsch," derived from the German word "menschlich" meaning "personable," with the connotation of "caring."

Dr. Carey was determined to do right by me. His first and primary concern was his patients. He was not out to preserve his ego or demonstrate his skill. I thought his name was extremely apt. For me he was Dr. Care-y! There can't be a better combination: a physician who excels at his craft while possessing outstanding bedside manners. This was what I found refreshingly different about Dr. Carey in contrast to some other medical specialists. Yvonne agreed with me, as indicated in this letter to our friends.

> *"… We are so grateful for the opportunity to make the right decision for ourselves; for having a surgeon who not only is highly skilled but who is also truly a "mentsch," a caring human being, who is there for us day and night."*
>
> *—Yvonne*

Dr. Carey's qualifications spoke for themselves. Apart from his M.D. degree and surgical training, he had earned his Ph.D. in chemistry at M.I.T. in Cambridge, Massachusetts. Consequently I knew I—and my private parts—were in good hands.

Ironically when my wife and I moved to Sarasota from Boston's North Shore in September 2006, we had vowed that in the event of a medical crisis we would return to the Boston area, hardly knowing a crisis like this would occur so soon. After all Boston is considered by many to be the "Mecca" of health care in America. And no wonder, given all its outstanding teaching hospitals associated with Harvard University's Medical School. Still, once I learned I had prostate cancer I wasn't inclined to go back to Boston. Happily it was as if Boston came to me in the person of Dr. Carey, who once lived there as a doctoral student at MIT and a National Institutes of Health fellow at Harvard. The old line rang true that, "If you can't bring Mohammed to the mountain, bring the mountain to Mohammed (or Moses)."

That's how and when the "die was cast." At the end of our hour-long meeting with Dr. Carey, my wife and I nodded to each other and told Dr. Carey that I would go the robotic surgical route with him. What was originally a complex set of possible treatment options suddenly became one of the easiest, most decisive moments of my life.

My story explains how I decided that robotic assisted laparoscopic radical prostatectomy would be in my best interest, although there's a lot more to tell. But I don't feel all prostate cancer patients should automatically come to the same conclusion I did. After all, everyone has a different set of concerns that must be satisfied and has to consider which alternative is the best fit. However, I do feel robotic surgery needs to be given a fair hearing on an equal footing with other treatment possibilities.

This was underscored by Dr. Paul Lange, Professor of Urology at the University of Washington and himself a prostate cancer survivor. To paraphrase him, whatever procedure you decide on, you need to trust in your doctor, ask him questions, consider different treatment options, talk to others who have gone through alternative prostate procedures, and get a second opinion on treatment. Once you've done this, don't search endlessly.[4]

I endorse Dr. Lange's view that there's no such thing as "one procedure fits all," especially if a person fears surgery and its outcomes, or may be too old or ill for anything invasive. But I disagree with Dr. Lange about a related point he makes in his book. He observes that a person with diabetes may have a shorter life span and should therefore be less enthused about surgery of any sort. As a gerontologist it's clear to me that medical advances have now enabled older individuals to live longer. As a diabetic I'm pleased to report that medical researchers have developed new methods for diabetic care. This should reassure millions who share these problems. Should they ever need surgery, they can generally count on added longevity, providing they take proper care of themselves.

I have only one other small quibble with Dr. Lange's views. As a prominent urologist, he could state authoritatively in 2003 that most physicians do not feel competent performing laparoscopic prostate surgery. For that reason he felt that standard prostatectomies may be the best way to go for patients who opt for surgery. I feel that this may well have been true four or five years earlier, when Dr. Lange published his book. After all, at that time robotic surgery for prostate cancer was still in its infancy. But in 2007 and 2008, while still "young," robotics was no longer brand-new and untested. It became a procedure that, like a recently acquired glass of fine wine, has been tried and proven in thousands of cases—pardon the pun! It is as beneficial as standard surgery, with a few added touches that for me made all the difference.

> *Robotics, like a recently acquired glass of fine wine, has been tried and proven in thousands of cases.*

At the time he made his remarks, Dr. Lange justifiably pointed out that simpler TV cameras inserted in a patient's body during laparoscopic surgery were not all that efficient. He noted in passing that as robotic laparoscopic procedures are developed, they might prove to be a much better way to do surgery.[5] In the absence of evidence-based medical studies, I don't think this can be demonstrated yet. But at the very least robotic surgery has clearly gained an equal footing with standard open surgery in terms of its ultimate effectiveness, while being less intimidating. As a matter of fact, it's become mainstream, now that half of all radical prostatectomies in 2008 are robotic-assisted surgeries.[6]

After meeting Dr. Carey I eventually read other medical doctors' views about this new technology. Some supported it and others viewed the new high-tech approach as extravagant, compared to older, equally efficient approaches. Such people have commented about all the "hype" about robotics and vehemently oppose it. Still others have rejected surgery of any sort as unnecessarily invasive and unwarranted. But all that did not matter to me. Once I met Dr. Carey and learned about his robotic device, I had made up my mind.

My confidence in Dr. Carey and his robotic methods turned out to be justified, as I'll elaborate later. During a post-surgical follow-up visit, I thanked him for saving my life. In addition I commented that, despite occasional discomfort, I was pain-free and stress-free before, during and after the surgery he performed.

I told him I was so impressed and inspired that exactly a week after the surgery, I had already begun to write a book about my positive experience.

I was determined to publicly endorse this cutting-edge technology—a truly apt depiction! On hearing this, the good doctor graciously volunteered to write down some of his thoughts along with mine. Accordingly, here are some of his impressions about our first encounter before my surgery and his approach to all his patients.

Doctors: How You Can Best Help Your Patients, by Dr. Robert Carey

As a urologic oncology surgeon and research scientist my primary goal has been to guide each of my patients through a prostate cancer treatment that provides the best possible long-term outcome for him. My goal in my patient's behalf is to obtain an effective oncological cure while preserving his continence and potency.

Every prostate cancer patient I've treated is different, physically and emotionally. For that reason I believe it's imperative to get to know each of my patients well, not just to know him as a particular case to be studied and treated.

With that in mind I initially assess every patient for age, Gleason score, tumor location and volume, prostate size, preoperative staging, lower urinary tract symptoms and erectile function. Equally important I assess each patient's overall performance status, family history and medical history. I feel it's essential to learn how well a patient functions cognitively and emotionally before I focus on the dysfunctional body part that concerns him at the moment. I am convinced that getting a patient's full history is the first step toward helping him resolve his maladies.

After getting the whole picture, I believe I'm in a much better position to help the patient assess how best to proceed. I need to take the time to provide a detailed explanation—whether or not a patient has already done a personal computer search on a popular medical website like WebMD, or has read the concise, but often dry brochures found in every doctor's office. Regardless of a patient's medical know-how, my working assumption is that many patients simply don't know what to do when they are first diagnosed with prostate cancer. Given the initial shock or confusion, it's important to help him figure out what's best for him and his family.

During my initial interview with Rabbi Weinsberg, I welcomed his bringing his wife Yvonne to my office, since in my view prostate cancer is as much a family problem as it is an individual concern. My chief objective was not only to tell them what I thought, but, borrowing from psychoanalyst Theodor Reik, to listen to their issues with "a third ear."[7] This is an approach incumbent on every doctor to best help his patients during any initial encounter or in subsequent meetings.

Like most patients I've met, the Weinsbergs had a pressing need to express what was on their minds regarding pre-operative considerations such as, "How long should we wait to take action?", and post-operative matters such as, "How much pain and stress might we expect, and how can we counter any impotence and incontinence?" They also raised peripheral but important matters like, "How long is it necessary to wear a catheter following surgery?" Only after they articulated these pressing concerns, was I ready to address these separate points and a myriad of unasked questions I sensed were on their minds.

After ascertaining the patient's background and personal history, I present my own personal history and background apart from being a scientist and a surgeon. I let them know more about me as a human being as well as a healthcare professional. I also make them aware that I perform over 200 robotic and laparoscopic urologic cancer operations per year, the vast majority of which are robotic prostatectomies. I inform patients that I have been performing da Vinci robotic-assisted surgery since 2003, and I encourage patients to carefully consider all their options for treatment prior to making their decision.

While conveying my area of expertise I do my best to speak in a light-hearted conversational tone with the least amount of technical jargon, to maximize communication. As I speak, I sit near the patient rather than behind a large desk. I do this to make myself more accessible, so the patient will feel comfortable asking questions while he and I critically evaluate each treatment option relative to the patient's specific cancer and overall health.

During the initial interview I look for signs that the patient accepts and understands his diagnosis and his options. We discuss existing treatment data available to him over a broad spectrum of prostate cancer treatments, including watchful waiting (active surveillance), radiation therapy, ablation therapy, androgen deprivation (castration) therapy, and standard surgery. I stress that it is more important for the patient to be fully informed and comfortable with his decision for treatment than it is for him to make a decision quickly or based solely on my particular expertise. With rare exceptions, a patient's prognosis is unlikely to change whether he is treated immediately or after some delay; so I emphasize there's no hurry to come to whatever conclusion he has in mind.

If surgery is an option, we usually discuss the specifics of robotic-assisted laparoscopic radical prostatectomy. I like to demystify the role of the robot. I start with a discussion of open, standard radical prostatectomy, which I and others have been performing more or less the same way for over twenty-five years. I emphasize that it's possible to get a large exposure to the diseased prostate when there's such a large open incision. However I point out that there are limitations to the vision and precision of dissection during standard surgery. In addition I indicate that while standard prostatectomy makes it possible to have direct tactile sensation with the patient's prostate, the surgeon's fingertips are 10 to 15 mm wide, compared to the required planes of dissection at the neurovascular bundles, which are sub-millimeter.

> *I like to demystify the role of the robot.*

I indicate that one of the benefits of using robotic technology is that I will not make a long abdominal incision up to 7 inches long. While that's often done in traditional open surgery, I will keep the abdomen closed. Instead I use small puncture sites 5, 8, or 12 mm large (the size of half a dime) to insert robotic or laparoscopic instruments. A robotic camera inserted above the patient's naval will magnify my vision by ten. The robotic instruments will be surrogates for my right and left hands. I explain the added benefit that the tips of the instruments provide sub-millimeter dissection precision. I use a diagram to show the relationships of the prostate to the external sphincter muscle (critical for continence), rectum, bladder, seminal vesicles, vasa deferentia, and neurovascular bundles (critical for preservation of potency). The prostate and seminal vesicles will be removed en bloc, placed into a small bag, and removed through a small extension of the camera port adjacent to his navel at the completion of the procedure.

I emphasize the necessity for preoperative awareness of Kegel exercises, which will be used postoperatively for continence training. We discuss the possibility of complications from the surgery and the relative risk specifically to each patient. I explain the value of a cautery-free dissection of the neurovascular bundles. We discuss the risk of transfusion, which in the hands of experienced robotic surgeons is reported to be two percent to four percent, and in my personal series one and one-half percent.

I explain the likely post-operative scenario. The majority of patients are discharged home on the first post-operative day. They will have a foley catheter in place for approximately one week, although this will be longer if the patient has a markedly enlarged prostate that requires revision of the bladder neck with extra sutures. Very few patients request home health care as they are usually ambulating and eating well, and the foley catheter is easy to manage. Patients are discharged with an antibiotic, a stool softener, and a narcotic pain pill to take if necessary. Some patients use the pain medicine, whereas others do not. Patients are expected to walk the same day of surgery and to continue light exercise each day.

I stress the need for long term follow-up, and I explain the role of the PSA test. Surgery is held to a higher standard than other local treatments, in that we expect the PSA to be less than 0.01 ng/ml in a supersensitive assay once the prostate has been removed. In comparison, the PSA for someone who received radiation will reach a nadir (lowest value) but may not reach undetectable levels. The initial PSA test will be obtained at three months from the date of surgery and there are usually two visits with the patient prior to that to discuss post-operative issues.

When patients leave my office after the initial consultation, I like them to know that there is more to a successful outcome than simply a technically correct surgery. The patient's understanding and participation is essential. I encourage them to lean on the experience of my office where we see patients with the same condition daily, and to seek counsel from other patients and other physicians as they deem useful. I also have no hesitation in providing patients with names and phone numbers of patients who have already had this surgery. Of course to safeguard HIPPA (privacy act) regulations, those I refer them to have indicated in writing that they would be more than willing to be contacted by others in their quest for solid results using robotic-assisted radical surgery. I'd also be happy to respond to our readers' concerns online at *www.ConquerProstateCancer.com,* with the assurance your name will remain anonymous.

4

How to Diminish
Your Pain
and Retain
Less Stress

"Experiencing postoperative pain is not a must."
—Jacques Chelly, Professor of Anesthesiology and a leading authority in acute pain care, University of Pittsburgh Medical Center, News Bureau release, 2004

The Surgeon as Healer—Pain-Control on the Cutting-Edge

I was one of the many lucky ones. Had I simply met a qualified, skilled robotics surgeon, who reassured my wife and me that all would be well, it would have been enough. Had he then successfully removed my cancerous prostate, it would have been enough. Had he just successfully cut away a large median lobe of the prostate that had grown deeply into my bladder and then reconstructed the bladder neck, giving me in effect "two surgeries for the price of one," it would have been enough. Had he done all this and spared the major nerve bundles on each side of the prostate, to prevent major incontinence and impotence, this surely would have been enough.

Had he also reassured my family and me after surgery that I was cancer-free, and prevented any post-op major pain or stress, that would have been more than enough. And yet he did all these things, using his excellent training in robotics and his innate surgical talent. For all this I thank God for my surgeon who came through for me and for his other patients.

Dr. Carey's skillful robotic method truly played a major role in reducing my pain and stress. However, it was actually my anesthesiologist who was the "point man" in making sure I continued to breathe without pain while I lay unconsciously on the table. That was his mission not only from the time he "put me under" until I woke up, but in subsequent days too.

A few hours after the surgery ended, I was back in my hospital room when I experienced extreme pain only once during a momentary bladder spasm. As soon as I notified the nurse, she rushed into the room and administered a simple injection of Toradol (ketorolac), a non-narcotic anti-inflammatory pain medication. Within thirty seconds the pain was gone. Other than that, I felt so good the first night following my surgery that I protested when another nurse routinely gave me two injections of Demerol and a Percocet as a preventative measure. She told me this medication would help me avoid pain from my surgical wounds. Just as she was about to "zap me," I said, "I don't feel I have any problem. Do you have to give me that stuff?" She left the room for five minutes and returned exclaiming, "I just phoned your surgeon. Doctor's orders!" With that I had no choice but to roll over so she could inject me in the backside.

The next morning, twenty-four hours after my surgery, my wife told me I looked as white as a ghost. I barely had any energy to go to the restroom near my bed. But I felt compelled to get there on my own, using a walker for added balance, with my large catheter bag hanging at my side. Later that morning a male aide came by to make sure I would get back on my feet. His upbeat attitude lifted my spirits and I didn't hesitate to go along with him. Again using a walker, I walked around the entire floor of the hospital's urology wing, accompanied by the young man. After the first circuit, I rested for half an hour. Then, without any further encouragement, I got up, and did two more rounds on my own, once again using the walker. I started off slowly, convinced that I would feel no pain or get off-balance, but taking no chances. Still, nothing went wrong. By the time I finished my walks, I was going at a pretty fast clip. After lunch, I went on the same walk twice, without the walker. I was able to ambulate on my own without any pain or imbalance, feeling rejuvenated and independent again.

Dr. Carey came to see me at 2:00 p.m. the day after the surgery. After checking, he said that the thin catheter bag hooked to the left side of my abdomen for blood drainage had done its job and could be removed. Still, in light of my bladder neck reconstruction on top of the prostate surgery, he invited me to stay at the hospital for another night if I wanted to. He offered this to assure a good long-term surgical outcome for me. However, for reasons I cannot explain, another burst of energy surged through my veins. Instead of feeling physically wiped out and emotionally drained, I felt so strong that I told him I was ready to go home. Besides, another patient down the hall had been yelling during the entire previous night, due to dementia combined with pain, and I and my wife, who had stayed overnight with me in an adjacent bed, were not prepared to take any more of that. So the doctor signed off on my request to immediately leave the hospital. Two hours later I was dressed and ready to go.

The Patient as Healer—What You Can Do To Alleviate Your Pain and Stress

Despite wonderful medical developments, there is another side to the surgical coin. As a patient I am convinced that physician-directed robotic laparoscopic advances are pain-relieving; however, they are not enough to help people remain continually pain-free or stress-free. The surgeon's main task is to complete technically correct surgery, but it is also his responsibility to see that the patient takes proper care of himself. Reducing or eliminating pain and stress is as much a matter of the patient's resolve as it is the result of scientific progress. Developing new medical equipment and enhancing physicians' skill-sets is extremely important, but we patients must do our part in the healing process. If we ourselves do not demonstrate a strong will, we may end up with a strong won't!

We patients must do our part in the healing process.

Precisely what can we do as patients? I believe that long before we might become ill we should develop personal practices to minimize pain and stress in our everyday lives. This goes well beyond the need for proper exercise—including practicing the **Kegel exercises** to strengthen the pelvic floor muscles to avoid having to void too often!

Anyone who shares my quest to reduce pain and stress might consider some specific suggestions I'd like to offer. Not only those who face prostate or other cancer surgery may benefit; other patients and healthier individuals might benefit as well. Many of these thoughts are based on my personal experiences, while other workable ideas can be found in books on mental health or on internet websites.[1]

All these methods share one objective: to enable you to recover from your illness by overcoming stress. These are specific steps a patient can take before and after robotic-assisted surgery and other prostate procedures, not to mention in the course of other illnesses or stressful life events. Some specific suggestions may be more useful than others in helping reduce or eliminate your pain, anxiety and stress, increase your immune functions, or gain a sense of well-being. After all, what works for you is an individual matter that varies from one person to the next. I encourage you to explore what works best for you, since there is no single magic formula for everyone.

There may be one exception that helps everyone rapidly reduce and eliminate pain and stress. This can be summarized in one word: **Breathe!**

> *To rapidly reduce and eliminate pain and stress: breathe!*

That's something we do instinctively all the time—at least those of us who are still among the living! But the key is to breathe more deliberately and consciously ... in and out ... in and out ... in and out. Start with three shallow breaths and then breathe in and out twice as slowly for three counts, before doubling the length of those breaths for three more counts. Concentrating on your breathing in regular patterns takes your mind off your pains, at least some of the time. Just ask any woman who has used the Lamaze method for breathing her way through childbirth.

Conscious breathing first helped me reduce my extremely high stress level a year before my robotic surgery. At that time I had outpatient surgery for a hernia in my groin. Four days later, when I was home, I experienced extreme constipation and a bowel obstruction—pardon my bluntness. My wife rushed me to the hospital Emergency Room, where a young male resident and female nurse took care of me.

First they administered an enema. Then they engaged in the unenviable job of using their gloved fingers to evacuate me. The pressure was exceedingly painful and stressful, and it didn't help that the nurse was both female and pretty. But I was able to set aside my extreme stress and self-consciousness by concentrating on breathing in and out multiple times. My conscious, deep breathing helped me park my mind elsewhere until the medical duo's work was done half an hour later. That was the only way I managed to just lie there without crying out in anguish.

Most patients, regardless of their maladies, can quickly learn to breathe in this manner. Almost anyone can adapt a breathing practice to offset whatever causes pain and stress before or after surgery.

Here's another idea: **stay busy.** One thing I did to reduce stress several weeks before my robotic surgery was to help edit parts of a newly minted manuscript for a book called *Grass Roots,* written by an acquaintance, Jane Gavin Sparacio. The book was slated to be published in fall 2007, and she had to submit the manuscript to her publisher by May 2007. As journalists say, she was "on deadline."

During the three weeks before my mid-April operation I quickly proof-read Jane's book and helped rephrase various paragraphs, while offering other suggestions for greater clarity. I did her and myself a favor, by staying constructively busy as I helped her edit her book. This reduced the sense of passive waiting that often besets many pre-surgical patients and made me feel less stressed. Some skeptics might consider a patient's dwelling on a project like that to be a form of escapism or denial. But I wasn't burying my pre-op anxiety instead of dealing with it head on. The work I did for my friend was a labor of love that kept me focused and calm. Meantime I consciously counted the ever-fewer days that remained until my surgery would end all outside activity.

Doing your favorite things in spite of your pain can also work wonders. You can rise above your pain by reading a good book, listening to your favorite music, or eating good food (but watch those calories!) You can also go for a swim or take a hot bath in a spa, like my wife and I have done from time to time on our lanai at the back of our house. The heated, whirling water helped reduce her severe back and leg pain due to her spinal stenosis and fibromyalgia. At the same time the water eased my tensions, including some post-operative issues I had in the weeks after my robotic surgery.[2]

Self-hypnosis is another means toward the same end. Not having any clinical training in hypnosis did not stop me from trying it. I believe that self-hypnosis is just a fancy phrase for planting a suggestion in your mind and following through. As such hypnosis can be directed by a trained clinician or self-directed by a person who intuitively knows how to redirect his mindset. For instance you can focus on beautiful images and hear music, or you can recall a beautiful film sequence and transport yourself to that scene. You can also concentrate your thoughts on someone or something you love very much or a beautiful sight you've seen, and keep it in mind until your stress or pain passes.

Of course not everyone is open to the power of suggestion, whether induced by others or themselves. So if you have prostate cancer or another illness and want to prepare for surgery, what's a fellow or gal to do? One of the best approaches to reduce and at least momentarily eliminate pain and stress is to **take every opportunity to laugh.** Tell jokes or watch funny TV shows or movies. Laughter doesn't always reduce pain, but it sure helps, as journalist Norman Cousins famously wrote while suffering from a painful degenerative spinal disease, described in his 1979 book, *Anatomy of an Illness.* This message is implicit in the ongoing *Reader's Digest* column, "Laughter—the Best Medicine." It's clear that laughter may not always be curative for the long-term, but clearly laughter can't hurt—unless you happen to suffer from broken ribs or severe asthma!

No matter what the disease—cancer, liver damage, brain injury, or spinal stenosis—laughter can reduce or eliminate pain at least momentarily, either because it kicks in endorphins or distracts us from our stress and sorrows. To illustrate this I'll offer a series of humorous one-liners about stress, which has been bandied about on the internet.

YOU KNOW YOU'RE STRESSED WHEN …
You get a "Runner's High" while attempting to sit up.
The Sun is too loud.
Trees begin to chase you.

YOU KNOW YOU'RE STRESSED WHEN …
You look into the possibility of setting up an intravenous espresso coffee drip solution.
You can hear mimes.
You say the same sentence over and over again, not realizing that you have said it before.

YOU KNOW YOU'RE STRESSED WHEN
You believe that if you think hard enough, you can fly.
You ask the take-out drive-through attendant if you can get your order to go.
You can skip without a rope.
You say the same sentence over and over again, not realizing that you have said it before.

Another example of humor that can get you out of the doldrums is jokes. For instance there's an anecdote about an older woman who was so out-of-shape, she literally felt disjointed. One day this woman complained to her friend, "I feel like my body has gotten totally out of shape. That's why I got my doctor's permission to join a fitness club and start exercising. I decided to take an aerobics class for folks who are 'over the hill.' When I finally got to the fitness club I bent, twisted, gyrated, jumped up and down, and perspired for an hour. But by the time I got my leotards on, the class I was going to enroll in had already ended."

An additional example of humor which helps people rise above their medical hardships pokes fun at death. For example, I recalled a story about reporters who interviewed a man who had just turned 107 years old. They asked him, "What do you think is the best thing about being your age?" His reply: "There's no more peer pressure!"

Poking fun at oneself eases tension and anxiety. Here's a one-liner that clergy like me have retold since our early seminary years: "Priests can be defrocked, but rabbis may be unsuited!"

When things look grim, telling a joke can reduce your stress and pain as well as break the tension between people. Humorous so-called "daffy-nitions" and anecdotes like these can revive your spirits and ease your pain even when cancer strikes. To be sure, while laughter is the best medicine, nobody can say it's a cure-all for cancer or any other illness—but it is a good start. To recover you also need a positive outlook, including a sense of purpose, a determination to live and live well, and the capacity to sustain your faith, love and hope.[3]

Many find they can reduce stress by **reciting prayers,** such as the well-known "Serenity Prayer." This prayer was attributed to 20th Century theologian, political analyst, and Protestant minister Reinhold Niebuhr, who before his passing taught at New York's Union Theological Seminary, across the street from the seminary where I was ordained as a rabbi.[4] However Reverend Niebuhr was unsure of its actual origins, which have now been traced to two Eighteenth Century deacons in the German town of Weinsberg— from which I am descended![5] Many who repeat this universally appealing prayer find momentary relief from various stresses and conflicts. Here's a version that is known and recited by millions around the world:

> *God grant me the serenity*
> *to accept the things I cannot change;*
> *courage to change the things I can;*
> *and wisdom to know the difference.*

Rev. Niebuhr's original prayer continued with other familiar phrases that refer to "Living one day at a time" and "surrendering to God's will", concepts that were later incorporated in Alcoholics Anonymous' Twelve-Step program.

In 1940 these four lines were co-opted by Alcoholics Anonymous and in 1951 they were published in AA's primary text, *The Grapevine*. AA's co-founder, Bill W., reportedly renamed this poem "The Serenity Prayer." It has become a reassuring mantra or pledge that helps release individuals from the pain and stress of feeling stuck on their life journeys.

One pundit wrote an anonymous take-off on the serenity prayer. If you allow your sense of humor to offset your worst anxieties about aging, you might appreciate this light-hearted sentiment, dubbed the "Senility Prayer": "Oh, Lord! Grant me the senility to forget the people I never liked anyway, the good fortune to run into the ones I do, and the eyesight to tell the difference!"

Unlike senility, serenity is often accompanied by a positive attitude, including the so-called "attitude of gratitude." When you're serene you can see your problems not as obstacles that block your way, but as hurdles to jump over. Even better look at them as stepping stones you can traverse until you reach the other side of your raging river safe and sound.

Whether I'm the first to tell you or not, remember this helpful insight: The Chinese word for "crisis" is formed by combining the Chinese letters that spell out "challenges" and "opportunities." When you have cancer, think about pain and stress as challenges to be resolved and as opportunities to garner strength. Opening yourself up in this manner can help put your plight in perspective and help you get on with your life.

Apart from serenity, we all need to **rely on our resilience,**—our inherent power to bounce back. I'm not suggesting you deny how difficult your life may be; rather I would encourage you to figure out how to respond with greater creativity and less passivity. Don't fault yourself or others for your illness or related problems. It may be tempting, but don't even fault your clergyman or God. Seriously! Instead seek your own solutions to your concerns. Commit to getting beyond the issues that bother you. Tell others openly what's on your mind. If you like to write, use a daily journal to write down your worries and your progress.

For some, **journaling** is worthwhile, although others may feel it is a waste of time. I recall saying as much over ten years ago at a Rabbinic Training Institute—an annual in-service seminar offered by the Rabbinical Assembly of Conservative Judaism in Poughkeepsie, New York. At that Institute I admit to lightly chastising a well-known seminary educator, a wise and patient professor named Rabbi Joe Lukinsky. "Frankly," I said, "for you to tell us rabbis or anyone else to take ten minutes to write a journalistic note in poetic form about one of our major concerns seems like an artificial exercise." Joe persisted so I reluctantly wrote the poem he asked for in the ten minutes allotted. When I read it aloud, as requested, I surprised myself. The impromptu poem I had written regarding a pressing concern was so lyrical and expressive that Joe applauded and all but said, "See, I told you so!"

The point is that "writing it out can help relieve ongoing sources of stress," as clinicians at Harvard's Mind/Body Medical Institute have pointed out. "It" can refer to your fears, anxieties, adverse feelings before or after surgery, or some other traumatic event you have experienced or anticipate experiencing in the future. Journaling can help you let go of your anxiety and ease your pain even if you spend just ten to twenty minutes a day in reflective writing. Months after my prostate cancer surgery, I admittedly didn't journal consistently. However in some ways writing this book was a form of extensive journaling. Rabbi Joe: You were right!

Those who don't care to write may **find other ways to relax listed** in a Harvard publication called *The Relaxation Tool Kit*. It advocates that one should literally smell the roses and use aromatherapy—although care should be exercised for cancer patients who are on specific medications. You can also drink your favorite beverage every day, read regularly, go to the movies and theater, or listen to your favorite music. Eating dark chocolate, within limits, usually won't hurt either! And, of course, hugging someone you love makes a big difference.[6]

In my personal experience those of us who are pet lovers can de-stress by **petting our cats or dogs** or other **pets** at home. My family has twin cats, Oreo—a girl, and Taski—a boy, which belong to our daughter. Just looking at such calm, magnificent animals gave me increased enjoyment and lowered my stress level before and after my robotic surgery. Rubbing their tummies until they purred was even more gratifying. All too often, we get along better with our pets than with people, and both we and our pets derive pleasure and relaxation as they curl up around us—or on top of us.

One of the most difficult questions is how to avoid the stress of a serious illness when it's accompanied by morbid self-pity. My only answer to this tragic occurrence is that it's really important not to identify with your illness. You are not a "cancer case" but a human being with cancer. For years I've found it abhorrent when doctors or nurses, standing in a hospital corridor, talk about the "cancer patient" or the "hip patient" or "heart patient" in a room down the hall. First and foremost we are people who have cancer or a hip or heart problem; we're not the disease itself. In turn, unfortunately, patients often incorporate such narrow-minded thinking into their own psyches. To reduce your psychological pain and stress, remember who you are—a vital human being who really matters!

Consider repeating glowing descriptions about yourself to reinforce your positive self-image. No matter how uncomfortable your illness or procedure makes you feel, **self-affirmations** remind you that you are more than a patient. For instance you might repeat the following, if it applies to you: "I am a clear thinker." "I have done a lot of good in my life, and will continue to do so whenever I feel better." "I have reared my children to become productive, helpful adults." "I took good care of my ailing, elderly parents," and so on.

It's also advisable to recall the slogan, "**Just say NO!**" When you don't feel up to doing something others insist on, just say, "NO!" When someone asks you to do something which is against your best interests, "Just say NO!" When you're challenged to stop an activity you really like, just say, "NO!" For example, if family members tell you you're really not ready to drive your car to a local ice cream parlor, don't yield to their judgment, unless you are truly unable to drive safely! Don't acquiesce to others unless it's really for your own good. If you are capable of doing things yourself, don't depend on others to do them for you. To do so might invite conflict, a sense of inadequacy and weakness, which will only add to your stress or pain.

On the other hand, **reach out** to your family for strength and guidance on your terms, when you feel vulnerable. Clearly supportive family, friends and co-religionists can be crucial to your healing process. Such people, if so-minded, can help transform a cancer patient's dismay into a more positive outlook.

And reach out and offer your assistance to fellow patients or others, when you feel you're up to helping them out. You can boost your chances of survival and renewal by accepting and reaching out to family and friends. Welcome your co-religionists who come by to visit you during your illness, as long as they're not obtrusive and you're not sick to your stomach! Such openness may help restore your religious faith in God's power to help you heal.[7]

As well as family and community support, I found **biofeedback** very useful. In the weeks after my operation biofeedback helped me overcome considerable stress over my moderate incontinence. Biofeedback is a marvelous high-tech means to reduce or eliminate pain and stress, as I'll describe in more detail later on. It simply involves attaching a small electronic monitoring device to your skin near your sphincter muscle below the area where the prostate was removed. This can help you become more aware of how well your involuntary sphincter muscles are functioning to keep you continent. In one to five sessions biofeedback can help you avoid incontinence, and it is something most patients can master in fifteen minutes a day. The only exception is a minority of patients who will need prescribed drugs or additional surgery to "stem the tide."[8]

Biofeedback helped me overcome considerable stress over my moderate incontinence.

The **practice of Qigong** can also enhance the positive outcomes of treatment. Qigong, which I occasionally practiced in a Tai Chi class that met at my last synagogue, is calming and does not strain the body. It certainly reduced any stress I felt, since it put me in a delightful trance-like state of mind. It has even been demonstrated that Quigong and similar techniques help avert such health issues as strokes and senility, while improving sex hormone levels and bone density. Who would have ever thought that an enhanced state of mind could have such a positive effect on your body?[9]

Other simple but helpful recommendations for reducing stress include: **meditating and visualizing; exercising** and moving around, even if you do so for as little as thirty minutes a day; **resting** and **eating sufficiently; going easy on alcohol; not eating excessively; not isolating yourself** from friends or others who are willing to lend their support; and **balancing work with play.**[10]

Some, although not all, of these pain and stress "busters" worked for me before and after my prostate surgery. You have to experiment in order to determine which approach works best for you. It's not quite clear why some avenues will raise your spirits more than others, but this varies from one individual to the next. Practice whatever method benefits your mental and physical health most. This will help you develop a more positive outlook, with heightened immunity and reduced toxicity.[11] These and other vital goals can be attained with the help of this book and its accompanying website, *www.ConquerProstateCancer.com.*

To sum up, it's important to take a proactive stance to reduce your pain and stress, supplemented by whatever relief your doctor may provide. Doing your share to control your personal well-being is in your best interest. No matter how ill you feel, it's largely up to you to make your life more livable.

Part II:

CONQUER PROSTATE CANCER BEFORE AND AFTER SURGERY

5

What Self-Help Guru, Tony Robbins, Taught Me About the Mind-Body Connection

"To defy external forces, to rise above circumstances is to proclaim the sovereignty of the human spirit."
—Chaim Weitzmann, 20th Century British scientist and first President of Israel

Transform Your Vision

Techniques for pain and stress reduction, such as those I've presented, rely on the mind-body connection. In preparing to reduce and ultimately eliminate surgical pain and stress, I recommend that you draw on the mind-body connection through guided imagery as well as associative thinking in ways suggested by Anthony Robbins. These are ways of thinking and doing that can help you conquer prostate cancer.

I have a vivid imagination. It's easy for me to visualize things, as it is for multitudes of so-called Baby Boomers, the oldest of whom are just a couple of years younger than me. My family got its first black-and-white TV when I was twelve years old. Most boomers were younger when there was at least one television in every house. They were light years away from previous generations, who had merely been promised a "chicken in every pot"!

Ever since I entered this world in February 1944, I've been at the vanguard of the Boomer Generation. With expanding telecommunications via television and computer screens, we are able to visualize people, things and words almost automatically while reflecting or meditating.

My ability is not simply due to being a rabbi who prays daily. My powers of visualization operate with even greater force in a secular setting. As an example, I can easily envision a map to help me drive to places I've never seen before. Similarly when I have lost something or I failed to recollect what I've heard, I tend to reorient myself by "seeing" the objects, words or related incidents that might otherwise evade me. To see or foresee things in your "mind's eye" is an intuitive gift, reinforced by our culture, and it can serve you well.

I strengthened my capacity to visualize during a summer vacation in July 1994. I attended a "Fire Walk" program in Washington, D.C., personally led by self-improvement guru Tony Robbins. In keeping with Robbins' style of presentation, that weekend conference was highly informative even though it had the feel of a pep rally! His talks were interspersed with loud, joyous stereophonic music, as many of us danced in the aisles. As we danced we got re-energized and bonded together before sitting down to hear more of Tony Robbins' spirited, thought-provoking comments.

That conference aimed to teach some 1200 participants in the audience how to eliminate fear and pain. Starting off quite simply, Tony asked all those in the audience to bring their right forearms behind their backs as far as possible. Many of us didn't get too far. Then he asked each of us to envision getting our right arm behind us much further than we did the first time. After this brief visualization exercise, most of us effortlessly managed to reach much farther behind our backs! Mentally stretching "to the max" revealed the power of the mind to help the body overcome minor, self-imposed limitations.[1] We were instantly able to transform our vision into action.

Tony Robbins also taught a more sophisticated skill that reduces stress through visualization. For instance, if your spouse or friend has a headache, ask her to transfer the headache to an imaginary ball in your hand. Then, as you toss his "ball of pain" way over the horizon, she may find that his headache has gone away. I tried doing this a few months later with my wife, who is generally quite skeptical about such efforts and is not given to hypnotic suggestions.

To my surprise, it really worked for her! Unfortunately I can't do the same for her now that she has more serious, painful neurological illnesses.

Social scientists theorize that when this neat technique works, it's because you're helping another person objectify her pain, thus enabling her to let go of it. Ultimately hypnosis is merely the power of suggestion. As a self-taught amateur hypnotist, I can't change anybody; all I can do is trigger auto-suggestions that can get another person to change himself.

Tony Robbins taught his "Fire Walk" participants yet another technique to transform pain to pleasure by using the art of visualization. First you imagine that you see an aura of hot orange surrounding some painful part of your body. Then you gradually allow the colored aura to go from a hot orange (reminiscent of a flame) to a cool blue. As a result of this approach, after only an hour of practice, I learned never to be afraid of that most feared of all professionals: the dentist!

For many Americans going to a dental surgeon is one of the most threatening activities, even though it is something most have to do regularly once or twice a year. However, after Tony Robbins' seminar, whenever I had to see the dentist for a cavity, I hardly ever experienced pain again. I simply changed the "color" of any initial pain in a tooth the dentist drilled, first "seeing" it wrapped in bright orange, then in dark, soothing blue, my favorite color. After that I never again had to ask for Novocain when my dentist worked on my teeth.

In accomplishing this, I amazed my wife and friends and even a dentist, who was one of my former congregants. I'll never forget how once, a few years ago, before water based laser dental drilling was developed, Dr. Fern actually begged me to take at least a small quantity of Novocain before a particularly arduous tooth procedure. As usual I refused saying, "I'll be fine." I then closed my eyes and took a "snooze" as she began to work on my teeth. Five minutes later I felt the tip of her Novocain injection in my upper gum. Awakened from my slumber, I demanded to know, "Why did you do that, when I specifically asked you not to? You know how much I hate the puffed up feeling of Novocain in my upper lip!"

In response, she answered, "I'm sorry, Rabbi, but I was worried about you. Could you at least do it for me, if not for yourself?" I paused and said "Okay," and then promptly went back to sleep![2]

Take Action by "Anchoring"

Another stress reduction method is association, or what Tony Robbins calls "anchoring"; connecting a specific hand gesture to a given behavior or thought. This is evident in marketing, such as featuring a pretty woman on TV as she places her hand on the latest vehicle for sale by your local dealership. In such a situation, because the average male viewer subliminally associates a car with the sexy woman advertising it, the man may think the car is sexy or attractive and be more prone to buy it.

> *Transform pain to pleasure by using the art of visualization.*

Most advertising focuses on a powerful, attractive reference point, which is then transferred to an object for sale. That object then becomes imbued with the desired quality of the original person or item the viewer first sees. As far as I can tell, this is standard operating procedure throughout the advertising world.

This is relevant in reducing pain and stress. It can "rev up" a positive flow of energy, which many people call "chi." Tony Robbins has developed a simple anchoring technique: while speaking before an audience, he will pound his right hand on his left chest every few minutes. As he once explained, he associates that repeated gesture with certain pleasurable moments he has previously experienced. Even when the specific pleasurable memories are forgotten, his chest-pounding generates a high level of energy. He has mastered the ability to elicit the same reinvigorating, pleasurable responses he once felt in an original scenario.

This is a variation of the stimulus-response syndrome, for those who are familiar with basic psychology. Most of us have heard of the scientist Pavlov, whose dogs salivated while eating their food placed in front of them. Later on Pavlov rang a bell while the dogs ate. In a relatively short time, even when no food was present, the dogs salivated whenever they heard a bell.

A few months after learning Tony Robbins' associative technique, I applied it to help my friend David, who had attended a wedding I conducted in a field across from my former home in Boston. Afterwards he returned to my house with the other guests. As we sat down to the sumptuous dinner, outdoors in my backyard, he appeared rather tense. Since I sat next to him

I couldn't help but notice how distressed and far removed he was from the festivities. When I asked him what was wrong, he answered that he had recently lost his job, and this was giving him grief. I took him aside and asked his permission to show him a technique I had learned from Tony Robbins to ease his mind. He said, "Why not?"

I directed him to recall the most pleasurable moment he had experienced in the past two weeks, but asked him not to share his thoughts with me. Suddenly he smiled and said he remembered something very pleasurable having to do with his wife. At that point I reminded him not to tell me anything more. Instead, I told him to close his eyes and recall the exact time of day, the exact place, and the ambience of the room where he was during that pleasant moment. I also asked him to think about the sights, sounds, smells, touches and tastes of that moment. Evidently he recalled everything in intimate detail, including all the sensory aspects of that experience. How did I know? Because I saw him grinning from ear to ear. At that point I asked him to take his right hand and squeeze the corner on his left shoulder, and he did so. That was the moment that anchored his positive experience in a single gesture.

Then David told me he remembered some other details of that event. Although he still didn't reveal what they were, he smiled once more, at which point I asked him to firmly squeeze his left shoulder again. After several rounds of this give-and-take, I asked him to open his eyes and asked, "How do you feel?" His answer, not surprisingly, was "Just great! Thank you very much! How did you do that?" Rather than answering, I said, "Why don't we take a few minutes to talk about some other things."

Five minutes later I noticed David had tensed up again, and I asked him to squeeze exactly the same spot on his left shoulder using his right hand once again. While doing so, he immediately flashed a grin at me. At my request he did that again ten minutes later and asked me once more: "Please tell me how you managed to make me feel so much at ease that quickly?"

In response I said, "David, in squeezing your left shoulder, you created an anchor linked to a bright, happy moment in your life. Whenever you're feeling down or stuck in some dark corner, just squeeze your shoulder exactly the same way, and you'll feel just fine!" He thanked me and went on to thoroughly enjoy the wedding dinner and reception. Later on that afternoon I saw David squeeze his left shoulder precisely the way he had done earlier, his face beaming.

There's no magic or mystery here; this was just a variation of associative anchoring Tony Robbins regularly practices to keep his creative, upbeat juices flowing. It will work on anyone who can practice what David did, and that is just about everybody, including cancer patients.

As for me, when I had to prepare for my prostate cancer surgery and after it was over, I tapped my heart with my index finger. Initially I did this while consciously recalling a very pleasurable time I had experienced long before the surgery. Eventually, just this motion alone helped me radically reduce my anxiety. If you'd like to develop such skills yourself, see *ConquerProstateCancer.com*.

Each of these approaches induces a stress-free response. Without a doubt, developing this capacity helped me prepare for my prostate surgery and do well during in the weeks and months that followed. Frankly I myself was astonished that what I learned fourteen years earlier at the Tony Robbins' weekend conference was still so effective for me. This is no doubt a tribute to his highly effective, mesmerizing teaching style. Ultimately this capability enabled me and most of the others at the long weekend gathering, to walk over hot coals painlessly, literally "walking the fire."

6

How to Visualize
and Relax
Before Surgery

"Aging is an issue of mind over matter
If you don't mind, it doesn't matter."
—Mark Twain, 19th Century American author

Mind over Matter: Is Pain Subjective or Objective?

The mind-body connection is reflected in Mark Twain's statement that "aging is an issue of mind over matter." What this means to me is that aging is largely subjective, since in many ways you are only as old as you feel.

Aging is also relative. That's what Supreme Court Justice Louis Brandeis meant when allegedly stating that, "To be old is to be fifteen years more than I am."

Of course there is a real physical aspect to aging. Of the various gerontological theories about why and how we age physically, I subscribe to the idea that aging is primarily the result of wear-and-tear. As the years go by, our bodies eventually wear down, making us more vulnerable to disease and death.

Similarly pain and stress are real, as measured by observable changes in brain waves when cancer patients react to various aches and pains that plague them. One of my friends, an experienced anesthesiologist in the Boston area, once informed me that Jewish boys' brain waves change momentarily as soon as their foreskins are ritually removed on the eighth day after birth. In his view this demonstrates that the rite of circumcision may be a powerful way to initiate a male infant as a member of Abraham's covenantal people, but it is an objectively painful moment for the young boy. This is so even if the *mohel* or ritual circumciser reassures parents that their newborn kid won't feel a thing. For this reason there are those who insist that ritual circumcision is barbaric, a view which I, as a rabbi, disavow.

Pain, like aging, is also not merely objective but is subjective and relative. That's why nurses and doctors often ask patients, "On a scale of one to ten (with ten being the worst), how much pain do you feel?" This is the nature of the subjective/objective relative pain continuum, measured by the Wong-Baker Pain Rating Scale and used at many hospitals. This allows patients to pinpoint whether they have no pain, moderate pain or extreme pain. Unfortunately the same scale has not been used to measure patients' stress levels.

Pain and stress are relative for a simple reason: when somebody says they hurt, you can always ask them how much, compared to how they felt before an operation or procedure, or compared to others who went through the same procedure. This is how I see it, not just as a rabbi or gerontologist, but as a patient who's been hospitalized more than once. I am just one human being among the world's six and a half billion people, whose aging processes and pain and stress thresholds vary considerably.

> *Your pain threshold can be affected by what you believe.*

As someone with a spiritual orientation, I am also convinced that your pain threshold can be affected by what you believe. If you believe you are still vigorous and pain- or stress-free, the power of your convictions can alleviate your symptoms. By the same token, if you believe that things are not going to work in your favor due to your age, pain or stress, there's a greater chance they won't. These self-fulfilling prophecies lead us to the "Relaxation Response," which merits some elaboration.

The Relaxation Response and You

The idea of "mind over matter" is not new. However, it has been formalized in contemporary terms by Dr. Herbert Benson, a pioneer in researching the mind/body connection through meditation and visualization for stress-reduction, pain-relief and healing.

I first heard of Dr. Benson and the Relaxation Response in the late 1980s, a few years after I began to serve my Boston-area congregation. At that time, one of his relatives, a former congregant, used to say with understandable pride, "Rabbi, you should invite Herb to lecture at our synagogue; he's world-famous!" As it turned out Dr. Benson is world-famous, so when he invited various Boston-area clergy, including me, to a conference at Harvard's Mind/ Body Medical Institute, I did not hesitate to attend. Years later I was to meet him again when he spoke at a Jewish Community Center.

Dr. Benson coined the phrase "Relaxation Response", explored in several of the books he wrote between 1975 and 2000. When meeting with me and other clergy, he illustrated how the Relaxation Response can easily be applied to reduce stress and pain. He asked us to visualize the well-known phrase in Psalm 23: "Yea, though I walk through the Valley of Death, I shall fear no evil for Thou art with me." As I recall, he told us to use our imaginations to "walk" through a very dark place, and emerge on the other side to bask in the light of God. Within minutes we moved viscerally from the personal pain of intense loss to the feeling of overwhelming well-being.

A trained cardiologist at Harvard Medical School in Cambridge, Massachusetts, Dr. Benson is now an Associate Professor there. But even as a medical intern, he sensed that you must consider a patient's mind and belief system when assessing his or her body. Through the power of belief, whether secular (as in "believing in yourself") or religious (as in "relating to God"), he asserted one could achieve a Relaxation Response.

In his second book, *Beyond the Relaxation Response,* Dr. Benson defined the Relaxation Response as the inherent ability to enter a special state of mind. The net effect is that you'll lower or slow down your heart rate, breathing, blood pressure and brain waves and metabolic speed. This offsets "the harmful effects and uncomfortable feelings of stress." Such easing of tension could often be triggered just by uttering certain words or phrases or by visualizing some relaxing scene.

In his book, *Timeless Healing: The Power of Belief,* Dr. Benson notes that the relaxation response occurs when "a bodily calm that all of us can evoke has the opposite effect of the well-known fight-or-flight response." Social anthropologists have long observed how, when faced with the potential loss of life or other stressful events, people usually resist or retreat, hence, "fight or flight." The Relaxation Response offers a third way for dealing with an enemy or crisis.

Even when there is no actual danger, but you perceive your life is in danger, you may choose to flee or fight. Dr. Benson recalled the movie *Lawrence of Arabia* and the effect it had on viewers when it first appeared in 1962. While watching the movie, many in the audience felt compelled to visit the concession stand in order to quench their thirst. When I saw the film, I too observed that some of the people who sat near me in the theater kept going out to the lobby and back to their seats again, paper cups in hand. As Dr. Benson noted, they did this despite watching the film in air-conditioned comfort. Obviously what stimulated their need for a cold beverage was that they projected themselves into the cinematic Arabian Desert, feeling exposed to its brightness and heat. In other words, their perception, not their reality, made them thirsty!

By the same token, I'm convinced that those who believe surgery will put them at high risk will have greater anxiety. Those who don't dwell on surgery's inherent dangers will be less stressed. I contend that such stress, while understandable, can be reduced or set aside, if a patient properly prepares for surgery.

If you prepare for surgery you are more likely to have the self-assurance needed to face an operation calmly and recover more quickly. This is something Dr. Benson addresses in two articles on surgery and the Relaxation Response. Both articles demonstrate that patients who were asked to elicit a Relaxation Response for about twenty minutes a day before surgery reported decreased psychological tension compared to other patients who were just given information.[1]

Relax and Heal

Two weeks before my surgery I read Peggy Huddleston's book, *Prepare for Surgery, Heal Faster*, subtitled *A Guide of Mind-Body Techniques*.[2] I also listened to her *Relaxation* CD. The book and CD focuses on helping patients face surgery by achieving a state of relaxation. Pre-op patients are encouraged to read her book, which only takes two hours, and to listen to her CD twice a day for several weeks before surgery. Others continue listening to her guided visualizations both before and during surgery. Her tranquil voice helps calm those who need to relax because of the pain or stress they anticipate or may actually experience. It certainly did this for me, even though I was only able to spend a couple of weeks, rather than the longer recommended period, listening to her recorded visualization/meditation. Her book and CD are effective for a variety of surgeries and have been recommended at leading hospitals across the United States.[3]

Essentially the book and CD enabled me to reignite the meditation and visualization skills I had developed over the last few decades. Those skills were not only a product of my interactions at the Tony Robbins' "Fire Walk" conference; they also emerged from my experiences for over five years as a facilitator of my last synagogue's monthly spirituality group.

Its primary leader, Dr. Harvey Zarren, specializes in alternative medicine. He has also become a nutritional expert on a quest to prevent childhood obesity and subsequent heart disease. As it happens, he and Peggy Huddleston were also acquainted with each other. Long before I encountered Peggy's work, I had grown to appreciate the visualization and relaxation methods they both utilized, since these were regular features of the spirituality group meetings.

Peggy Huddleston developed five steps to prepare for surgery and reduce pain and stress. They are: 1) relax to feel peaceful; 2) visualize your healing; 3) organize a support group; 4) use healing statements; and 5) meet your surgical team in advance, especially your anesthesiologist, whose job is to reduce or eliminate your pain.

I followed her advice closely. I used her CD well in advance of surgery and later on during the precise moment the surgeon directed me to lie on the operating table. I imagined my body filling with light. I visualized recovering quickly after the surgery and getting back on my feet the same day. I even "saw" myself getting back to my regular routines within a week of surgery, which in fact would happen to a large extent.

I also contacted my colleagues at the Rabbinical Assembly, an international association of Conservative rabbis to which I belong, asking that they post a prayer for my complete healing online and in our printed international newsletter. I also informed various people in at least three different congregations of my forthcoming surgery, with a request that they pray for my quick recovery as my surgery began. I did the same with individual family members and friends.

Some people actually volunteered to pray for my recovery without being asked! This reminded me of an anecdote about a rabbi who was visited in the hospital by his synagogue president while the rabbi recuperated after a heart attack. The president, speaking in an appropriately soft, reverent tone, told his rabbi, "I'm pleased to tell you that while you were in the hospital the temple Board took a vote. They decided 18 to 9 in favor of your having a speedy recovery!"

I heard many encouraging words from congregants, colleagues, friends and family, by phone or e-mail, both before and after my prostate cancer surgery. Their thoughts reassured me that many people really cared and were actually praying for me. The individual whose book I helped edit in the weeks leading up to my surgery, actually went out of her way to her hospital chapel to pray for my recovery. She got to her chapel at 7:30 a.m. on April 12, 2007, just as my surgery was about to begin. I learned about her prayerful activities after I sent her an e-mail following my hospital discharge. Here's how she responded:

> *Hi, Ed!*
>
> *What a surprise to hear from you just days after your surgery. As promised, I went to Chapel last Thursday morning, April 12th, as your surgery started, and focused on you. Oh, the power of prayer! You have made my day! You were so prepared for surgery and thus you are healing faster. Bless you my friend!*
>
> *—Jane Gavin-Sparacio*

Prior to my surgery I recall using some healing statements suggested by Peggy Huddleston at the end of her book. Minutes before the operation began, I handed her book page called *Healing Statements for Surgery* to my main surgeon, Dr. Robert Carey, and to my anesthesiologist. On that page I had a written request for both doctors to utter encouraging words to me toward the end of my surgery, when I would remain unconscious. These thoughts included sentiments like, "Ed, you're doing great; your operation has gone very well."[4]

Simply getting the doctors' consent to recite these affirmative thoughts aloud had a calming effect on me. Later, during the actual surgery, I could only trust that I might hear their utterances at some level, and that this would permeate my mind. This reassured me further that I would be fine after their work was done.

An hour before the operation, I remembered that one of Peggy Huddleston's Healing Statements invited patients to write down what they wanted to eat after surgery. I simply stipulated, "I would like a glass of water and some toast when I wake up." After I was brought back to my hospital room hours later, the food service personnel came by to ask me what I would like for dinner. Without hesitating I immediately asked for water and toast! Minutes later I slowly drank the water and easily ate the soft buttered toast without any ill effects. This was quite surprising, considering that I had a tracheal tube down my throat to help me breathe during the entire three-hour-plus operation. Ordinarily you might think that would make it hard for me to swallow, but that was not the case.

Above all, I followed Peggy Huddleston's guidance in advance of my surgery by imagining myself healing quickly with a minimum of pain medication, yet without pain or stress. Lo and behold, by following these steps I was out of the hospital and back home the next afternoon, thirty-five hours after my surgery. I accomplished this quite readily, despite some bladder issues that complicated my prostate surgery.

Even my appearance immediately after the surgery seemed remarkably relaxed and alert, as I was wheeled from the recovery room to the hospital room for my one-night stay. I know I looked relatively good, because later on I saw a photo my daughter had taken of me on her cell phone camera. Subsequently my appearance was a cause for worry, but on the whole I was fine.

Peggy Huddleston points out that "85% of all medical problems are caused by stress. Stress-related symptoms range from tension headaches and migraines to lower-back pain, insomnia and hypertension," which "diminish the activity of your immune system—your body's natural defense system against illness."[5] Knowing this was true, I followed her instructions to "believe your treatment is a healing agent by making it your friend, seeing it as a potent healing ally, and imagining it as sweeping your body clean."[6]

Taking these steps in preparation for my surgery, I was able to reduce my stress through relaxation. Rather than resist (fight) or try to escape my surgical situation (flight), I faced it head on and sailed through surgery with flying colors. I went through the trauma of my radical prostatectomy with virtually no pain or stress. Without a doubt, through the guided mind-body and support techniques I utilized, I healed far faster than others who went through prostate cancer surgery, whether robotic or a standard procedure.

These observations are augmented by additional pain control tips at *www.ConquerProstateCancer.com.*

To be sure I felt the strain of stitches later on, and occasional fatigue continued to slow me down for nearly a week afterwards. It was also undeniable that general anesthesia during the operation eliminated any pain or stress, as I was blissfully out of it. I also took three post-op injections of strong pain medicine, and one Percocet, to stop pain in its tracks. Nonetheless I would need no other pain pills during my thirty-five hours in the hospital.

> *I was living proof of the power of the mind to overcome just about anything.*

Equally important, in the two days after I left the hospital, I felt no need to take all the Extra Tylenol pills I was given for potential pain. As a precaution I took a total of three doses over the next two days, but I totally discarded the Percocet that had been handed to me. By the third day I was only a bit uncomfortable but not in any pain whatsoever, so I stopped taking any pills. I had every confidence that I would remain pain-free—and that's exactly what happened.

Of course I benefited from having an excellent surgeon who applied cutting-edge robotic laparoscopy that is inherently less invasive than traditional prostate surgery. Even so, in fully preparing for my surgery, I was living proof of the power of the mind to overcome just about anything.

Yea, though I would walk through the Valley of Death, I would fear no harm … and it came to pass that I felt no pain or stress at all.

1

Going Under the Knife
Doesn't Have to Be Scary—
Robotic-Assisted Surgery
Revealed

"First do no harm!"
—Hippocrates, 5th Century B.C. Greek Physician

The Patient and Doctor as Teammates

"With a little help from your friends" became my mantra as I got ready for surgery. My careful preparation involved eliciting the support of my family, friends and the operating room staff. Such comprehensive support helped me envision a pain-free and stress-free healing process not just for a short duration but for the long-term.

By initiating these steps before, during and after surgery, I went from being a passive patient to becoming an active member of the surgical team. This is what Peggy Huddleston prescribes in her book *Preparing for Surgery, Heal Faster.* In a way the physician's oath, "First do no harm!" became my own vow. I was determined to do no harm to myself, physically, emotionally or spiritually.

The first good decision I made was selecting robotic surgery and a surgeon who gained my trust. I was fortunate I made this choice, as my wife underscored in a letter to some friends.

Ed decided to go the surgical route rather than use radiation to eliminate his prostate cancer. That decision most likely saved his life. Some of his other treatment choices might have easily missed the large median lobe and high pressure bladder which the surgeon was able to resolve robotically. Without surgery Ed might have been left a urologic cripple.

—Yvonne

> *You can participate actively in your recovery.*

When a patient actively participates in his surgery and its aftermath, another classic truth may apply: "Physician, heal thyself." However, this applies only if you're convinced you can participate actively in your recovery and you truly expect to be relatively pain-free and stress-free. It is not a matter of luck: it is a matter of will.

The message here is that you can conquer prostate cancer, especially if you take control of your destiny even when you're in medical territory that's foreign to you. You can pursue an active role even when you decide to go under the knife as a recipient of high-tech surgery's "cutting edge." As long as you and your surgical staff act as members of the same team, you'll avoid the prospect of viewing your doctors as helpful adversaries to whom you must passively submit. This outlook may help you achieve a better outcome, although there never are any guarantees.

The Surgery I Will Never Remember

Two days before my prostate surgery I followed the doctor's explicit instructions to eat only soft foods. The day before surgery, as instructed, I only drank liquids and clear jello, capping that off with a self-administered enema two hours before going to bed—and emptying my bowels. I've put this as delicately as possible, to spare the reader further details. Then I showered with the astringent liquid soap I was told would help avoid infections.

The day of the operation, I got up at 4:00 a.m. and took another shower as instructed, using the same antiseptic soap. Exactly an hour later I drove to the hospital, as my final act of independence, accompanied by my wife and our daughter. We got to the hospital at the pre-arranged time of 5:30 a.m.

By 6:00 a.m., I had totally disrobed and put on a hospital gown. Then a male nurse shaved my lower chest as well as my stomach and below in preparation for the surgery. Meanwhile a female nurse prepped two IVs on each of my forearms, for an infusion of glucose and the anesthesia mix that awaited me. The two nurses were upbeat, spoke in friendly tones, and explained each step of their procedures in advance. They did everything to ease my tension while making me comfortable. What they didn't know is that I was already quite comfortable and probably could have done without their reassuring professional manner—but it didn't hurt either!

At 7:30 a.m., I was wheeled into the operating room on a gurney. I knew that the moment of truth had arrived when we came to a double set of large metal doors. That's when two other nurses pulled my gurney into the operating theater with considerable haste, while putting on their surgical face masks. This was it: Showtime! I'm convinced that had I not prepared myself as described—and admittedly if a sedative I was given had not taken effect—I would have had an anxiety attack on the spot. Instead I felt totally blissful. I was able to put my mind elsewhere by focusing on one of my favorite things, our affectionate little dog, Misty, who had been a member of my family for sixteen years before her death. Focusing on a loving pet was also based on one of Peggy Huddleston's recommendations.

When a nurse assisted my transfer from the gurney to the operating table, I was not afraid at all. I was so "comfy" that I remembered an anecdote about an elderly hospital patient, who when asked by his nurse, "Are you comfortable?" answered, "Yes I'm comfortable. I make a very good living!" The truth is that I felt just great. By then my Relaxation Response was in full swing, with no thought of flight or fight.

After that, I remember absolutely nothing! It seemed that only seconds later I was transferred from another gurney to my hospital room bed, even though the operation took longer than the typical one-to-two hours needed for most robotic surgery—plus an additional two hours in the recovery room. Those six hours flashed by in a blink, without my being aware of anything. It was a surgery I will never remember.

While I remained unconscious during the surgical procedure, my wife Yvonne and our daughter Elana were alert as they sat with increasing agitation in the family room. They could hardly wait for the surgery to end, as Yvonne told me the next day. "The surgery took a lot longer than we had been told," she said, "and Elana and I were sweating buckets waiting for the surgeon to finish and come talk to us. Thank goodness our friends kept us supplied with Starbucks coffee and cookies. Forget healthy stuff: This was a time for comfort food!"

Because I was totally "out of it" during the operation, my primary surgeon, Dr. Robert Carey, has agreed to describe what transpired in those missing hours. At my request he refers to the technical side of what was done to remove my prostate and fix my bladder, and also describes his thoughts and emotions before and during the surgery. He wrote this clearly aware that the practice of medicine is both a science and an art. More importantly his thoughts were those of a caring human being with a mission to "do no harm."

◇◇◇

The Surgeon Fills in the Blanks, by Dr. Robert Carey

I love the sights and sounds of the operating room in the morning. Circulating nurses and surgical technicians carefully prepare each room for the procedure to be performed. Coordinators and supervisors ensure that all details and each surgeon's preferences are accounted for. Surgeons greet their patients and answer any final questions. Soon thereafter they can be seen at their individual scrub sinks in deep thought, a solitary pose reflective of the accountability each has as they enter their respective rooms.

Although I may have performed a surgical case hundreds of times before, each patient is unique, each new day an isolated impression of surgical skills and reputation. It is an honorable discipline. I have worked all of my life in preparation to be a part of this morning scene and it is a privilege that no surgeon can take lightly.

As I went through my morning routine, I knew that Rabbi Ed Weinsberg's surgery was going to be difficult. He was presented to me not only with prostate cancer, but also with severe lower urinary tract symptoms of urgency, frequency, and waking up multiple times each night to urinate. His prostate, three times larger than normal, was likely to have grossly distorted anatomy with a large median lobe intruding into his bladder and disrupting the shape and fibers of his bladder neck.

In addition to having documented bouts of prostatitis (prostate inflammation) in his history, he had previously and needlessly been given a shot of Lupron for androgen deprivation by another urologist, thus increasing the fibrosis and inflammation around his prostate. He had previously experienced not one, but two sets of prostate biopsies. I knew that his bladder would be thick-walled and under high pressure, thus making him at high risk for future continence problems.

> *It was up to me to give him renewed life, renewed vitality.*

I fully realized that the work ahead of me in the operating room required far more than a successful cancer operation. What was called for was a successful reconstructive operation to give my patient the best chance at a long-term satisfactory result. I wanted to be sure that once the operation was over, he would function as normally as possible in his day-to-day activities. In many ways his life was in my hands. It was up to me not only to give him renewed life, but renewed vitality for the long-term.

During my preoperative greeting and exchange of words with Rabbi Weinsberg, I was moved at the depth of his spirituality and stoicism. I remembered the long journey he had made from the time of his first negative biopsy two years earlier and his positive biopsy three months before today's surgery. I remembered the limited choices that his complex presentation afforded him and his unique risks.

He had prayer requests for me and for his anesthesiologist. As unusual as that seemed, we were more than happy to comply. While reciting affirmations during the surgery, as requested, I and the others assisting me became even more aware of the humanity of our patient and the risks he was prepared to take in our operating room. This intensified our resolve to uphold our professional oath to do him no harm. Beyond that we were more determined than ever to help bring him back good health with his functions intact.

Once Rabbi Weinsberg was sedated and wheeled into the operating room, the gurney where he lay was placed adjacent to the da Vinci robotic device. Then the attending anesthesiologist induced his general anesthesia. After that

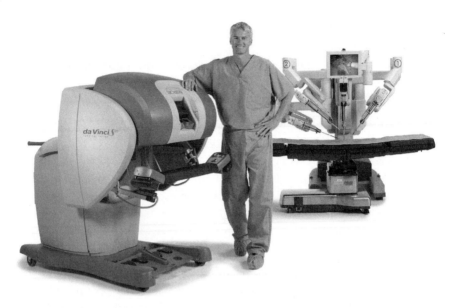

A surgeon stands next to the da Vinci console, where he will control the movements of the robotic device.
© 2008 Intuitive Surgical, reproduced with permission

I personally led the positioning of the patient. The circulating nurse prepared him for surgery as I scrubbed, gowned, and gloved. Each of the laparoscopic entry sites were made, and once all of the robotic trocars (portals of entry) were placed, the da Vinci S robot was docked without complication.

I sat down at the console's high definition monitor and attached the control sticks to my wrists and fingers before commencing the surgery. As I exposed my patient's prostate and associated tissue, I was struck by the amount of inflammation that was present. Upon opening his endopelvic fascia (layers of tissue in his pelvic region), I found the expected contraction fibrosis (adhesions) usually present after a man with a very large prostate has been given Lupron. The tissues had to be separated millimeter by millimeter to ensure a bloodless field. His large dorsal vein, the source of much bleeding in open procedures for prostatectomy, was tied off with suture twice as an extra precaution. The anterior urethral tissues were supported to his pubic arch to help assure his future continence.

When I opened the patient's anterior bladder neck, I found, as I had suspected, a large median lobe of the prostate protruding deeply into his bladder. There was asymmetry to the intrusion. As I went about incising his

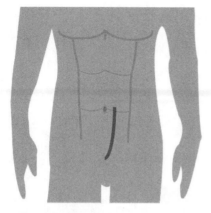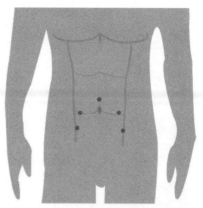

Open Prostatectomy Incision   *da Vinci* Prostatectomy Incisions

Five dime-sized incisions (four approx. ¼ inch and one approx. 1½ inches) are made in the patient's abdominal area instead of a single 4" to 7" vertical incision required for open surgery.
© 2008 Intuitive Surgical, reproduced with permission

bladder neck, I was careful to note and preserve each of his ureteral orifices, where each tube, the ureter, enters the bladder carrying urine downward from each kidney. I was careful to spare each muscle fiber that I could from the bladder neck.

As I continued my dissection posteriorly, I identified, dissected and ligated (tied) his bilateral vasa deferentia and seminal vesicles, which in his normal life would convey sperm from the testes to ejaculatory ducts and produce the majority of his ejaculatory fluid respectively. I then entered the space between his rectum and prostate and dissected this area from the base of the prostate at the bladder neck all the way to the apex.

This area was filled with inflammatory, fibrotic tissue usually seen in patients with a history of prostatitis or lupron injection. I then identified his neurovascular bundles and proceeded to meticulously separate each side from the posterolateral edge for the entire length of the prostate. The prostatic pedicles, containing the main artery and veins to the prostate, were ligated with clips and severed. The urethra was identified, dissected for maximal length and incised sharply. The prostate was then placed into a bag inside his body and the bag completely closed.

Each step had been harder than usual but, despite the fibrosis, was achieved according to plan. I then proceeded with a bladder neck reconstruction

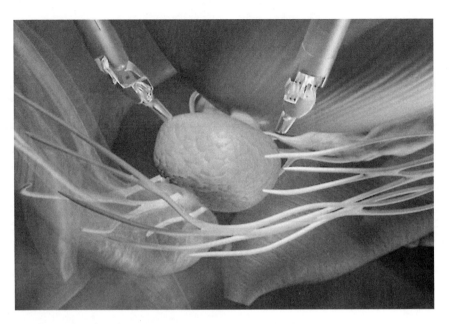

Two robotic arms prepare to extract a prostate.
© 2008 Intuitive Surgical, reproduced with permission

and tubularization, a surgical technique that I have always performed for patients with large prostates, whose bladder neck is distorted beyond an acceptable level. This required that the bladder neck, which had been invaded and disrupted for years, be reassembled in the shape of a funnel toward the urethra prior to making the final connection or "anastomosis." This proceeded well and at the completion of the procedure, the indwelling foley catheter was irrigated and aspirated in the bladder without any leakage of fluid.

At that point I undocked the robot and proceeded to remove his prostate through an extension of his camera port in the midline of his stomach area. Meanwhile I directed my associate to place a small drain on the patient's left side, adjacent to his anastomosis. All of his robotic ports were closed, and the anesthesiologist then began the process of bringing Rabbi Weinsberg out of anesthesia to awaken him safely. Once my patient had been transported safely to the recovery room and I knew that he was stable, I dictated the details of his case, gave the nurses post-operative orders, and proceeded to the family waiting room to speak to Yvonne, the rabbi's wife.

When a case is more than twice as difficult as normal, it is impossible to hide this fact from the family. As a surgeon, you simply express your sincere appreciation that the procedure had been accomplished without complication and that everything we wanted to achieve had been achieved: the cautery-free sparing of his neurovascular bundles, the successful bladder neck funneling, the urethral sparing, and the watertight anastomosis or reconstructed urethal connection. I conveyed to Mrs. Weinberg that even though her husband had lost twice as much blood (250 ml) as I usually see during a robotic prostatectomy, it was much less than is lost on average in an open prostatectomy and was nowhere near that which would require a transfusion.

As the rabbi lay in the recovery room, I also discussed his bladder neck reconstruction with his family. I described its advantages in terms of the likelihood it would assure an earlier return to continence and protection, as opposed to the long-term incontinence high-risk patients might ordinarily experience. I pointed out that he would have to keep his catheter in place much longer than normal for most robotic patients, to make sure his suture lines around the mold of his catheter would heal properly. I depicted his expected post-operative course and answered all questions. I reminded his family that the expected recovery period is a marathon, not a sprint.

My patient, who had entered the operating room that morning as Rabbi Edgar Weinsberg, would from that time forward instinctively become "Ed" to me. This would remain the case as we would work together to reach the post-operative milestones he desired, and achieve the good long-term outcome we both wanted for him. From the time of our first mutual interview, through the surgery and afterwards, we had bonded physically and in human terms. It was a doctor-patient bond, and a person-to-person human connection that could never be severed.

◇◇

A Surgical Patient's Afterthoughts

Before my surgery I had tried to inject a bit of added reality into my visualization exercises. I tried to envision the surgeon with his robotic machine gently cutting its way into my stomach. While I conjured up an indefinable red mass, I wasn't able to get into any detail, and maybe that was for the best. Seeing a film of another prostate cancer patient's robotic surgery might have been a bit daunting, although for some it could lead to an even quicker recovery. I'll never know since it was months after my operation that I checked out an internet video on robotic surgery.[1]

Many patients might feel acutely uncomfortable or even threatened if they previewed a documentary film or photos of a procedure they're about to go though. Hearing their doctor's verbal description before their surgery might be enough. However, seeing a photograph of a patient healing just weeks after surgery could have been helpful. I know it would have enhanced my ability to get beyond the operation itself. I'm no different than most people: for me a picture is worth a thousand words.

Naturally I prefer seeing the glory rather than the gory, since I'm hardly a masochist. However, it's my belief that you can speed up your healing process if you visualize going from an inert, incapacitated state back to full consciousness as you renew your life. This powerful image might help a number of patients quickly regain complete control of their bodily functions.

My thinking is based on the thought pattern I described about visiting my dentist. On those occasions I had to acknowledge my pain before muting it with the help of colorful, cooling images. I was then able to "walk" away from any pain without medication. Why can't it be that what's good for the teeth is good for the prostate?

> *"Meditation augments medication."*

I believe in the power of integrative medicine, which combines standard Western practices with alternative, complementary approaches. Hence the way I see it, meditation augments medication. I don't advocate visual reflection as a substitute for anesthesia during major surgery; however, a well-honed ability to foresee recovering well can help a patient make it through. It might enable his doctors administer only a minimal amount of pre-op sedatives or post-op pain medication to keep him calm and comfortable.

Developing such mind and heart power will not only help bolster your confidence that you will bounce back to full health. It may actually enhance your resilience and strengthen your resolve to get up and going again.

For exercises to help you hone these skills, see *www.ConquerProstate Cancer.com*.

Home, Sweet Home—Recovering from Post-Surgical Stress

*"To fully heal, one must release the memory of
pain from body, mind and soul."*
—Anonymous

Why "No Pain, No Gain" Makes No Sense

Looking back it seems incredible that I began to write a rough draft of this chapter in July 2007, only three months after my surgery, having spent the previous months writing chapters 1 through 7 at top speed. What motivated me was my need to convey the message that like me, you too can clear your body of immobilizing pain and stress before and after surgery. I'm convinced you can do so by applying the various insights and techniques I've already offered and those I have yet to present. Perhaps you'll eventually develop your own effective techniques which you can then share with the rest of us.

Although I've noted numerous approaches to release tension, that doesn't mean I've managed to completely get away from the day-to-day stresses most people face. For instance, like most loving couples who have been married for many years, my wife and I still had our occasional spats, usually based on some miscommunication. Our family tensions intensified due to my reduced libido primarily because of the Lupron I was given before surgery.

Pain and stress are major concerns of most hospitals. Just before leaving Sarasota Memorial Hospital the day after my prostate cancer surgery, I finally noticed my hospital unit's memo about pain regulation. I was particularly impressed by the insistence that, "We make every effort to ensure that you or your loved one's pain is made tolerable. Occasionally for various reasons, this may not be possible, but please be assured that we are trying. Your comfort is extremely important to us."

I read that memo after my head was clear of the anesthesia administered a day earlier. I no longer had any pain symptoms. Apart from my doctor and my visualization exercises, the hospital ward staff gets a lot of the credit for making me pain-free. My nurses were so reassuring that it helped minimize my stress too.

So I was surprised when I read page two of the Patient Discharge Instructions, typed in bold font: **"CALL YOUR PHYSICIAN IF YOU DO NOT GET RELIEF FROM THE PAIN MEDICATIONS PRESCRIBED, OR IF THE INTENSITY OF PAIN INCREASES, OR IF PAIN IS INTERFERING WITH ACTIVITY OR REST."**

At first I didn't know whose pain this notice addressed. Certainly not mine since I didn't have any pain! I was informed much later that the reason for this warning is that if there were to be a hemorrhage or problem with an internal collection, it could show up as increased pain.

To be sure, the surgery immediately resulted in anticipated short-term side effects like impotence and incontinence. It also produced sporadic fatigue that lasted for nearly two weeks. Besides this I became acutely aware of a raw feeling where the prostate had once been, especially after sitting down for prolonged periods of time.

My fatigue, which generally popped up in the early afternoon, was easily resolved. I simply lay down for a couple of hours and slept it off! The rawness between my legs was another matter, but I was able to mostly ignore it as I healed. I was so inspired by the painless outcome of the surgery that less than a week later I felt compelled to write this book about my robotic experiences, from an informed patient's perspective. I was raring to go and couldn't be stopped.

As noted previously, the spot where my prostate had been removed felt increasingly tender after I sat at my computer for hours on end (pun unintended). I did only one thing to counteract this: I asked my wife to go to a nearby medical supply store to buy a cloth and foam "donut." That spongy blue pillow with a large, round hole helped me sit in relative comfort on my big leather chair as I typed away. I was able to forge on, bolstered not just by my soft chair and pillow but by my enthusiasm.

Because physical pain was not an issue after my operation, I wrote my friend and fellow-author, Jane Gavin-Sparacio, two weeks after my surgery:

April 25, 2007

Dear Jane,

The good news is that today I walked two blocks (slowly) because I was getting a bit sore and quite depressed. Now I'm in better spirits, especially because of your good wishes. Let's stay in touch!

—Ed

Jane's response was reassuring:

Hi, Ed!

Great minds run on the same track. I was just sitting here thinking about you while I worked on my book! Don't' worry about the depression. This often occurs after any surgery. Just think, ten years ago there was no such a thing as robotic surgery for prostate cancer. How blessed we are to live in 2007!

Positively,
Jane

What my friendly correspondent got right was that I needed some cheering up. However, my depression was not about any soreness that came from the surgery—there was no soreness from that source other than from sitting at length at my computer. What I was depressed about was my inability to move at a faster clip, due to my peripheral neuropathy that affected the soles of my feet—which, as in the two years before my surgery, continued to feel like pins and needles with some burning. That ongoing condition and some short-term bladder concerns were at the root of my depression.

My gait was even slower due to bladder complications discovered during surgery. Once the surgery ended, the doctor insisted that I should wear my catheter bag for eighteen days before getting it removed. Now I'll elaborate on how I quickly managed to overcome any incontinence with the aid of biofeedback once the catheter was removed.

The First Eighteen Days after Surgery

I'm an exception to a rule, and this time I don't say that with pride. Generally, when recovering from robotic-assisted or open surgery, a robotic surgery patient needs to use a catheter bag for about four to seven days, but rarely for an extra week beyond that. The catheter, with its narrow plastic tube placed into the urethra, allows urine to drain directly from the bladder into an attached leg bag, which is periodically emptied. This is needed until a patient regains muscular control over his bladder and resumes his full urinary functions. Virtually all surgical patients, robotic or standard, become incontinent until the bag is removed, usually a week or two later, and about five percent remain incontinent. For most patients, then, this is more of a temporary inconvenience than a major source of stress, although at times it can be pretty dicey.

When the doctor told me I'd have to wear a catheter bag after surgery, not for a week or less but for eighteen days, I uttered an audible "Oy"! I was fortunate that he didn't tell me to wait out the entire month until he would remove the catheter.

The reason for the eighteen days, he reminded me, was that I had been subjected to both prostate and bladder neck surgery. Wearing a catheter and leg bag was a precaution that made it possible for me to heal and "hold it in" better. Most patients can gain self-control in about a week, but my case was not typical. Was I upset or stressed out when I learned about this? Not at all! Instead I marveled that a doctor like Dr. Carey could do a double round of major surgery while remaining seated at his console. To me this was a credit to the pliability of both the man and his machine.

"Of course," said Dr. Carey, "Greyer hairs than mine would insist on your wearing a catheter for at least three to four weeks after the way things worked out, but I am of a different mind." In other words, as a contemporary, "new school" doc, he was more willing to count on my youthful energy, even at age 63, to hasten my healing process. As it turned out, he was right. Besides, his reassurance eased my mind and helped me keep on going.

It's important to note that the catheter, known as a "foley catheter," was inserted in my urethra while I was still blissfully "out of it" during my operation. As such it was never a source of pain or stress from the get-go until it was finally removed on April 30th. To be truthful, though, I did count the days as they passed, one by one. To have a five inch plastic tube traveling down my urethra through my penis into a plastic tube and bag attached to the outside of my leg was not a hardship, but it was definitely not a pleasure.

Perhaps I should say "bags," since before I left the hospital, a nurse had to instruct my wife and me how to attach my catheter tube to a large bag at night and a smaller "walking bag" during the day. It looked something like the illustration below.

Frankly I was surprised that I was given no advanced notice before my surgery about having to wear this bag. Of course it's possible that either I wasn't listening or it slipped my mind. No wonder, given all the other issues I had to absorb at that time. The upshot was that I didn't take the opportunity before my surgery to visualize getting through this phase of my post-op experience. I would have preferred to visualize myself working toward full recovery and independence without suddenly finding I would be a continual "drip"! Had I been clearer about this earlier, I would have been better prepared mentally and physically. On the other hand it was nice not to worry about

running to the "pot" several times a day. My pre-op days of doing so due to prostatitis and an enlarged prostate were over.

I can only thank my wife (again) for helping me retain the necessary information the nurse gave us about changing and cleaning the catheter bags. I owed my wife big time. If there was ever an indication that a wife loved her husband, it had to be this: each morning and night during those first eighteen days at home, my wife washed out my interchangeable catheter bags with white vinegar. That's not only love but fortitude!

The day after I got home I was allowed to shower every evening, while wearing the walking bag. Then I dried the outside of the bag thoroughly, emptied it, put it in a basin for cleaning, and replaced it with the larger nighttime bag which my wife had already rendered germ-free.

Man wearing a foley catheter walking bag.
Drawing courtesy of Sarasota Memorial Hospital.
Photo Credit: Herb Paynter

If you ever need to wear a catheter bag, perhaps you can learn from a series of mistakes I made during that phase of my recovery. For instance, when bearing down as I sat on the toilet, I noticed that sometimes drops of urine would seep directly into the toilet bowl instead of traveling through the catheter tube into the bag. I asked the doctor if this was good or bad, and he told me it was perfectly normal. What I didn't tell him is that I bore down deliberately because I felt this would actually reactivate my sphincter muscles sooner, enabling me to "keep it in"! It turned out that my assumption was incorrect and could have been potentially harmful. Nobody should exert themselves that way during the week after surgery. With the bladder walls still exceptionally weak this could be hazardous for your health!

I made a few other mistakes that are worth noting if you are headed for surgery that requires you to wear a catheter bag afterwards. I know a lot of people are squeamish about important, yet delicate matters like this, but bear with me. Here's what I learned after-the-fact about what patients need to know and do:

- After you empty the catheter bag, don't forget to close the bottom of the bag before walking off.
- Don't risk infection by forgetting to use special disinfectant soap when showering daily. Use two washcloths, one for your "private parts" and another for the rest of your body.
- Don't forget to watch your watch, and empty the catheter bag before its four hour capacity ends.
- Wash the vinyl plastic leg bags inside and out, morning and night, with a cleaning formula of a half-cup of vinegar to two cups of water.
- Don't push too hard when excreting. This is especially tough on you if you have a weak stomach or hemorrhoids.
- Only lift things that are less than five to ten pounds, until you're really ready for something heavier.
- Don't distance yourself from others because you're embarrassed due to wearing a catheter.
- In short, if you ever need a catheter bag, don't follow my example! If you repeat my errors you may well cause needless, self-imposed stress.

On the eighteenth day, the doctor finally removed the catheter. To borrow an old phrase, he saw I was able to "piss in his pot" and easily stop on demand. At that point he acknowledged I had successfully regained complete bladder control. I needed only eighteen days after surgery to get back to normal, although I still feel I could have done this sooner.

Once I was catheter-free, I was more comfortable. But even then I made other mistakes which I advise others to avoid. First of all I didn't get enough exercise for general physical reconditioning. More importantly I didn't immediately start doing Kegel sphincter contraction exercises, to strengthen the pelvic floor muscles that help maintain continence.

Continence Again: Biofeedback Does the Trick

In the months after my catheter was removed, I cannot claim that I experienced total bladder control. I soon detected a new pattern: my capacity for holding off going to the bathroom was exactly four hours, day or night. If I sat at the computer while working on this book, it was inevitable that by the fourth hour, I had to go. If I slept four hours, I had to go. And if asleep, I "went" in my shorts only to discover my mishap the next morning. In subsequent weeks, when I felt the pressure I would wake up after four hours, knowing beyond any doubt that I simply couldn't hold it in anymore At that point I would run to the toilet and make it just in time—usually.

> *We human beings can't seem to shake off our instinctive needs any more than Pavlov's dogs!*

Later a second pattern emerged. About two months after the surgery, except for some light dribbling (and I don't mean basketball), I was able to "keep it in" until I got to the bathroom. But as soon as I saw the toilet I occasionally began to "take a leak" before meaning to do so. I guess it was that old stimulus-response thing again. We human beings can't seem to shake off our instinctive needs any more than Pavlov's dogs! In my case, not only seeing the toilet but anticipating the sound of it flushing (like a bell) made me "go" before I intended to.

Some of my acquaintances who had prostate cancer surgery used adult diapers. I could have done that, but I chose not to. This was not because I was embarrassed, but because I did not want to habituate myself to urinating in my pants at any moment of the day. When I mentioned this to Dr. Carey, he approved, since he felt it would help me regulate myself more quickly. Still,

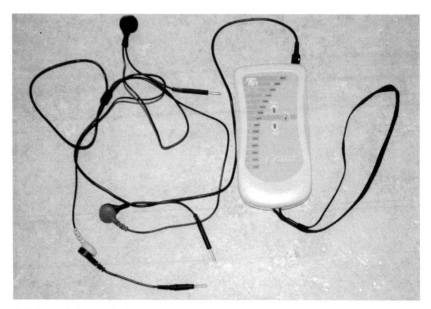

A U-Control electronic handheld biofeedback device. The electrode lead wires are connected to the perineum—the area behind the scrotum. The pain-free device reinforces Kegel exercises that strengthen the pelvic floor muscles. This can reduce and prevent incontinence while enhancing potency.
Photo credit: Herb Poynter
© 2008 Thought Technology (Montreal, Canada), reproduced with permission

my occasional mishaps bothered me enough that I consulted with the doctor again and asked him, "Do you think I'm a candidate for biofeedback?" His response was that it couldn't hurt.

Earlier in this book I referred to biofeedback as one of many examples of technical progress for prostate cancer patients. In my experience using biofeedback is one of many stress-busters that can help a patient regain control over his bodily functions. After speaking to Dr. Carey I conferred with one of my other specialists, a physiatrist. He in turn referred me to a local physical therapist named Pablo, who specializes in biofeedback at Excel Rehabilitation in Sarasota, which he co-owns with his wife Anna.

As directed by Pablo, I lay down on a soft cushioned table. Pablo placed some conductive electrodes midway between my rectum and scrotum, with a wire attached to a small hand-held device, called "U-Control." In the middle of this device, which resembled a TV remote, was an LED which lit up every five seconds. After seeing an amber light blink twice, I was to squeeze my buttocks together and upwards, as if withholding a bowel movement or urination. A set of ten lights on the "U-Control" would light up as I squeezed. The harder I pressed, the more likely it would be that I would reach a light at the top of the meter illustrated above. Five additional lights indicated the level of difficulty I could achieve.

With repeated use, biofeedback would train me to gain more self-control over my functions, supplemented by special home exercises. Specifically biofeedback would help me become aware of my pelvic floor muscles while strengthening them. By both feeling and seeing this action, I would become attuned to the so-called "Kegel response" needed to hold urine in. All this would take place in four sessions held two days a week, for twenty to thirty minutes per session.

How well did I do? Here's what happened to the best of my recollection:

Session One: Pablo, my physical therapist, set the resistance to Level 3. I contracted my pelvic muscles when the amber light in the center of the biofeedback hand-held device lit up. Each time (a duration of about ten seconds), I got to 8 or 9 out of 10. The session ended thirty minutes later.

Session Two: Pablo set the resistance to Level 3 again. I pushed my backside together when the amber light lit up. I couldn't get past 5. Talk about going backwards! The session ended thirty minutes later. Pablo said either I forgot the Kegel method or his machine needed a new battery! I should go home and practice doing up-and-down squats against the wall, to strengthen my mid-section. Better yet I should do the Kegel exercise while standing. This is technically known as a pelvic floor contraction, devised sixty years ago by Dr. Arnold Kegel.[1]

Pablo told me I could also do some "bridge" exercises, by lying on my back and then arching my pelvic area for a few seconds. He ended the session with the well-worn phrase we all abhor: "If you want to improve, you have to do your homework every day. See you next week." I wasn't home-free yet; not by a long shot! (Pablo's other comments can be found at *www. ConquerProstateCancer.com.*)

Session Three: Pablo set the resistance to Level 3, once more. I managed to do the Kegel exercises better.

Session Four: Pablo set the resistance to Level 4 and then Level 5. I got to 8 and then 9 in both cases. At long last I finally knew I'd become a "regular" guy once again!

Best of all, these four sessions weren't the least bit embarrassing. I point this out since it might have been otherwise, had I gone to the computerized biofeedback unit at the local hospital. There, instead of placing a wire on my perineum, the skin's surface behind my scrotum, female technicians would place a wire directly in my rectum. I suppose some men don't mind if a professionally trained woman places something in their rears. Many men really don't care, much as the stereotypical older gents who like pretty young "things" to administer their enemas. But I admit I'm a bit staid and uncomfortable about such matters despite female technicians' total professionalism. At any rate, once I finished handheld biofeedback with Pablo's guidance, I realized that the best part is that it didn't humiliate or hurt me at all. Most importantly, once biofeedback helped me train myself, I was able to "hold it in." By eliminating all incontinence, I felt I had conquered a major side effect of prostate cancer treatment. At last I felt like a new man!

Part III:

CONQUER PROSTATE CANCER THROUGH SEX AND FAITH

9

Sex Again,
When You're Up for It,
Part I

"Your marriage is in trouble if your wife says,
'You're only interested in one thing'—
and you can't remember what it was."
—Milton Berle, 20th century comedian
and TV personality

New Views about Sex

I do not claim mine is a perfect marriage. Like any other couple, my wife and I have our ups and downs. Perhaps, though, our determination to keep "our boat afloat" is what makes our marriage strong and enduring. Equally important, we are determined to keep open our lines of communication. As a result, despite my illness and Yvonne's health issues, we remain unconditional friends and lovers. That is the way it is and should be, no matter how often either of us can be a "pain in the butt."

If you've been married for a decade or two or three or more, you can understand why for us every anniversary is not just another day; it's an accomplishment! Sure every anniversary is a blessing, but it's also a time to pause and wonder, "What new challenges will we have to face next? What new adjustments will we have to make to keep this relationship going?"

The way we were—prior to our 34th anniversary, September 3, 2006, less than five months before learning about the prostate cancer.
Photo credit: Herb Goldberg

You simply never know what lies ahead, even though you are determined to face it together.

We live in an era where sexual mores are constantly changing, due to increasing openness about such matters. I believe that in many instances these changes are positive. You could argue certain behaviors are too open, and that all too often people are overly confrontational, publicly airing things that are better left private. However, many people I know, at various life stages, appear to interact in a more upfront, open manner.

Newspaper advice columns challenge husbands and wives to communicate more directly about their individual needs, generally and sexually. Influential books like *Men are from Mars, Women are from Venus,* by former monk John Gray, demonstrate that openness about sexual concerns is the best policy. Television sit-coms and dramas increasingly reflect the trend that people are willing to articulate their innermost concerns. From my point of view it is a good thing when individuals communicate their intimate thoughts with refreshing honesty, as long as they remain considerate of each other's feelings.

Many husbands and wives, as well as unmarried companions, lead sexually healthy lives. Such people manage to openly verbalize what they want from each other. In my mind this can reduce family stress. It certainly beats allowing your spouse to feel ignored and unwanted. It almost seems as if two fundamentally opposite symbols—the marriage counselor's couch and the divorce attorney's conference room table—have conspired together: either explicitly negotiate your circumstances to get what you need out of your relationship, or reconsider whether you have a future together. This is the new marriage contract.

When a spouse has an illness like prostate cancer or breast cancer, it's even more vital for a couple to be as open with each other as much as possible. It makes a big difference if they communicate their needs and wants clearly and unambiguously. If they can't resolve their issues on their own, due to complications from stressful illnesses, they should consider professional intervention in order to get through the rough spots. I'm in favor of taking any step that

> *Marriage is a merger between two people.*

leads two consenting adults to be increasingly open with each other about private matters. When two people have taken the time to develop a long-term marital commitment, that's the least they can do for each other.

Prostate surgery and its side-effects can threaten the stability of your most personal relationship, due to potential incontinence and impotence. At such times it helps to reassess fundamentals. To paraphrase Alfie, a popular film and song from the 1960s, we need to ask core questions about marriage like, "What's it all about?"

Marriage is a merger between two people. Each member of a marriage has agreed to accept compromise for the sake of maintaining and enriching themselves and their relationship. Benefits of such a merger include physical nourishment, emotional support, and sexual stroking. Without question there are various economic and psychological components, some implicit and others explicit and contractual, but all very real. As I once told a couple under the *huppah,* or wedding canopy, "Marriage is no mirage!"

Marriage can become a dependent or co-dependent relationship, where you can't be you without the other. Ideally, marriage evolves into an inter-dependent rapport between two individuals, where neither loses his or her individual identity. That's the case even though being part of a couple is the foundation of the family unit, which in turn is widely regarded as the basic unit of society. Even when people remain single, the centrality of the family is a view shared by anthropologists and religious authorities alike.

Where mutual openness is accepted and implemented, marriages tend to remain healthy; otherwise a marriage is not likely to last or remain viable. This is particularly so if you and your partner avoid ongoing communication and explicit but friendly give-and-take. In such a scenario, even good sex is not likely to help prevent a marriage from deteriorating or dissolving.

My wife and I own a delicate three-square inch cameo which depicts a man and woman sitting next to each other, literally joined at the hip, as they turn to embrace. To the left of this picture are the words, "Not only do I love you, but you're my best friend." More than just romance, the cameo illustrates how physical intimacy fosters a couple's connection and camaraderie.

Portrait of Love and Friendship

Despite our infirmities, Yvonne and I have sustained and nurtured our love and friendship ever since we got married. To illustrate this, here's an entry from a "Love Journal" I've begun keeping ever since my robotic surgery.

◇◇

Love Journal: September 3, 2007

It's just over four and a half months after the prostate surgery and it's our 35th anniversary today. Hard to believe that Yvonne and I are nearly 62 and a bit more than 63 years young, respectively, and have spent over half our lifetimes together!

We went out last night to an early dinner with our son and his wife, now in their early thirties, whose seventh anniversary coincides with ours. Today we're lying low, since I was hospitalized this past week for three days due to Sudden Hearing Loss Syndrome and am "buzzing" with an unpleasant Prednisone "high." Besides, Yvonne is getting ready for major back surgery three days hence.

For all that, we're in pretty good shape for the shapes we're in. She still looks slim and sexy in her tight-fitting red sun-skirt with Garfield the cat emblazoned on the front. It's as short and tight as the light brown suede micro-mini skirt she was wearing when we first met in October 1971 at a Manhattan family social work agency, where I was trained in pastoral counseling. Still looking goo-ood, Yvonne!

At 6 feet tall, I don't mind saying that I'm also a pretty decent physical specimen. The pot belly that used to peek over my belt has all but disappeared as of two years ago, when I realized I had diabetes. Since then, losing weight, in my mind, became a matter of life or death. So I now weigh in at only 175 pounds, 35 pounds less than when I got married at the age of 28.

Despite our sustained mutual attraction over the years, this is the first anniversary in a long time when we haven't ended up celebrating our relationship with the joyful act of S-E-X. Of course this might have also occurred on one or two past anniversaries; I just can't remember that far back any longer!

What's going on to make us less "frisky" than we once were? I have to admit that a quick recovery from prostate surgery, even without pain or stress, does not guarantee an immediate return to full desire or normal sexual relations. That's especially true because I had some erectile dysfunction a few months before the surgery itself, due to the impact of diabetes and related neuropathy, and because of other complications such as libido-lowering responses to certain medications. There was a time I thought that would never happen to me, a three-times-a-week-minimum kind of guy for so many of my younger years!

Still, I am grateful for the ongoing intimacy between us at this stage of our lives. This morning Yvonne handed me an anniversary card. The card portrays a dignified, pleasant-looking couple in their early sixties propped up by their oversized, comfy pillows as they lie in their queen-sized bed. Covered up to their necks by a quilt, they wear a happy, yet surprised look on their faces as both the husband and wife sneak a peek under the bed's quilt in the direction of the gentleman's genitals. He seems impressed but bemused, and she is taken aback but delighted because evidently, he's more "alert" than usual!

The printed message inside the card reads, "We may still have a few little surprises left! Happy Anniversary, Honey!" My wife's written message continues: "I agree, and maybe with time there will be many "big" surprises … Love you lots, and always will! Can't wait for our 70th. Hearing aids, canes, walkers and all that. … But we'll do it together! Love, Yvonne"

That night when we go to bed, I whisper in my wife's ear, "Another 35 years is really possible, since by then I'll be 98½ and my mother has lived thus far until 93. But if it's okay with you, why don't we aim to stay together another 57 years when I'll be 120? After all, scientists predict that 120 (if not more) may eventually be the average lifespan of people if cancer, heart and other diseases are eliminated. As it happens that's how long the biblical Moses got to live, and that sounds good to me—at least for now!"

◇◇◇

The Impact of Impotence

Love can endure even when impotence strikes. That was so in my case, before and after my robotic surgery for prostate cancer. There's no question, though, that impotence can have a major impact on any loving couple, even if it doesn't have to be the end of the world. It's obviously a significant let-down, not only for men who are impotent but for their wives or others they are intimate with.

The key problem with impotence is that it can ignite performance anxiety, especially for those of us who think we're sexual failures. By impotence I mean what people over the last decade have politely called "erectile dysfunction." The distinction is important because impotence is not a matter of "all or none," but involves a range of sexual problems. Erectile dysfunction can mean a male sex organ is always limp to not quite rigid. It can also refer to a male organ that doesn't become firm spontaneously, but only with prescribed medicines or erectile devices. In my case, during the month before my surgery, I only had occasional firm erections. However I was frustrated by sporadic impotence because of my medications and health conditions noted earlier. Then too I suffered from an enlarged prostate and prostatitis. For me, and I imagine many others, intermittent burning sensations were a disincentive to sexual enjoyment. Perhaps the prostate cancer, even before it was identified, was another factor that contributed to my not feeling up to having sex.

Before my robotic surgery in April 2007, I was assured of nerve-sparing and little likelihood of impotence, but the latter did not pan out. To know I would most likely retain or regain the capacity to have erections was music to my ears; however, in my case it was hardly reassuring to hear I might get back to where I was before the surgery. After all I was hardly at my peak then.

I'm reminded of the story of an orthopedic doctor who tells his patient that after surgery he'll be as good as he was before. "You'll be playing tennis again just as soon as you heal," he said. His patient answered, "Doc! I never played tennis before. What makes you think I'll play tennis now?"

I was hardly like another younger prostate cancer patient—a young "stud" whose thoughts were published in an interview about his experiences during the summer of 2007. Before his operation he had been told that he needed to prepare properly, if he wanted to be sexually functional once he healed. What did he do? According to an anonymous interview he had sexual relations with his girlfriend every day until the day before his robotic surgery. In his mind this is what enabled him to get back to intercourse sooner after the surgery, in contrast to others who were less healthy or who had less frequent sex beforehand.[1]

My increasing inability to sustain an erection on my own, months before surgery, was coupled with a growing loss of libido. My sense of failure morphed into a sense of defeatism, as I told myself, "What else can you expect of a man whose prostate complications, added to other previous maladies and medications, have squashed his sexual desires?"

Ironically the knowledge that after surgery I would only be able to have "dry" orgasms was fine by me and did not stress me out. That's because it made sense: after all, without the prostate and seminal vesicles, I could no longer produce semen. However, in my case, this almost became irrelevant. I had the sense that since I was impotent just before surgery, it might be more difficult to return to potency afterwards. I was not so sure that I would experience an erection or orgasm again without some extra help.

The only silver lining is that localized, early prostate cancer survivors like me can potentially have a recurrence of erections and orgasm within a year or two after surgery. This can happen if the surgeon succeeds in sparing their nerve bundles adjacent to the prostate—as was done in my case. Beyond this a patient needs to practice "keeping it up," once he recuperates. How that works was something I learned later.

To offset our anxiety we men must remind ourselves that even if we reluctantly give up on having sexual relations with our male organs for awhile, it does not spell the end of our sexual relationships. It does not mean our companion or spouse has lost all physical and emotional desire for us, nor we for them. It also doesn't mean we have to throw out the proverbial baby with the bathwater—or sexual steam! But what's a fellow or couple to do when a man's desire is so low? Conversely what can a man do, if the menopausal woman in his life shows no more sexual interest in him, even though she still loves him?

Along these lines, months after my robotic prostate surgery, I recall kidding my wife that as my libido was already low she should get a dildo, especially if nothing I had to offer got better. A bit put-off, she stated, "Look, even if your desire is low—due to your diabetes, meds and recovering from surgery—I refuse to settle for a dildo. I want you!"

> *If it's going to be artificial, I don't want anything at all!*

That conversation reminded me of another anecdote about an attractive older woman at the beach. After getting a bit warm, the woman wanders out from the beach and jumps into the water. Suddenly she realizes the waves are rough. As she begins drowning, she yells, "Help! Help!" A handsome lifeguard nearby rushes into the deep waters, risking his own safety to bring her to shore. After dragging her to the sand, the lifeguard puts the woman on her back and hesitates as he begins to assess her condition. A crowd gathers around and someone yells, "Put your mouth on hers and give her artificial respiration!" At that point the woman's eyes open and she cries out, "Wait! If it's going to be artificial, I don't want anything at all!"

I was truly supported and comforted when my wife rejected anything artificial and instead reached out to and for me. Still, just for extra measure, I asked her to explain further. With explicit candor she said: "I want to feel **you** inside of me, not some foreign object!" I guess the longer you're married and remain in an honest, wholesome relationship, the more open you can be with each other! That too is a good reason for staying the course of marriage.

This conversation brought to mind our pre-op sex therapy session which stipulated that erections are not all there is to a sexual relationship. Sexual desire, or the libido, begins in the mind.

I focused on this issue earlier but it's worth elaborating here by referring to some noted sex authorities. Dr. Ruth Westheimer of radio and television fame points to this matter in one of her more recent books, *Sex After 50: Revving Up Your Romance, Passion and Excitement (A Best Half of Life)*.[2] The title of Dr. Ruth's first chapter is "Your Brain is Your Most Important Sex Organ." The rest of her book enables readers to take whatever steps they deem appropriate to carry out their sexual and romantic fantasies, thus living a more fulfilling life with their partners or on their own. What she recommends for the general population of fifty and older, also applies to prostate cancer survivors, whatever their age.

It is a truism in all but the most repressed circles (which includes large pockets of the population) that what is not allowed in the boardroom is permissible in the bedroom. Dr. Ruth exemplifies this in her books as well as her radio and television presentations. I particularly enjoyed her upbeat suggestion in *Sex After 50* for couples of all ages to consider so-called "sex-swings" in the bedroom, if they can afford them. As she indicates, such devices should be approached carefully since they require some athleticism. They supposedly have the advantage of heightening male pleasure while inducing clitoral stimulation, which enhances his spouse's enjoyment at the same time. I haven't tried it, since I'm not all that strong, but I'm sure there are those who might like it!

Many widely respected, nationally known sex educators like Dr. Ruth and Dr. Laura Berman, just like our short-term sex therapist, have suggested that couples may decide to watch explicit videos to arouse themselves into lovemaking. Dr. Ruth makes a valid point that while such films may be tantalizing, they should not be considered illicit, as long as they are not criminal or abusive in any way. To put it differently, nudity is undeniably graphic, but it is certainly not pornographic!

Numerous sex manuals and books are available. Two that might be of particular interest to adults with prostate issues, or those who are healthy but are fifty and above, include *All Night Long: How to Make Love to a Man Over 50* by noted sex therapist Barbara Keesling, and *The New Love and Sex after 60* by pre-eminent psychiatrist and gerontologist Robert Butler and his wife Myrna Lewis. There are many others listed in this book's References.[3]

While America's youth culture tends to overemphasize the joys of physical sex both outside and inside marriage, older Americans should not be denied the physical pleasures of erotic love. Having been younger ourselves, those of us in our sixties or above must reclaim our right to establish a mutual physical connection, however expressed, as the glue that reinforces emotional intimacy.

The various references I've reviewed underscore that sexual desire can be actively expressed even in view of health obstacles, whether among younger or older adults. Such health issues, as in my case, can include prostate abnormalities like BPH and cancer, diabetes, neuropathy or depression; or as in my wife's case, back pain, post-menopausal concerns, fibromyalgia and chronic fatigue. Similarly the side effects caused by medical prescriptions for these health concerns can at times be offset to allow for the expression of human sexuality.

> *Many of us want to reinvigorate our relationships with more, not less sexuality as we get older.*

Whatever happens to us, our strong need for intimacy and physical interaction remains, although perhaps at a low ebb. This means that even when our health has been compromised by illness, many of us want to reinvigorate our relationships with more, not less sexuality as we get older. Sexuality can be expressed through any symbolic or suggestive act, even a wink and a nod. Sexuality can be conveyed through embraces, physical caresses and kisses on the face or more private body parts. If given no choice, this may suffice, since, as stated over and over again, sex begins in the mind.

Still, when vaginal penetration, either digitally or by the male organ, is still feasible, that generally remains the ultimate choice for love-making, bar-none. How a husband and wife can pursue this proactively, despite erstwhile or permanent impotence, will be covered in the next chapter and in various postings at *www.ConquerProstateCancer.com*.

10

Sex Again, When You Can Get It Up, Part II

"Children today know more about sex than I or my father did."
—Bill Cosby, 20th–21st Century comedian, actor and educator

Ways to Get It Up Quickly and Effectively

During August 2007 I had to spend three days at the hospital for an infusion of Prednisone in an attempt to restore the sudden hearing loss that affected my left ear. Although the intravenous procedure was in vain, I used my time in the hospital to good advantage as I hovered over my laptop, working on material for this book.

While I was typing away, a cleaning woman in her mid-sixties entered my hospital room. Curious, she asked me what I was typing. I replied I was reviewing part of my book manuscript about prostate cancer and sex. With an air of recognition she said, "Oh! Are you writing about that penile implant?"

I smiled and said, "Well that is one way some prostate cancer survivors get "it" back up so they can resume sexual intercourse; but a man doesn't have to go to such extremes to function sexually after a prostate cancer procedure."

"I know," she responded. "My late companion, who was five years older than me, corrected his erection problems by using injections in the front or base of his penis. The problem is that one time, he wanted it firm for me, and he over-injected himself. We had to rush to the hospital because it hurt him so much! Boy was it awkward as he lay in the Emergency Room, what with all those nurses going off duty and slowly walking by to see what was going on with him!"

Even after thirty years of pastoral counseling, I was still amazed I could be approached so openly by total strangers. It was gratifying to meet folks who felt free to tell me everything on their minds—even when I sat in my own hospital bed! More important in terms of this book, this refreshing, brief interchange reminded me of two methods currently available for sustaining an erection.

For some who have found no easier, more natural, or spontaneous method for getting an erection, the penile implant is a welcome surgical approach. Once in place, you simply push a button or two that has been surgically inserted in the scrotum to raise the "flag" to full-mast, allowing for sexual interplay. There are various types of penile implants that can be surgically put in place, with a reasonable shelf-life of ten to fifteen years. The types of penile implants include semi-rigid, inflatable, and three-piece prostheses. An implant is a highly convenient way to make both the deflated male organ and the corresponding deflated male ego soar once again![1]

Unfortunately, as with any surgery, things can go wrong. For instance a more advanced prosthesis can sometimes develop mechanical problems that require repair. Sometimes an infection occurs, especially among diabetics. Replacement parts may be needed in simpler prostheses too. Still this book's medical advisor, Dr. David Kauder, has performed many penile implants in patients of various ages. According to him this is a relatively safe technology and penile implant surgery can lead to excellent results.

Citing Dr. Kauder, "Having inserted many penile implants in patients, after robotic or conventional surgery or after radiation, I can say that it is a viable and useful option. Remember that oftentimes the nerves are intentionally removed by a surgeon because of the position of the cancer. Even if the nerves remain on one side there can still be significant problems that may warrant a man's and woman's decision to consider a penile implant."[2]

Prostate cancer patients, their life partners and others ought to keep their eyes on new technological developments like this that can help them cement their sexual relationships. Even at an advanced age, individual patients who have not found a suitable alternative would do well to consider a penile implant. I know of one case where someone age 80 eagerly made that decision and it worked out to his satisfaction. While not elaborated in this book, I refer here to a fairly recent decision made by "Rev. Paul" (mentioned in Chapter 15) to undergo surgery for a prosthesis. Penile implants have been available for the past 30 years, ever since American Medical Systems and the Mentor Corporation manufactured some of the earliest versions. It's claimed that by 2005 at least 250,000 men had surgically implanted penile prostheses. Over the decades both the hardware and surgical procedures have become increasingly refined.[2]

The self-injection procedure is an alternative widely advocated by urologists for those patients who find it helpful. This is usually a moderately painless approach, although some bruising can occur. Men who go this route have to learn how to properly inject themselves and abide by the doctors' recommendations.[3] Injecting FDA-approved Caverject, or paperverine with phenpolamine, is to be limited to no more than twice a week.

Over-injection at any one time is not recommended, although sustaining an erection for one hour or so is acceptable. Certainly, after four hours one must call the doctor immediately. A prolonged chemically induced erection constitutes a medical emergency, regardless of age!

The most spontaneous means to aid a man's erection are obviously oral and hands-on help from one's partner. A considerate, loving man would do well to reciprocate such activity by lubricating his spouse. This is so even when menopausal or post-menopausal women use hormone replacement therapy (HRT) supplements such as Estrace.

A man's spontaneity is aided by Cialis, Levitra or Viagra, the little blue pill. These prescribed medications are known as phosphodiesterase type 5 (PDE5) inhibitors. They can create a large, firm penis prior to intercourse, if a man or his partner helps stimulate his penis. This subject became more open in American society in 1999, when Senator Bob Dole, a prostate cancer survivor, agreed, in his own words, to become a "poster boy for Viagra." He entered into a contract with Pfizer, the drug manufacturer, to participate in widely dispersed television advertisements of Viagra about a year after its 1998 FDA-approval. This was a win-win-win approach that filled his and his sponsor's pockets and eased the minds and relationships of millions of men and their spouses or partners.

In society today, among both the younger and older subpopulations of sexually dysfunctional males, America's prescription drug culture means that the blue pill truly "rules." This applies with equal force to those whose health has been compromised by prostate cancer or other conditions. While there are other correctives for impotence, a temporary antidote in pill-form is the easiest to use for most men, despite the potential for unpleasant side effects like headaches or facial flushing.

Another synthetic material that can be used to rejuvenate the sexual "juices" is testosterone developed in a laboratory. I met with my urologist, Dr. Carey, in July 2007 for a follow-up visit after my robotic surgery, to discuss the possibility of my taking synthetic testosterone. That was after he reminded me that the hormone Lupron might account for much of my low-libido and inactive sexual relations, as it had chemically neutered me.

In a lab test the doctor ordered in July, three months after my surgery, my body's natural testosterone was one-fifth of the normal level for most men. As determined by a blood test my testosterone score was 46 ng/dL (nano-grams per decileter). That was castrate level. I was well below the normal range for testosterone, which is defined as ranging from 241 to 827ng/dL. This was primarily the effect of the Lupron administered two months before my robotic surgery. It was only by November that my testosterone level was 277–low normal. It had climbed very slowly to 351 when I took another blood test on February 25, 2008, ten months after my surgery and ten days after I turned 64. Talk about a great birthday gift!

During the immediate post-op phase I felt fortunate that my stomach and chest didn't become as flaccid as my penis. One of my acquaintances, also on Lupron hormone treatment for prostate cancer, reported that his breasts grew, and that really hurt his ego. While this did not happen to me, my lowered libido was a biochemical fact and hardly a figment of my imagination.

Due to my particular circumstances, my surgeon and co-author, Dr. Carey, at one point indicated he might be willing to consider prescribing testosterone. He thought my prostate margins were so low it might not be too risky to test testosterone's positive effect on building up my sexual desires and potency once again. After further thought he and his colleague, Dr. Barzell, concluded this would be too dangerous for me. There has been some talk about testosterone treatment for men with a zero PSA five years or more after their prostate surgery. But, to quote my friend Dr. Kauder, "It would take a very brave urologist to give testosterone replacement therapy to a prostate cancer survivor."

Dr. Carey was not eager to induce supplementary testosterone into my system. As I recall, his analogy was that a fireman doesn't go into a raging forest fire and put it out, only to come back again and spray the fire with new oil! In other words there was a possibility that increasing testosterone might well lead to a recurrence of prostate cancer, if any prostate cells remained undetected in my body. He told me that instead I would probably have to wait at least a year until Mother Nature would allow me to "prime my pump" spontaneously with no outside testosterone. Meantime other devices or approaches were more than welcome!

Impotence is more pervasive than many people think.

I was perversely relieved to learn from my readings that nearly one in three American men above the age of thirty experiences impotence at one time or another in his life. This is associated with aging, depression, medication, alcohol, sleep-deprivation and other factors, not just those who have a disease. Dr. Laura Berman suggests that women take their partners' occasional impotence in stride, and offers valuable suggestions on what to do when this happens.[4] Others point out that impotence is more pervasive than many think: ten percent of men in the general population (approximately 15 million men) currently suffer from ED And it's been reported that some forty million Americans have a "no-sex or low-sex" marriage.[5] This last statistic includes some 40% of women, both pre- or post-menopausal, who may experience a degree of sexual dysfunction.

A sizable number of men will have to cope with this problem and reflect on how to sustain intimate relationships, perhaps focusing less on our physical sexual functioning. Meantime most of us should expect that eventually we'll come back into our own, with a renewed capacity for sexual intimacy. Where that's not possible, we and our partners need to be realistic and get on with our lives, relishing whatever is still possible in our interactions.

We Must Do Our Sexercise

Within the year after my surgery I began to come back into my own, as far as having bouts of increased sexual desire. However infrequently this occurred, it appeared that Dr. Carey's optimism was warranted. He was right that my nerve-sparing robotic surgery might eventually end my post-operative impotence within a year or two, especially once the hormone Lupron was out of my system. The fact that my testosterone reached low normal and moderately normal the following November 2007 and then February 2008, meant I managed to cross that magical divide between "can't" and "can." To borrow from a beloved Country Western song, I was "on the road again."

Immediately after surgery I decided to heed the doctor's advice to wait and see what would happen, but I refused to wait passively. Towards becoming a more active participant in my own rehabilitation, I followed the doctor's directions to use a penile vacuum erection device he had prescribed in conjunction with one-fourth of a Viagra pill an hour or two earlier, as needed. This enabled me to obtain and sustain an erection within ten to twenty minutes. The result was sufficient for sexual intercourse when my wife and I were up for it, which frankly was still not all that often. Generally I was not as firm as I once was, but at times I was firmer than ever—with the help of Viagra and manual stimulation.

My urologist had prescribed Viagra since I do not have a personal history of heart disease, although my father, a physician and dental surgeon, died of a series of heart attacks in his mid-fifities. It should be noted that Viagra, Lavitra or Cialis are counter-indicated for anyone on nitro-glycerin heart medication. This would lower one's blood pressure so radically it might be fatal. The use of one-fourth of a pill rather than a whole pill is nonetheless a medical precaution. Others have suggested two longer-lasting Levitra pills a week, interspersed by Viagra, as a cost-cutting way to maintain penile blood flow and the capacity for an erection.

Whereas some people don't have sex because they purportedly have a headache, Viagra is known to cause men a real headache and facial flushing when they do have sex! Recently before intercourse, I ingested a whole Viagra pill and felt lucky I had no side-effects, but I preferred not to take such chances. Besides, at the cost of $10 per dose, splitting the pills saved a good chunk of change!

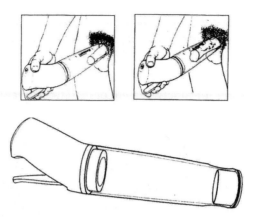

Osbon ErecAid Esteem Vacuum Therapy System
Courtesy of Timm Medical Technologies © 2008, reproduced with permission

Some of you may be wondering about my use of the vacuum erection device. To take the mystery out of this kind of contraption I'll need to get a bit graphic. The main purpose of the vacuum pump was to help me begin what I would call my new daily "sexercise" program. The pump was necessary to reinvigorate my penile blood vessels, so they would not become atrophied. It was simply a matter of "use it or lose it."

The vacuum pump Dr. Carey routinely prescribes is a system called the Osbon ErecAid™ Esteem Vacuum Therapy System, manufactured by Timm Medical Technologies, Inc. It's available by prescription only, as opposed to many other over-the-counter vacuum devices. I purchased it a month after the operation with a co-payment of $180, since my health insurance company paid the brunt of the cost. They did not authorize my using the device that features an electrical button, but the less expensive version that has a manual pump.[6]

I had some hesitation in using this device because of my long-held hang-up about masturbation. Jewish and Catholic religious traditions generally regard masturbation as wasteful and sinful. Similarly American popular culture, even today, generally regards masturbation as shameful, although various surveys demonstrate that the vast majority of men and women in their teens and older masturbate in secret. Even though I knew I had to follow "doctor's orders," my hang-up still prevented me from freely using the vacuum device or hand-stimulation to achieve an erection.

In time I learned to re-frame what was required, increasingly looking at this activity not as masturbation but as self-stimulation for promoting good penile health. You could rightly ask, "What's the difference?" but it made sense to me. I was also glad to learn from the leaflet in the vacuum device package, that it works for ninety percent of men with Erectile Dysfunction. And after trying it as directed, I thought it was great that I was not among the remaining ten percent!

Later on I discovered that there are scores of companies that manufacture variations of this vacuum. Most of these are listed on the internet under vacuum-constriction devices, or they can be found in several books.[7]

During the next couple of months I tried using not only the Osbon ErecAid pump, manufactured by Timm Medical Technologies, but also another one manufactured by Bonro, called The Vacurect™. Both are FDA approved. For reasons I'll mention shortly, I ended up preferring the first for rehabilitation or "practice" and the second for actual use before engaging in intimate relations. At least I felt that way for the first two months of using these devices. In time I felt that only Timm Medical's Osbon ErecAid pump was superior for both preparation and actual intercourse, because it is sturdier, relatively safer, easier to use and more effective.

I first got the hang of both pumps in the privacy of my master bathroom. The Timm Osbon ErecAid (above) is a see-through plexiglass tube with a wide opening at both ends. To operate it, you insert a handheld plastic device at the opening on one end and then insert the flaccid penis in the other end. Under the hard plastic piece is a pump handle that, when compressed, builds up suction for erecting the male organ in the tube. An upgraded version of this pump operates electronically at the push of a button, which avoids any possible hand or wrist strain.

Before using the device, the ErecAid, like the Vacurect, requires the application of special KY gel or a similar lubricant on the inside lip of the device's opening, as well as on the tip of the penis. With the ErecAid model you then press the handle repeatedly, a couple of times in a row, to add further suction that draws blood into the penile veins and makes for greater length and firmness. In the course of about fifteen to twenty minutes, the penis is erect. After practicing this enough times comfortably, one can transfer the included rubber constriction band at the end of the vacuum to the base of the penis closest to the body and remove the vacuum tube. You are now firm and ready for vaginal penetration after allowing for foreplay and other forms of lovemaking.

Once I tried the ErecAid device several times, I realized that initially each of the four available constricting bands felt too tight when placed on the base of the penis to build up penile blood supply, even though this is what made the device so conducive toward creating an erection. You see, with practice the ErecAid was so effective my post-op erection became as large as in the years before my robotic prostate surgery!

It was due to the initially mild discomfort of the ErecAid that I ended up purchasing the second vacuum device, the Bonro Vacurect system, which I used for a couple of months. It turned out that this worked in less time—less than three minutes, and was easier to set up since it's pre-assembled and there are no separate parts to work with.

The Bonro Vacurect system more closely resembles a short tube within a larger tube, with only one opening at the end. Before inserting one's penis, all that was needed was to apply the gel. Moving the smaller outer tube back and forth over the larger tube helped create suction. In many ways this device resembled the type of tube sent by vacuum to and from a bank teller and his drive-through customers. At first this vacuum device seemed easier to use because it was completely pre-assembled, but in time it proved more difficult due to hand exertion.

In my assessment the Bonro Vacurect's constriction band was broader and not as tight as the Osborn ErecAid band, and therefore did not pinch as much. If Timm Medical used a broader band for its sturdier product, it would be that much more comfortable, quicker and easier to use.

Given the extra level of comfort of the Bonro device, the penis seemed to retain more body warmth and sensitivity. As the company's advertisement accurately stated, because it is a one-piece system it is safe (although here I have to add that it's not as safe as it could be), simple and compact in design, and it requires no extra effort to utilize, or so it seemed at first. In other words it is quicker and less stressful for the user, who can make use of it in bed, rather than first placing the device on a flat, firm surface. This means it can be used in bed in the last moment when most needed, followed by initial foreplay, and it helps create the illusion of spontaneous intercourse.

The appeal of interacting as naturally as possible with one's partner before applying this device is undeniable.

A note of caution is important here. Practicing with the Timm/Osbon system has its advantages, as it may be safer than the Bonro system. That's because, unlike the Bonro tube, the Timm device has a vacuum release button in case of sudden strain or pain. In addition it won't inadvertently pull your testicles into the suction tube, when you choose not to use a constriction band. There's more danger of this happening with the Bonro device, and that can hurt. Ultimately, despite any mild discomfort, that's why my decided preference is for the Timm ErecAid vacuum system.

> *You have to choose what's most comfortable for you and experiment before deciding what suits you best.*

Selecting a vacuum device is a highly personal, individual matter. You have to choose what's most comfortable for you and experiment before deciding what suits you best, including which size constriction bands to use. Only you can tell what suits you best.

The advantage of both vacuum devices I tried was that they do not necessarily need to be augmented by medication like Viagra, Levitra and Cialis. As noted earlier, these can be helpful to sustain a firm erection with a vacuum device, but are not strictly required. Both companies also offer a free advisory phone service and will replace the ointment and vacuum parts discreetly through the mail.

Dr. Carey, as my urologist, encouraged me to use the vacuum erection device (V.E.D.) after surgery as soon as I was ready. Evidently many surgeons counsel their patients to wait at least six weeks to allow for healing. Other surgeons feel two to three months should pass until sexual intercourse is attempted. I know of two instances where urologists who did prostate cancer surgery (one robotic and one a traditional prostatectomy) did not even tell their patients that they might consider a V.E.D. When I told one of my minister friends about my preference for the Timm ErecAid, he tried it just one month after his surgery, with satisfactory results for himself and his wife. However his urologist learned of this and vocally disapproved, asking him to hold off for another two months until his wounds had time to heal.

This eager beaver friend of mine was disappointed but did as he was told. Obviously different doctors and different surgical outcomes make for varied advice! That incident reminded me that I am only an educator who can offer information, but I'm not licensed to practice medicine. That's best left to each person's physician.

On that point Dr. Carey told me that it took him some time to convince a prominent physician at the Mayo Clinic's department of Urology that waiting too long could be more problematic than not. It was only recently that this leading urologist finally concurred, but many others still demur.

There's no doubt that the penile blood vessels of someone who has had his prostate surgically removed need to be engorged with blood regularly, to prevent fibroids or collagen from restricting the blood vessels and in order to facilitate intercourse. That is why, even with my lowered libido and loss of interest in having sexual relations, I knew, at least intellectually, that I must do my "sexercise."

Readers may wonder how well this worked for me and my wife. To be perfectly candid, knowing we could proceed with my doctor's blessings was helpful to both of us. In fact we enjoyed two evenings of satisfactory intercourse three or four weeks after my prostate removal. However by the third time I used the Osborn ErecAid I grew a bit leery of its pinching effect, which caused me to become "limp." But this is to be attributed as much to my lowered libido as anything else.

I have to confess that during the first nine months after my surgery using a vacuum erect device was a bit hard…on me! For one thing it seemed artificial and planned, in contrast to the old days of spontaneity. Second, as I elaborated earlier, it is a "hands-off" form of masturbation. While I eventually came to see nothing morally wrong with masturbation to regain body functionality, masturbation is not something I have favored for myself over the past few decades. I felt quite strongly about that even though I occasionally masturbated before marriage. I hasten to add that I've never had any real objection to others who feel masturbation is a helpful sexual outlet for themselves. In fact I feel that what others do is none of my business!

At one point this matter troubled me so much that I consulted with Rabbi Dr. Elliott Dorff, a professor at the American Jewish University in L.A., and a friend who is a leading expert in Jewish sexual and medical ethics. Only then did I fully realize that, despite the predominant disapproval of traditional Judaism, physical and emotional health considerations should nullify any inhibitions of patients like me. Masturbation is an appropriate emotional and physical outlet that preserves the health of individuals, young and old alike.[8]

In time I completely accepted that a vacuum erect system was worth using to counter ED But with or without the device, the frequency of sexual intimacy decreased not just due to my low libido but because of my wife's back pain. I could not countenance adding to her pain by putting my body weight on her. I simply felt I did not want to impose on her while she was suffering. Actually it scared me to think I might be adding to her difficulties, and my fear for her well-being lessened my ardor for love-making. She insisted otherwise, and pointed out that sexual intercourse was a healthy distraction from her woes; but this did not persuade me.

My outlook briefly brightened somewhat months after my wife's successful back operation in September 2007, five months after my own surgery. Once her capable neurosurgeons had successfully fused two of her spinal discs, her pain level eventually diminished. Like me she used some of Peggy Huddleston's *Relaxation* CD's before and after surgery to begin the healing process, and she applied some of my relaxation techniques as well. Remarkably she began to bounce back within a week of the operation, although later she had an extended relapse of acute pain for three months and diminishing pain for the next seven months. Knowing how slowly she recovered from her grueling pain made it difficult for us to resume frequent sexual relations.

Perhaps that led me to the dreams I had about waking up with an erection. Without elaborating, I will say that I envisioned the kind of hard-on I had not dreamt about since my college years. If Sigmund Freud was right that dreams are wish-fulfillment, I guess I was on track toward eventually returning to the way things once were, long before I opted for robotic prostate cancer surgery or my wife needed back surgery.

In the months since Yvonne and I both recovered from our respective surgeries, I've grown more confident that we would in time become increasingly intimate. To be sure, we knew that the absence of intercourse did not mean the end of sexual relations. We could pleasure each other physically in various ways, limited only by our personal proclivities and imaginations. We could do so knowing that we might enjoy achieving an orgasm (mine or hers) even if complete erection were not to become an option in the near future, or ever. Besides, even without erections, I experienced occasional dry orgasms which were delightfully pleasurable.[9]

I vividly recall two subsequent moments of exquisite sexual intimacy. In one instance my wife conjured up a highly romantic scene, involving fragrant massage oil and colorful, flickering candles she lit in our darkened bedroom. That inspired moment, early in December 2007 (eight months after my robotic prostatectomy), led to mutual sexual arousal. It left us both wanting more, even though I was still not able to go "full-throttle"! Still, for the first time since surgery my libido re-emerged in a way I thought it never would.[10] Subsequently I had a couple of "relapses," but at least I was on my way!

The other exceptional sexual encounter between us occurred late in January 2008, shortly before I finished the first draft of this book. In that case I can only say "Thank you" for the positive outcome of a whole Viagra pill I took, supplemented by the unbelievably effective use of my vacuum erect system. Then again, it might have been my wife's new lacy underwear, the candles once more burning romantically in a darkened room, the fragrant body oil and the erotic background music my wife put in motion without first telling me. Men, like women, love surprises … sometimes. I could not have become firmer … but more you don't want or need to know.

I mention these last two incidents simply to indicate that with time, post-operative sexual satisfaction is possible for most men who have had robotic-assisted or other surgery, not to mention different procedures to treat prostate cancer. This is at least true for those whose prostate cancers were localized before being eradicated and whose nerve bundles were spared. I myself experienced at least limited sexual satisfaction after surgery, despite earlier chemical castration due to the hormone Lupron, despite the neutering effects of my disabilities and the effects of medications to treat them, and despite my wife's health limitations. If it happened to me it can happen to most men who have the opportunity, means and motive!

A Quiet Sexual Revolution

From my account thus far, it's clear that having sex again after my robotic surgery was hardly a routine matter for me. Still, in revisiting this issue, my wife and I were reminded of some important fundamentals. The first, which I emphasized earlier, is that love and physical intimacy need not include physical intercourse. This was so even though American culture advocates intercourse as the be-all and end-all of sex, a perception all too many of us have internalized.

Second, for both of us intimacy in the form of mutual physical pleasuring of any kind has remained indispensable to our relationship. This is one of several powerful ways to enjoy each other. Still, Yvonne and I admit we prefer intercourse as a key mode for personal expression, not just for the enjoyable physical sensations. Sexual intercourse clearly makes for intense interpersonal bonding. Like countless other couples, it has brought us emotionally and spiritually closer.[11]

While current insights for handling complex sexual relations are helpful, they don't necessarily provide a permanent solution to interpersonal quandaries. For now we can only overcome our sexual frustration and disappointment by doing the best we know how—through other forms of physical contact and by maintaining mutual trust that we are right for each other as a couple. Whatever you do, you also need faith that some things will sort themselves out in the long run. As one of my favorite Bible professors used to say, "You have to leave a little to God."

We had no doubt that, however we chose to make love, we would do so only in the framework of sacred, rather than indiscriminate sex.[12] This means acting on our basic instincts, while providing the mutual care and nurturance which brought us together in marriage to start with over three and a half decades ago.

There's another point that prostate cancer patients need to acknowledge, along with others who seek intimacy as they engage in life's struggles. Whether we're healthy or not, it helps to know we are not alone. In specific terms, even by the most liberal guesstimate, no more than half of the two million prostate cancer survivors in the United States today have active sex lives, which is also true for older Americans in general. This means that half engage in sexual intercourse on an average of at least once a month and more often in various other forms of sexual play, but half do not. Given the disparity in sexual desire among husbands and wives, the general population also has to deal with similar concerns. Clearly men and women are often not in the same place when it comes to mutual desire and seeking sexual fulfillment.[13]

I base this hypothesis not only on self-reports and case studies, but on the first comprehensive national study of older adults' sexual attitudes, behaviors and problems summarized in the August 2007, *New England Journal of Medicine*. That study of adults ages 57 and older is significant since it includes the oldest members of the Boomer Generation, those born between 1946–1950, apart from other individuals in their sixties, seventies and eighties, born as early as 1920.

The national study, conducted by University of Chicago researchers, does not mention specifically how much benign and malignant prostate problems beset this population; however, it refers to older people in general, who to an extent are increasingly subjected to illnesses that are obstacles to sexual intimacy. In my opinion it's clear that the men in this older age group are among those most likely to be confronted by enlarged benign prostates or with prostate cancer and its treatment side-effects. Accordingly it comes as no surprise that this study reported that the most common problem among these men was erectile dysfunction—thirty-seven percent, a proportion that's comparable to men with at least sporadic ED in the general population, as discussed earlier. As we've also noted, erectile dysfunction is a problem for men with diabetes and other illnesses and can be a side effect of certain medications. Besides this, many men, not just women, may have a negative body self-image that can cause sexual dysfunction.

The most stunning fact that surfaced from this national survey was that three-quarters of those with partners were sexually active, defined as engaging in sexual intercourse at least once a month. This was the case as well with younger couples in their forties and fifties, while many of both age groups engaged in intercourse at least two or three times a week. In addition half to three-quarters of older married men remained sexually active at least monthly, if not through sexual intercourse then orally and in other ways.[14] These findings may be proof-positive of a quiet, unnoticed sexual revolution that has gone on for decades, if not for centuries.

The reality is that it is not only lack of desire, but illness and the absence of opportunity that often hampers human sexual relations. Such opportunities are thwarted due to widowhood or because of medical problems of the kind I have noted in my own personal life. Yet it's clear that a majority of men who remain married manage to sustain their sexual drive until they approach death.

To me this indicates that the drive for sexual intimacy is a lifelong pursuit. It clearly demonstrates the old adage that where there's a will there's a way. It certainly means that it's within our power to act decisively to attain our most personal objectives. If we are guided by heightened awareness, patience, and mutual acceptance, many of us will find that the sexual intimacy we crave will be ours at any age. If you'd like to share your response to these issues, I would welcome your comments at *www.ConquerProstateCancer.com*.

No matter where you are in your quest for reigniting your sexual life, I'd like to end on a cautionary note. Specifically I'd like to suggest that prostate cancer survivors, whether younger or older, try not to "jump the gun" and expect too much of themselves sexually. Remember that you, and your partner, are works in progress.

Now more than ever, you have to act in concert to get where you want to go. To avoid disappointment, spell out your needs to your partner(s), rather than asking them to second-guess what's important to you. Be clear but gentle, and maintain the give-and-take relationship that can endear you to each other, the way my wife and I have—most of the time! And should you prefer your "singlehood" to togetherness, because you've learned the art of living by yourself, consider yourself blessed. There is no judgment here!

Above all we prostate cancer survivors should avoid self-recrimination. We should not put ourselves down for our inability to function as the "studs" we once were—if ever! After any cancer treatment, how can we expect to have sexual intercourse again until we are truly up for it?

Ultimately there's only one way to conquer prostate cancer: we have to own up to our limitations while acknowledging our capacity to prevail.

11

When Medicine and Faith Meet

"Call on God, but row away from the rocks."
—Indian Proverb

How God Provides

Comedienne Ellen DeGeneres was at her funniest when she did a take-off on the creation story in Genesis: "In the beginning, there was nothing. Then God said, 'Let there be light.' And there was light. Which made the nothing a lot easier to see."

Navigating the shoals of nothingness in this world stands in sharp contrast to our being guided by the light of religious faith. "Faith," as used in this book, partially refers to my trust in God's goodness in helping me get through surgery in order to cure cancer. My faith was also evident in terms of the trust I placed in my surgeon to help me become cancer-free.

I also had faith in myself that I could conquer prostate cancer by proactively eliminating my pain and stress. Last I had great faith or trust in my family and friends to support me and be there for me.

Fortunately the cure I prayed for came rapidly. I did not have to torture myself with an old Jewish saying that, "God provides. But if only He would provide until He provides!" For me it was nothing short of miraculous that my prostate cancer was diagnosed at an early stage in January 2007 and was speedily eradicated through pain-free robotic surgery three months later. For that reason I had ample reason to thank my doctor and God for taking me from scare to care in such short order. I know there is a 10 percent chance of recurrence within ten years and nearly 25 percent within fifteen years, but the odds of that happening are in my favor.

While my religious faith points to a providential God, for me this does not mean God personally provides for my well-being or looks out for me. Frankly I should be so lucky that God would take time out of his busy schedule just for me, instead of ministering to the rest of the six-and-a-half billion people on the face of the earth. And God only knows how many other earths there are like ours! Given the unending natural and man-made catastrophes in the world, I don't believe God routinely acts in a supernatural manner by reaching out to a suffering humanity. In my view God acts through trained, caring human beings who, having been created in God's image, carry out God's will.

> *Physicians hone their God-given abilities to save lives.*

By the same token, the doctor is not the ultimate source of the cure for a disease. Instead, from a faith perspective, physicians hone their God-given abilities to save lives and become vehicles through which God operates, in my case quite literally! It's true that there's a stereotype that doctors act as if they were God, and there's some truth to that when a physician acts in an authoritarian manner. In a religious sense doctors are God, or more precisely, are an extension of God, imbued with divine healing powers.[1]

Of course we could say this about most individuals in the helping professions, such as social workers, nurses and even the clergy. The core idea, in rabbinic Judaism and other religions that emphasize stewardship, is that all human beings are God's partners in the ongoing process of creation. I hasten to add that in both Jewish and Christian tradition we are not God's peers but only God's junior partners! In that respect my resilience was both my doing and God's doing.

During the six months after my surgery, my wife agreed with me that my positive outcome was the result of my proactive search for the best care available. She realized I had networked in my typical manner in order to find a skilled physician. At the same time she thought it was a combination of plain luck, coincidence and the active intervention of God in my life. Here are her own words as to how real-world factors and a more sublime faith intersected to rescue me from our distress.

> *With the help of doctors, family and friends, our own initiative and a series of coincidences we made it through. However, I think God was very much around and within us in helping make a decision. Leave it to my husband, who lets himself be guided by both knowledge and faith, that we chose to go the route of robotic laparoscopic radical prostatectomy.*
>
> *It turned out that Sarasota Memorial Hospital had recently acquired the newest surgical robot. The hospital staff, in conjunction with a private urology practice, then managed to convince one of Miami's top robotic surgeons to work here in Sarasota. What luck! Dr. Carey moved to Sarasota only a couple of months before we did.*
>
> —*Yvonne*

Timing, Survival, and Spiritual Healing

Like many people I've often felt that timing is everything. In terms of detecting and taking care of my prostate cancer, timing worked in my favor. It doesn't always. Within six months after we purchased our new home in Sarasota, Florida, the house was devalued by over twenty-five percent, due to a major local and national economic downturn. In that situation timing worked against us.

As for luck, I've always felt that by and large you make your luck, more often than being a passive recipient of whatever luck bestows on you. That no doubt is why the earliest rabbis in Jewish history declared, "It makes no sense to rely on miracles," (Hebrew: *"Ayn somcheem al haNes"*), and added that "if you change your location, you can change your situation." (Hebrew: *"Shanah mikomo, shanah mazlo."*)

On the other hand, a recent news item about two Florida State University anthropologists confirms that luck is actually a factor beyond our control.

Two professors finished their archeological dig earlier than expected in a mountainous part of Peru. Six hours after they left, a devastating earthquake struck in that precise locale, killing many local inhabitants, including those praying in a church. Had these two Americans not left the site six hours earlier, they too would have perished in the rubble. If they were religious folk, they might simply have said that God was not ready for them. If they were secularists they probably thought their number just wasn't up yet.

A key element of faith which was crucial in my recovery was my belief in spiritual healing, specifically in the healing power of prayer. Earlier I mentioned that I took every step possible to make others' aware of my plight, and to pray for my speedy recovery. I had some sense that their prayers on my behalf might have some intrinsic power, but, frankly I wasn't truly convinced of that. What was important to me is that their prayers for me were ample proof that they cared, and this knowledge had a healing impact on me. My goal was to experience pain-free and stress-free surgery so that, despite my physical wounds I would quickly heal in both body and soul. Knowing that hundreds of synagogue and church-going friends used their traditions of formal and spontaneous prayer in my behalf, helped facilitate my healing process.

A traditional prayer fellow Jews offered was one I used to regular intone on behalf of others in my years as a congregational rabbi. Just as I had comforted them with this prayer, it now comforted me.

"May He who blessed our ancestors Abraham, Isaac, Jacob, Moses, Aaron, David and Solomon, bless and heal Rabbi Dr. Edgar Weinsberg. May the Holy One Praised be He mercifully restore him to health and to vigor. May God grant him health of body and health of spirit and mind, along with all others who are stricken. Let us say: Amen."

I cannot prove the existence of God, nor would I even try. I can only say that my convictions are genuine although mine is not blind faith. This is obvious given my reluctance to affirm that God directly intervenes in our lives whenever a crisis occurs. I feel I am in good company since the biblical Abraham questioned God's decision to wipe out Sodom and Gemorrah, and Moses himself challenged God's stated goal of eliminating the Israelites after the incident of the golden calf. However, for me God is an independent spiritual being (Hebrew: *"Ruach"*) infused in, yet beyond the universe. (That's why one of God's other names in Hebrew is *"HaMakom"*—"the Place" of existence.) In short, for me God is the indispensable, dynamic organizing principle which gives life coherence and significance.

Can Scientists Prove Prayer is Effective?

A major question that has been raised remains largely unanswered: Is there any way to scientifically prove that praying to God for your recovery from an illness such as prostate cancer has anything to do with your recovery?

Whether the efficacy of prayer can be demonstrated scientifically has been a subject of debate for some time.

Dr. Dale A. Mathews, M.D., an expert on contemplative Christian spirituality, assessed the connection between prayer and illness in his book, *The Faith Factor.* One example he used was a 1972 study of 91,000 subjects in Maryland, which concluded that active church attendance correlated positively with disease prevention and recovery as well as longevity.

As Dr. Matthews noted, some intervening variables may have been that church attendees smoke and drank alcohol less and were therefore less prone to cancer, suicide and sexually transmitted diseases.[2] Dr. Matthews added that the Mormon hierarchy had a better health record than those in the rank-and-file of the Church of Latter Day Saints, and adherents of the Seventh Day Adventists had better health records than other groups. Once again a healthier lifestyle may be credited to the belief system of these religious groups.

Dr Ellen Kreidman, Ph.D., a woman imbued with faith, also believes in the power of prayer to heal the sick. As a noted marriage counselor, she has lectured around the country and appeared on the Today Show, CNN, The View, Montel Williams, and Oprah Winfrey. She has also written articles for *The New York Times.*

Dr. Ellen, as she is called, has pursued her arduous career in between bouts of breast cancer complications over the past decade. Despite her intermittent ailments and close calls with death, she has remained a deeply believing Christian.

As a highly educated woman, Dr. Ellen has neatly summarized a few of the research studies that attempt to validate prayer as a tool for healing. In citing some studies she briefly referred to research by Dr. Larry Dossey, M.D. With her permission I've reproduced her thoughts from her website, *www.lightyourfire.com,* where she states that even if double-blind scientific proof were not available, prayer has a beneficial impact on the lives of religious adherents.

Here is Dr. Ellen's summary (abridged) of some studies on prayer and the human body, prayer and blood cells, and prayer and mood:

◇◇◇

1. The most widely publicized study on prayer-based healing is the one performed by cardiologist Randolph Byrd. He studied 393 patients admitted to the coronary care unit at San Francisco General Medical Center between August 1982 and May 1983. Using a computer generated list, he randomly divided the patients into two groups. The first group consisted of 192 patients, who were prayed for and given standard medical care. The other 201 patients were just given the standard medical care and were not prayed for.

None of the patients, hospital staff, doctors or nurses knew which patients belonged to which group. The people who prayed for them were given the patient's first name, diagnosis, and general condition, along with updates on their condition. Prayers were offered daily until the patient was discharged from the hospital. All patients signed a consent form letting them know that they may or may not be in the group that was being prayed for.

The results of that study were dramatic and surprised many scientists. It showed that the patients who were prayed for suffered less congestive heart failure and pulmonary edema, were five times less likely to require antibiotics, had fewer episodes of pneumonia, had fewer cardiac arrests, and were less likely to have tubes inserted in their throats to assist breathing.

2. In his 1994 book, Healing Words, Larry Dossey, M.D., cites a number of studies that have researched the effects of prayer and healing:

At the Mind Science Foundation in San Antonio, Texas, researchers took blood samples from 32 volunteers, isolated their red blood cells (RBCS) and placed the samples in a room on the other side of the building. Then the researchers placed the RBCS in a solution designed to swell and burst them, a process that can be measured extremely accurately. Next the researchers asked the volunteers to pray for the preservation of some of the RBCS. To help them visualize, the researchers projected color slides of healthy RBCS. Praying significantly slowed the swelling and bursting of the RBCS.

3. In another study at the Mind Science Foundation, volunteers in a room on one side of the building were asked to visualize volunteers in a room on the other side of the building becoming calmer or more agitated. Meanwhile, the "receivers" were hooked up to biofeedback-type equipment

to gauge their reactions. The results showed that the "influencers" exerted a statistically significant effect on the receivers' moods.

The Healing Impact of Prayer

The healing impact of prayer is increasingly an issue for faith and science. It is a matter of faith for those like me, who believe that their prayers, or those of their friends, can bring healing. It becomes a scientific matter when the effectiveness of prayer or meditation is subject to scrutiny and verification. For instance, Professor Herbert Benson and others have clarified some basic issues. He helped design a study of 1802 people at six different hospitals, from Oklahoma City to Boston, in which social scientists could examine the effectiveness of praying on heart bypass patients.

This was a longitudinal study of patients who enrolled in a prayer program as early as 1998 through 2001. Those conducting the study determined scientifically that praying, under certain circumstances, does not help people of varying Christian or Jewish backgrounds. Indeed, a slight majority of people who knew they were prayed for actually fared worse over time. Some of the ground rules included praying for the same amount of time and reciting the same message for a quick recovery with no complications. This scientific inquiry was called "STEP": "The Study of the Therapeutic Effects of Intercessory Prayer." While it verified that prayer under certain circumstances does not work, most religious believers feel prayer helps relieve anxiety in times of crisis.[3]

One could argue that this study was limited, since it only involved several small groups of Christians who prayed for specific patients with heart disease before an operation. And this is only one study among many more that should be undertaken. It may be that any group of patients prayed for by that particular group involved in this study could have an unwanted outcome. At any rate disproving that prayer for cardiac patients is effective does not refute the sense that prayer can reinforce positive feelings among those who are prayed for.[4]

In the fall of 2007 several rabbis discussed the original heart study of 1988 that was contradicted by the 2006 study by Dr. Benson. These rabbis, like me, are affiliated with the Rabbinical Assembly of Judaism's Conservative Movement, and as colleagues gave me permission to cite their views. A few of them pointed out that the original study, to which Dr. Ellen referred, was suspect since it could not be duplicated by other social scientists. However the lack of scientific proof did not explicitly obviate their collective view that faith can heal.

◇◇◇

Rabbi Paul Teicher (New Jersey and Florida): "The author of the study, Dr. Byrd, posted it in the July 1988 issue of the Southern Medical Journal. The study involved hundreds of cardiac patients on the west coast, and they were prayed for (or not) by a Christian group, who had a list of patients to be prayed for, knowing none personally, and knowing them only by first names. Similarly, the physicians who checked and reported on the patients did not know whether or not a patient was prayed for, just as the patients themselves had no knowledge of which group they were in and whether they were prayed for or not.

Although the published results of that study seemed clearly statistically valid, there have been no similar findings since then. That suggests not a lack of trying to duplicate it, but either of fraud, self-deceit, major error, random luck (studies need a 95% confidence level, not 100% proof), or God changing her mind about allowing science to investigate religion!

When the Byrd study was still considered valid, I proposed to our son the cardiologist, that he run a similar study, comparing the efficacy of prayers by Lubavitch (Hassidic) and by other Orthodox and by Rabbinical Assembly (Conservative) members. He declined, saying essentially, 'No thanks, I'm a diagnostician, not an investigator of mass phenomena.'"

Rabbi Stephanie Dickstein (New Jersey and New York): "There is certainly material suggesting that the social component of religious life seems to be beneficial in terms of health and even possibly longevity. This is particularly true for older Jewish men at morning minyan (daily prayers services), since retired men often don't have the same continuity of social support and interactions that older women do. However, when I share this information in the context of talks I do on Jewish healing and prayer, I also recall how a fellow congregant reminded me, after such a talk, that his father-in-law was hit and killed by a car walking to morning minyan. I think we have to be very careful in prescribing prayer and even other religious practices for cure or prevention. Even as we have to take medical facts and healthy living recommendations as good ideas, they don't necessarily keep us from getting sick and dying. Nevertheless, prayer can be helpful in many ways when we face illness."

Rabbi David Abramson (Massachusetts): "In the medical community there is a growing area of interest and research looking at correlations between religiosity and physical health variables. While there appears to be relationships between religious variables such as direct-active prayer (the Byrd study focused on intercessory prayer), religious attendance, hopefulness, and physical health variables, the research is still in the early stages of development ... Much of the research is still struggling with ways to operationally define religious constructs and separate overall religious observance from general healthcare behaviors."

Rabbi Daniel Goldfarb (Israel): "Some five to ten years ago, I saw an article by Prof. Jeremy Kark, an epidemiologist at the Hebrew University- Hadassah Faculty of Medicine, which reported a study of the comparative health of two sets of kibbutzim—collective settlements, religious and non-religious. As I recollect, the data showed that the religious generally live longer, were healthier, more relaxed, satisfied, etc."

Rabbi Sue Fendrick (Massachusetts): "I'm far less interested in the effect of the double-blind intercessory prayer and more interested in the effect of prayer on people who know they are being prayed for. For example, what if one thousand random Jewish patients who agreed to participate in the study were assigned to two groups of five hundred people, and were told whether they were in the group or not who were given a prayer for a complete recovery. A certain number of synagogue rabbis would agree to add this particular group of people (as a group—not all five hundred names!) to their synagogues' get-well lists. The outcomes of the two groups would be compared.

What would be even better would be to find one thousand self-identified atheists, and get five hundred of them to agree to have synagogues all over the world to pray for them, or randomly assign five hundred of them to the group and see what happens. I have a feeling that even people who don't "believe" in prayer would find their well-being affected by the knowledge that people were praying for them."

<><><><><><><><><><><><><><><><><><><><><><><><><><><><><><><><><><><><><><><>

While the individual views of these rabbis varied, there seemed to be a consensus that religious faith and behavior can have a beneficial impact on health and longevity.

Negative Doctors and Doubting Believers

Whether intercessory prayer can directly help heart patients recover, like those discussed earlier, is doubtful to my mind and in the view of many. However the value of such intercessory prayer is widely endorsed by others, including those who believe that God works through the prayers of his people. Others believe that concerted prayer by others can alter people's destinies.[5]

> *What doctors say can influence their patients' recovery.*

To me it's self-evident that prayers and other types of positive affirmations can have an impact on the healing process of surgical patients. A corresponding impact of negative statements is also apparent. This is illustrated in an episode of the popular TV series, "Grey's Anatomy," where an obese young women hears her surgeon's thoughtless, cruel comments about how fat she is. This causes her to shut down and lose her drive to live. Unfortunately this dramatized episode reflects reality. Words can have a lasting impact, whether such utterances are included in healing prayers, positive affirmations or derogatory comments.[6]

According to psychotherapist Peggy Huddleston in her book *Prepare for Surgery, Heal Faster,*[7] considerable research has been carried out on the healing effects of physicians' affirmations in behalf of their patients. Her emphasis is on words uttered by doctors during surgery, when patients are unconscious but often can still hear what the doctors say to them. Huddleston concludes that what doctors say can influences their patients' recovery long after they wake up.

I'd like to add that even from a religious viewpoint, faith and prayer are problematic. After all there are no guarantees that pious people will have a good life, no matter how much they pray for it. This was illustrated as long as 2500 years ago in the biblical story of Job, who suffered despite his piety. In this parable Satan challenged God to test Job's faith, after indicating Job was a believer because his life was blessed with abundance. When Job then lost his health, wealth and family he still did not curse God. If anything his ordeal challenged him to broaden his perspective, rather than causing him to lose his faith in God's goodness.

At the end of the biblical tale he consistently refused to give in to three friends' admonition to admit he deserved God's punishment. At that point his friends were directed to apologize with sacrificial offerings, while God favored Job with twice the wealth and many more progeny than he had before Satan and God first tested him. The reader may suppose that Job hardly forgot his previous losses of family, health and wealth. However, he ultimately became as content as he was at the beginning.

The prophet Jeremiah too suffered, when joining the Israelite people during the first exile after Jerusalem was destroyed in 586 B.C. At that juncture the prophet asked the eternal question we still raise today: "Why is it that decent people are decimated, while wicked people flourish?" My colleague Rabbi Harold Kushner's internationally acclaimed book, *When Bad Things Happen to Good People*, addresses this troubling question in contemporary terms.

People of faith, including myself, believe that healing is an on-going process that comes from within, and that verbalized prayer is a means to elicit one's own healing or that of others. Just as important, healing comes from beyond us—from our doctors and other caregivers, and ultimately from the Universal Healer. Regrettably that sort of healing is something we can never fully count on. Put another way, even if God always answers our prayers, all too often the answer is "No!"

Prayer, Hope and Love

Throughout this chapter, the kind of prayer we've talked about is intercessory prayer, that is, a plea for divine as well as human intervention. Prayer in various religious traditions is also equated with praise, acknowledgment, thanksgiving, reaffirmation and vows. Such prayer, whether directed to ourselves, to others or to our Higher Power, has the potential for easing people's spirits and calming their souls in a reassuring manner. As someone who has a balanced view of the role of religion, Dr. Herbert Benson has pointed out that those who maintain religious convictions are often imbued with an extra layer of hope when in need of healing. Still, as he acknowledged long ago in a clergy seminar I attended, non-religious, but spiritually-oriented people often exhibit humanistic beliefs that are likewise curative.

But for many who lack religious or more generalized spiritual convictions, we can assume that prayers are probably less helpful, if at all. An exception is found in the old saying, "There are no atheists in foxholes." A major crisis like impending death can make many devout atheists think about God and perhaps lead them to cry out for divine salvation. Such a new-found faith can have a salutary effect, however short-lived.

This is illustrated in a story about a 79 year-old atheist, who lies on his deathbed in a hospital. The aging atheist calls for the hospital chaplain. When the chaplain arrives, the patient asks him to pray for his recovery. "I'm surprised you called for me," said the chaplain. "I heard you are an atheist and you don't believe in God or an afterlife." The dying patient responded, "I am an atheist; but Reverend, I just didn't want to take any chances!"

Even when there's no crisis, God is often invoked. To exemplify this we need only recall George Bernard Shaw's famous comment in which he declared, "I'm an atheist, thank God!"

All-in-all, if we were to ask whether prayer works, the answer would be: "Of course!" But this is so only if you believe the words you say, even if it's just a momentary expression of your fears and aspirations. Just as there is truth in advertising, you must be truthful with yourself for the short-term, and better yet for the long-term, as you examine your convictions and crystallize your outlook. It's also important to be clear about how you might best reach your goals of overcoming the obstacles before you. This is especially critical when health care issues like cancer arise.

One final issue should be addressed here: if God and prayer, or science and mind-body techniques, fail to help, is there anything else that does help? Millions of people, of various faiths or outlooks, have suggested that at such moments the Beatles were right: "All you need is love!" But is it really true, in this instance, that all a prostate patient needs is love? Is love all you need to be restored to good health? Is romantic love or even a broader form of humanitarian love all you need when push comes to shove? If you, or others, maintain a proper, caring attitude, will that be sufficient to resolve your greatest difficulties?

I'd like to suggest the obvious point that by itself, "All you need is love" is simply not true. You require a whole lot more than love to sustain good health and life, whether yours or someone else's.

More than love, you need the commitment of others to fulfill your needs. This includes physicians and other caregivers, who are willing and able to apply their skills to heal you. It includes personal friends who will offer physical and emotional support. And it includes strangers on whose kindness you can rely, to borrow a phrase from Blanche Dubois in *A Streetcar Named Desire*. In addition, you need a degree of self-awareness to discern what's in your best interest or that of your family. Finally, and far more mundane, you need a decent health insurance policy and the financial means to sustain yourself.

In my view these are indispensable, along with pain- and stress-reduction techniques and support group interactions. These down-to-earth realities should be augmented by faith in yourself that you can make it; faith in advancing medical sciences to develop ever better health alternatives; and for those who are so inclined, faith in an eternal deity or some Higher Power to help people and things come together for you. These issues and related subjects are discussed further at *www.ConquerProstateCancer.com.*

Combined with love, these are a powerful set of factors that—with a little bit of luck—will enhance your life for many years.

Part IV:

CONQUER PROSTATE CANCER BY CONNECTING WITH OTHERS

12

Why Family and Friends Make All the Difference

"A real friend is one who walks in when the rest of the world walks out."
—Walter Winchell, 20th century radio newscaster

Going It Alone—a Global Perspective

"Going it alone" is rarely a good idea. For that reason, even somebody who chooses to climb Mt. Everest solo needs a "sherpa"—a local native mountaineer as his guide to assure he'll make it to the summit and back. An Olympic gold medal swimmer like Michael Phelps or a golf champion like Tiger Woods has to score big on his own, but he can achieve his goals only with a great coach. The most powerful CEOs, including the President of the United States, can't do it alone either. They need their business and political consultants, even though, as Harry Truman famously put it, "The buck stops here."

On the other hand, learning how to live on your own, completely independent of others, is purportedly the goal of those who value their sense of self. As a one-time Boy Scout patrol leader and former Cub Scout Master, I've always felt that the motto 'Be Prepared' means the ability to be totally self-reliant. As a long-time religious leader I've identified with Abraham and other biblical leaders who acknowledged their personal commitment to a cause when declaring, "I am here." (Hebrew: *"Hineni."*) Individual self-reliance of this sort is as much a mark of maturity as is the capacity for teamwork.

For me, and I would guess most people, going it alone for a while may be helpful, but not if you do so indefinitely. Isn't that why so many people take a chance on marriage in spite of the high divorce rate? As the Good Book declares, "It's not good for a person to live alone." (Hebrew: *"Lo tov hehyot ha-adam livado"*—Gen. 2:18) By definition aloneness isn't good if you'd like to develop intimacy with others. It won't help if you wish to develop a family or if you seek a broader circle of friends, or want to be connected at a deeper level to the community at large.

Going it alone is also not in your best interest if you'd like to live to a ripe old age. This was demonstrated by a six-year Swedish study involving over 17,000 people. In that study the most isolated and lonely were four times more likely to die earlier than others who had more social supports. This conclusion was validated by a nine year California study where the death rate increased by two to three times among those who had fewer communal and social bonds. These and other research efforts confirm what most of us assume, although the relationship between social isolation and early death needs to be explored more fully.[1]

Aloneness can be a great gift, when you are overcome by the crush of humanity. However loneliness is a terrible curse, particularly for those who do not genuinely prize their solitude. This point is dramatized in one episode of the acclaimed science-fiction television series, "The Twilight Zone." The episode shows a man who had to contend with the daily hassle of New York City's subway system. For some time he wishes with all his heart that the crowds would simply disappear. Waking up one morning, his dream becomes a reality as all those folks suddenly vanish! Quite content, he strolls onto an empty subway train car, sitting wherever he wants, and he gets off without being jostled once. After a few days, he can't stand the horrible, sterile isolation anymore. All he can do is wish for his life to be the same as it once was.

Similarly when a person learns he has prostate or some other cancer, he may wish to be left alone to adjust to his or her new reality or wallow in his misery. Days later, the same person may emerge from an initial state of shock only to crave the support of family and friends. This occurs when a crisis like prostate cancer or some other serious illness arises.

Sharing our pain is both expedient and comforting. Why expedient? Because you can get better more quickly when you know that others will be there for you, standing by your side. Why comforting? Because when you share your pain with others, you know you are not alone. Connecting with others, it turns out, is essential to conquer prostate cancer.

It's ironic that communicating with like-minded people is supportive when, to some extent, their empathy may cause them to suffer with you. Perhaps it's not coincidental that the German word for "empathy" is *"Mitleidung,"* which literally means "suffering with" another. You may even discover that your peers, including family, friends or acquaintances, have suffered like you. When those you know struggle and manage to overcome their problems, their successes can be an impetus for your own recovery, or at least help you adjust to your new circumstances.

Connecting with others is essential to conquer prostate cancer.

The notion that we can't live without each other goes counter to the ideal of the rugged, independent American, fostered by the likes of Emerson and Thoreau in 19th Century New England. Perhaps those gentlemen prized their solitude more than the people they encountered! I suspect though that they preached the importance of self-sufficiency because they had learned the rare art of living with themselves. Could it just be that they were exceptions that proved the rule that, when it comes to humanity, one plus one equals more than two? After all society is more than the sum of its parts.

It can be argued that many of us in 21st Century post-industrialized America have witnessed a resurgence of self-reliance. Since the early 1990's the internet information era has helped women break the "glass ceiling," because brains and energy, more than brawn and bravado, rule the day. Many women and men, have demonstrated that climbing the corporate and entrepreneurial ladder can pay off. Those who work their at-home businesses, while managing to lead active family lives, can succeed because they know how to "work smart, not just hard."

Feminist leaders have proclaimed you should stand on your own two feet and not depend on others, especially men, for your financial well-being. As Leslie Bennet says in her book *The Feminine Mistake: Are We Giving Up too Much?*, women need to be more accountable to themselves. This is so, not only because of the increasing number of divorces, but because women continue to outlive men. Besides, previous assumptions that the right man will eventually come along and support them often do not pan out. In some ways this harkens back half a century ago, when Betty Friedan took up the cause of women in her book *The Feminist Mystique.*[2]

Apart from a resurgence of self-reliance, another promising current development is the ethical ideal of what 20th Century philosopher Martin Buber called "interdependence." This is the state of relying on each other without being co-dependent.[3] I believe that a social-business ethic for the 21st century has begun to emerge that is based on interdependence. For instance multimillionaire businesswoman Loral Langemeier's approach to entrepreneurial team-building seems to be gaining momentum. Women and men alike are beginning to realize they can make it on "their own" if they work with other professionals in "master-mind seminars" in order to reach their individual goals. The whole arena of joint ventures for mutual as well as individual gain is ample evidence of this new modality of far-flung, shared global business practices.[4]

By the same token, collaborative efforts now dominate the publishing industry. For instance one of the most popular and profitable series of books, *Chicken Soup for the ... Soul (College, Teenager's, Mother's, Pet-Lover's, Jewish, You-Name-It!)*, is a huge collaborative effort. These books are the cornerstone of the billion dollar-plus empire of its two founders, Jack Canfield and Mark Victor Hansen. As of April 2008 they have published 112 million books and more than 170 *Chicken Soup* titles because they were able to get other expert speakers to edit each new volume. Each of those editors in turn has produced fabulous anthologies of uplifting true tales by attracting many more captivating authors. These books, translated into 41 languages, continue to enthrall people around the world.[5]

What is true in a global economy applies to the business of life. It is increasingly less desirable and less practical to live life apart from others. To attempt to do so is to miss numerous opportunities, socially, emotionally, and financially.

The distinction between being alone and being lonely is important, but is often blurred. Increasingly people are looking less and less to social, institutional and civic organizations like bowling leagues, fraternal clubs, churches, or synagogues for social outlets, as underscored by Harvard's Robert D. Putnam in *Bowling Alone: The Collapse and Revival of American Community*. Institutionalization has taken a back seat to individualism, and it appears that spirituality has become decentralized. However the realization that this is going on has spurred new efforts to bond people together as reflected in Putnam's subsequent volume, *Better Together: The Book*, co-authored with Lewis Feldstein.[6]

People seem to be on individual spiritual quests while seeking solace in each other. I believe this is so because we have a deep-seated desire to belong somewhere. We know that by remaining socially isolated, we risk staying uninformed and incapable of finding solutions for resolving our problems. In not reaching out to one another, we suffer demoralization, depression, social ostracization, or worse—as indicated by the growing rate of suicide among the very young and old.

In not reaching out to one another, we suffer demoralization, depression, social ostracization, or worse.

Recognizing the negatives of social isolation can account for the explosion of support groups. There's an endless range of online and off-line personal discussion groups or "chat rooms" whose members seek to resolve matters of pain and stress. Such support groups are worth consulting, but should not be your only means of support. Internet forums may have administrative moderators but usually don't have professional facilitators or mentors. In addition, networking with total strangers may not be as secure or helpful as other venues. However these groups can be beneficial, if participants engage in informed discussion about coping with common problems. Barring the availability of other outlets, the internet can unite an on-line community of caring people.

Various chat rooms are dedicated not only to patients with cancer, but diabetes, neuropathy, fibromyalgia, weight gain, bipolar disorder, severe arthritis, spinal stenosis, migraine headaches, heart disease, asthma, sleep disorder, ADHD, and a host of other abiding concerns. This list of maladies applies to my immediate three-generational family alone! You can only imagine what additional illnesses can be addressed online for the population at large.

Examples of online emotional health support group "chat room" comments can be found at *Every Day Health,* a Harvard University website. The categories there include: (1) stress, depression and anxiety; (2) kids' health; (3) living with bipolar disorder; (4) therapist issues; and (5) sleep health. The American Cancer Society Survivor's Network delves into more specific cancer-related topics on its on-line interactive website.[7]

Millions of Americans suffer with multiple problems that demand answers online or off-line on a daily basis. Such answers require close communication between patients and their peers, and between laymen and professional caregivers, whether in person or anonymously. In many cases it's not important that personal family or friends or internet correspondents are unable to prescribe medicine. What's needed is for them to lend an ear or a hand. At the least they can share enough experiences that might help others find appropriate solutions, greater stability, or tranquility.

> *We reach out to one another for the sake of making our lives healthier, as we live stronger and longer.*

Many of us seek to end our loneliness because we know Barbara Streisand had it right: "People who need people are the luckiest people in the world." But there is another dimension of equal importance: we reach out to one another for the sake of making our lives healthier, as we live stronger and longer.

According to yet another recent study, loneliness does not have a major impact on the health of younger Americans as much as it does on the health of older subjects. The negative impact of loneliness among adults ages 50 to 68 was noted in terms of higher levels of epinephrine, higher blood pressure and greater difficulty in dealing with stress, along with a greater risk of incurring poor sleep, immunity, heart problems, suicide and Alzheimers disease.

These issues were noted by Dr. Sheldon Cohen of Carnegie Mellon University in Pittsburgh, Pennsylvania, who concluded that being part of society enables individuals to live longer. Similarly, in *Cancer Talk,* authors Selma Schimmel and Barry Fox pointed out that patients in support groups tend to outlive patients on medications alone.[8] Loneliness or friendship can spell the difference between life and death. This is true in the global economy where the isolation of large populations from the rest of the world has led to the slaughter of millions. This applies as well on a smaller scale in urban and suburban settings, whenever the need for companionship is spurned by individuals or by society-at-large.

We have to do more to reach out to people who seek our help. At the same time those who are neglected must do what they can to call attention to their concerns. That is the point of a fictional story about two former friends, Joe and Moe, who happen to meet on the main street of their small town. Joe sees Moe and says, "Why don't you say 'Hullo!' to me anymore?" Responding, Moe says, 'Because you never ask me how I'm doing." At which point Joe asks, "So tell me, how are you doing?" Moe snaps back, "Don't ask!"

If we cut ourselves off from others we end up as losers. We lose the support of people we could otherwise count on. And we lose the opportunity to overcome pain and stress. If we emerge from the cocoon of isolation, rather than going it alone, we will have what it takes to quickly conquer prostate and other forms of cancer and the disruption they bring into our lives.

Unconditional Love versus Passing Friendship

One of the most important questions a person with cancer (or anyone) can ask himself is, "Who are my friends?" I mean real friends! Not mere acquaintances who will say "Hullo!" when they happen to see you at a community function. Not passing friends, who occasionally invite you to a dinner party or the theater.

The friends I'm talking about are the ones who are there for you when you and your family first learn of your cancer. True friends will also be there for you when you have it treated and in the months and years that follow. Such friends are with you whenever you suffer any loss or celebrate a joyous occasion. These are people who are the first to lend a hand if there's work to be done or a problem to be solved. They are also the last to leave your house or the hospital when you still require the "milk of human kindness."

A real friend is one who offers you unconditional love, which you offer them in return. Such a person can be relied upon in good or bad times. He or she is not a fair-weather friend, who appears only when conditions are ripe or the living is easy. Real friends love you for no reason other than the value they place on their relationship with you, not because they can gain something from you, like wealth, power, influence or sympathy. A genuine friend does not fear getting tainted by a disease. He or she may be careful if you are contagious, but will not be daunted when you have cancer, which is hardly communicable.

When I was a twelve-year old kid I had two such friends, Arnie and Ray. We would play together, come rain or shine, whether we were sick or healthy, and nothing could keep us apart. We enjoyed each other's company when biking on the sidewalk or working together on school projects at each other's homes. In college my best friends were usually my roommates. We cried over girlfriends who broke up with us, or yelled at teachers in absentia when they gave us bad grades. We were elated when we "aced" a final exam. We always stood by each other.

For what is now some thirty-six years, I've been fortunate that my best friend has been my wife, Yvonne. Whatever our ups-and-downs, through sickness and health, we've been there for each other. Her pain is mine, and mine is hers. My joy is hers, and hers is mine. Frankly, whether your best friend is your spouse or your partner-in-life or your current boy- or girl-friend is immaterial. Everyone needs a best friend. Having one is great. Two are unusual. Three are rare. Four are exceptional.

Nobody should assume that one's spouse or life partner is automatically one's best friend. I learned this the hard way as an undergraduate at UCLA. I was one of sixty students chosen out of six hundred applicants to attend a student-faculty conference on "The Art of Loving," based on Eric Fromm's book of the same name. I will never forget how in one discussion group a female professor voluntarily told a large number of students that she found herself talking more to women faculty friends than to her own husband. When she paused for questions after her presentation, she told us we could ask her about anything, so I raised my hand. When she called on me, I asked her whether she meant her husband was not her best friend. Immediately she lashed out, "That's none of your business!" and added, "Next question!" That rude reaction told me more about her than any direct denial or bald-faced lie.

By definition your best friend loves you unequivocally. That person can and will do his or her best to help you get through prostate cancer or other crises. Sure, you can get upset once in awhile by things your significant other says or does, and vice versa, but that's true in every relationship. What's important is that you and your best friend know you will overcome your temporary doubts because you realize you can count on being there for each other. I believe this realization has a curative value: It can reduce your aches and pains and sundry stresses, as you try to conquer challenges like prostate cancer and its side effects.

Make no mistake: unconditional love does not come easily. All too often in my professional career, I've devoted myself to my congregation at times to the exclusion of my family. Even after retiring after thirty years of "pulpiteering," I've often isolated myself to finish various projects, including this book. Yet my wife, however begrudgingly, has relinquished her time with me so I could meet, counsel and console others. This is what she had to say when I was about three-fourths done with this book:

"Ed has just finished Chapter 12 of his seventeen-chapter book on prostate cancer. He decided to write the book based on his experiences as well as those of others. He has been researching, talking to people, etc. I'm delighted that he has found a way to give back; a way to help others and their families, confronting similar and somewhat broader issues. His enthusiasm is catching. What he has written is amazing. However, it's getting harder to get his attention these days...a little like the old rabbinic days when he invested more time with his congregants than with us. Still, his experience has reminded him how we all need him. He is there for us just as we are there for him."

—*Yvonne*

One of the silver linings of prostate cancer or surgery of any sort is that it confirms that your friend's love is unconditional—or not. When you have to check into the hospital at 5:30 a.m. and your wife or significant other willingly gets up two hours earlier to go there with you; when she watches you "go under" the anesthesia and refuses to leave the waiting room during the four hours of an operation; when she sits in your room as urine flows into the catheter tube, smelling up the place; when she insists on staying that first night in the adjacent bed (with the hospital's permission), just so you're not alone; when she willingly wakes up every time a nurse walks in to check on you; when she listens to you grouse at home as your body rebels against your new stitches during the first two days after surgery ... you just know her love is unconditional. That kind of love should never be taken for granted.

The same can be said about the unconditional love of one's children. The last faces I saw before being wheeled into the operating room were those of my wife and daughter. The first faces I saw upon waking up from surgery were those of my wife and daughter. When I was back in my hospital room, my wife handed me a collage of photos from my son. The photographs displayed him, his wife and their infant daughter, currently our first and only grandchild, who at the time of the operation was just ten months old. Knowing my son and his family were a fixture in my existence made my heart soar, not sore. This too was mutual, unconditional love at its best.

Realizing you are part of a family that can turn to each other in your time of need is priceless, whether it's the younger generation relying on the older generation, or the older relying on the younger. Indeed this scenario is played out in a biblical vision according to Malachi, the last of the prophets. He proclaimed that one day Elijah, an earlier powerful prophet of God, will return from his heavenly sojourn, to usher in the messianic era. That end-time, proclaims Malachi, will be marked by the intergenerational reconciliation of sons with their fathers (Malachi 3:13–24). In my view that's a vision each of should not only espouse, but enact as often as possible in our own lifetime. Too often the opposite occurs, since ours is a "throwaway generation," particularly with regard to our elders. I describe this in a recent posting at *www. ConquerProstateCancer.com*.

It's evident that passing friendship can be very energizing, but by definition such a relationship is momentary, be it days, months or even a few years. Whether it is a pleasant conversation with a hospital staff member or an interchange in a support group, or an association with a neighbor while you're still in the neighborhood, tentative friendships assure us that we will not be turned away for the short-term.

Unconditional love can't be beat; but interim friendship, even of strangers, is reassuring. It doesn't matter whether you're in touch with an occasional acquaintance, a one-time visitor or letter-writer, or if you interact with your nurse during her eight- or twelve-hour shift while in the hospital. Each of these count for a lot, especially when you don't have a genuine, long-term friend you can count on, or if your constant friend can't be there at that moment—which happens. In many circles this is known as "friendly visiting," even when it's the first time the visitor meets the patient.[9]

Years ago, before my wife and I had children, I remember opting for a vascular operation to increase my semen count to raise my fertility level.

Following the operation my cousin and some acquaintances visited me at the hospital. I was surprised how buoyed up their visit made me feel, given the elective nature of that operation. Still, I'm convinced their visit helped me bounce back more quickly to full health.

All of us need the support of family and friends. Without a doubt unconditional support and love offers the best form of assurance. However, it's the better course of wisdom to rely on the individual and collective support of others, even if it's just for the interim. Simply put, I would take it any way I can, and I'm sure you would too!

13

Support Groups
Near and Far

"You give but little when you give of your possessions.
It is when you give of yourself that you truly give."
—Kahlil Gibran, 19th–20th Century Lebanese-American author

Are Support Groups Indispensable?

One of my acquaintances, a man I'll call "Otto," went through robotic prostate surgery about four months before me. It was through attending a support group—a small, facilitated gathering of prostate cancer patients and survivors—that he first heard of robotics, explored it more fully, and felt it was for him. He never regretted attending those meetings and continued attending the weekly sessions less than a month after his operation.

Otto divulged the details of his operation to me when I called him. His account was so encouraging it helped spur my resolve to follow suit. Later on I interviewed Otto for more details, which led to a supportive dialogue. I eventually wrote his profile for this book (in Chapter 16). Otto clearly represented two sides of the same coin: the need for group support and individual support.

Others have told me they dislike formal groups and don't do well in them. They emphasized that when they have questions or issues to resolve, they prefer one-on-one individual conversations with other knowledgeable, empathetic prostate cancer survivors. Some patients prefer to make phone calls or engage in hot-line discussions instead of face-to-face meetings. Such conversations are useful, even necessary, when family members are unable or unwilling to communicate openly with a patient to discuss his cancer with him. Even if a relative of a patient is willing to talk with him, many patients prefer more dispassionate discussions with individuals who "have been there" and can more directly address their concerns.

I myself did not even consider a support group before my surgery, and looking back I believe that was probably my loss. I might have found the necessary resources to cut through the confusion my first urologist instilled in me. In presenting a large menu of treatment options, cafeteria style, like all too many doctors, he overwhelmed me because he, in effect said, "Here! Choose one of the above!" Support groups, while not prescriptive, can do better than that. Its members can help you weigh the pros and cons of different treatments with an insider's first-hand description of what to expect.

I attended my first support group meeting about three months after my operation, more out of curiosity than need. I had previous experience in spirituality support groups and in Alanon, but I had no idea what a prostate cancer support group could offer me. After all, my recovery was so swift and pain-free I was not sure whether I needed any further help. What I found out is that when people from all walks of life gather, there's always something to be learned. Just as important, there's always something you can share that will benefit the others in the group.

When I walked into my first meeting of the Southwest Florida Wellness Community prostate cancer group and sat down, everybody was a stranger to me, but all were quite cordial and accepting. The group facilitator was a down-to-earth, laid-back psychologist who directed The Wellness Community location where we met. As was his custom in behalf of newcomers, he made sure to ask each participant to briefly introduce himself by his first name and his last name. To my surprise nobody remained completely anonymous. I took this as an indication that, unlike Alcoholics Anonymous, there is generally no social stigma in having prostate cancer, even if some of the particulars that come up in discussions are quite intimate. I should emphasize that this is the outlook of this particular Wellness Community; other prostate support groups may ask only for first names to protect privacy.

As those present introduced themselves to me, each of them summarized how long they had their disease, at what stage it was diagnosed, if there was a recurrence, and the nature of their current treatment. I immediately surmised that these group meetings were primarily about sharing community resources as well as new testing or treatment approaches group members had come across in their outside conversations or readings. The tone was friendly and positive. Nobody cried, wailed, or bemoaned their fate, although some quietly expressed their chagrin when pointing out an adverse turn of events. Before long it occurred to me that such groups are valuable for those who have no other recourse for openly expressing their concerns. They are also of value if you don't live an environment that's generally free of emotional outbursts or confrontations.

The support group I attended was not one where each person described his innermost anxieties. Group members, thankfully, did not offer so-called "constructive criticism" when responding to another group member's current concerns. Rather this was a group where each individual shared where he was in his medical journey, with comparable comments uttered by his fellow-travelers. The tone of the group was one of hope and empathy.

Take for instance one gentleman who reported how years after surgery, the recurrence of his prostate cancer compelled him to try radiation seeding, also known as brachytherapy. Initially he conveyed his doubts about the value of this method. Weeks later, when he saw brachytherapy's positive results, he expressed his exuberance. Given his success his remarks at the group meeting were met with a round of applause. We were all glad for him that he had "licked" his cancer for the moment, and our outward expression of support meant a lot to him, judging from his facial expression. It simply didn't matter that many of us would not have chosen any form of radiation for ourselves.

> *A support group is yet another vehicle for conquering prostate cancer.*

In its literature, The Wellness Community promotes a "patient-active philosophy," with the belief that "in actively fighting cancer those suffering from it may improve their odds." In other words, a support group is yet another vehicle for conquering prostate cancer.

While the group I attended dealt primarily with the sharing of resources, groups at other locations might address more intimate concerns on a regular basis. Even at my local Wellness Community's support group, there have been a few occasions when our members decided to address a particularly sensitive issue that revealed the vulnerabilities of some participants. Such topics included sexual functioning, incontinence or the fear of death.

Some prostate cancer support groups are purely expressive—that is, a member shares his problems and the rest of the group seeks to address his issues. I've devised a mnemonic that may be useful in guiding group dynamics for these more interactive personal discussions. Using the letters S-U-P-P-O-R-T GrouP can help every member grasp the group's purpose and process in a memorable way.

- S—Speak and communicate openly and clearly: don't yell or whisper, conceal, or over-reveal.
- U—Understand fully what others are saying before you respond.
- P—Passion—speak from the heart; emotions are allowed and encouraged.
- P—Principle—respond with thoughtful content and from integrity.
- O—On target—stay on topic.
- R—Rapport with others must be maintained; no antagonism, no judgment ("friendly eyes"; not even "constructive" criticism).
- T—Time-limited comments are expected, so others can respond or speak their own thoughts.
- GrouP—The Group must be Pliable when a member asks permission to start a new discussion thread.

An expressive support group follows a predetermined group process, with a facilitator's guidance. It becomes increasingly indispensable, as its members will keep learning from each other and not be distracted from the collective goal of growing as individuals. To be sure, a lot depends on the group leader's style: it makes a big difference if he is more directive or more laid back; if he sees himself more as a group member than a group facilitator; and if he feels that there are certain areas that need to be addressed, rather than letting group topics evolve on their own. In turn it can make a difference if discussion topics are based on group consensus, determined at a group meeting, or if a topic comes up when an individual member gets the sense of the group that it's okay to move on to something new.

Although I attended meetings at The Wellness Community twice a month, I also went to two other area locations. One is a Man to Man meeting I attended, which like other Man to Man gatherings around the country is funded by the American Cancer Society. In the first hour a group of some ten men held a personal discussion at a lunch table in Sarasota Memorial Hospital's main cafeteria. An hour later they gathered with other men and with wives or female companions for a community education session in the hospital auditorium. The purpose of the male-only groups was to give men a chance to openly discuss their intimate concerns, especially those involving sexuality.

To convey a sense of the Man to Man support group dynamics, it's worth describing how three newcomers to the group, including me, were first introduced to the "old-timers." As it happened, none of us "newbies" had known each other previously, yet we'd all had robotic-assisted surgery within the last six months, courtesy of Dr. Carey. Each of us stood up and told what the chairman would later call our "success stories."

The first gentleman, about 45 years old, reported that for the past thirty years, ever since his teens, he had suffered from a severe case of diabetes. As a result his robotic surgery was more complicated and it did not help him avoid near-total incontinence for the duration. He explained that his weekly visits at a computerized bio-feedback lab for a three-month period were gradually helping him to regain what I would call a "gladder bladder."

The second gentleman, age 69, explained that he had never had any previous health issues. To my surprise he indicated he was unconcerned that he might never have sexual relations with his wife again, should that be the long-term outcome of his surgery. He was simply happy to have his cancerous prostate completely removed. He told us he was equally pleased that he was able to leave the hospital within twenty-four hours of surgery, and return to his daily routines a few days later. His only complaint was that after the operation he suffered from excess stomach gas. As in all robotic-assisted surgeries, gas was deliberately inserted into his stomach area by the anesthesiologist in order to more effectively separate his prostate from other internal organs. This was done to allow the surgeon to see and do more precisely what needed to be done.

After the first two men finished speaking, I was asked to summarize the nature of my quick, pain-free recovery after robotic surgery earlier that year, when I was still 63. I gave credit to robotic technology, the surgeon, and my mental/spiritual preparation. I found it striking that the three of us were at different stages of our lives, as reflected by our age spread of 45 to 69 years; we had vastly different health backgrounds, orientations and ways of coping with surgery; yet we unanimously felt that our robotic surgery was a great success.

Incidentally a couple of weeks later, when attending yet another Wellness Community support group meeting, another member asked me to explain how meditation can eliminate stress before surgery. At that point I gave a two minute summary of how I breathed deeply in and out several times, followed by visualizing my body gradually filling with purifying, uplifiting light from head to toe, while using my other senses to relax each part of my body. The man who asked me about meditation had a one-syllable response: "Heh!" By that I gathered he was suitably impressed but didn't have an inkling about how to go about this on his own. Had I been the group leader I would have preferred not just to talk about this meditative practice but to demonstrate it by inviting others in the group to experience it for themselves; but that was not on the agenda!

A different Wellness Community patient support group I attended involved men and women with a variety of cancers. There too the tone was cordial and upbeat. I was particularly impressed by an older woman who had survived breast cancer for ten years. She told us that five years after her initial surgery, her cancer came back and metastasized, affecting her arms and legs, causing her legs to distend and making her bones brittle. She bore all this with grace, wit, and perseverance, and as she spoke a smile never left her lips. Her concern, she told us, was more for her husband than herself. I was totally buoyed up by this support group session because this woman was an inspiring, first-rate human being. What keeps such people going is their faith in God, in their doctors, and in themselves, and above all, their faith in the value of life.

In view of my support group experiences, it may surprise some to hear that I do not feel these groups are indispensable, even though they can make a real difference. By this I mean you can recuperate from prostate cancer without relying on the resources of a formal group. In fact you can manage quite nicely, providing you have other formal or informal supports in place, such as a doctor's supervision, family members to talk with, and friends to rely on.

However, a support group of peers who, like you, have experienced prostate cancer can add a lot to the quality of your life if you keep an open mind and an open ear. This is true of any well-run cancer group, cardiac care support effort, or Alcoholics or Gamblers Anonymous group. Support groups are not essential for survival, unless you're totally on your own, but they are extremely helpful for patients, survivors and their families.

While support groups are not essential, I advocate them because they provide a safe environment that fosters renewed hope. At the same time they often allow patients to vent and express their fears, frustrations and despair. Furthermore, as implied by research findings, support groups, when coupled with appropriate medication, can add years to your life and life to your years.

> *A support group of peers can add a lot to the quality of your life.*

To borrow from Barbara DeAngelis, a group makes you realize you are not different, you can do it, and you are home.[1] As such, support groups can effectively help you conquer prostate cancer.

Support Groups You Can Turn To

An almost unlimited number of virtual and in-person support groups serve the needs of all cancer patients and survivors, including those who have had prostate cancer. Such groups may be found at web sites useful for those who can't attend a group in person or for those who wish to supplement actual attendance at a support group. One example is a talk-radio cancer support show called "The Group Room," billed as "the world's largest cancer support group."[2]

When you tune in to "The Group Room" you can hear the voices of survivors, therapists, doctors, and others discuss patients' emotions, coping skills, dealing with treatment side-effects, and managing work and insurance concerns. Others describe moving on with their lives once their cancers have been treated. A book that collates many previous broadcasts has been published under the title of *Cancer Talk: Voices of Hope and Endurance from the Group Room* as noted earlier. The show is available throughout the world on XM satellite radio and is featured on regular radio broadcasts in about twenty states, generally on Sundays from 4:00 to 6:00 p.m., Eastern Standard Time. For telephone access one can dial 1-800-GRP-ROOM/1-800-477-7666, or you can go on-line at *www.vitaloptions.com* and hear current and archived broadcasts, such as those in which this book and I were featured during June and September 2008. *Cancer Talk* was edited and reproduced in a book by cancer survivor and advocate Selma R. Schimmel with Barry Fox, Ph.d.[3] Selma is the show's weekly moderator at a radio studio located in Los Angeles.

The American Cancer Society website offers a Cancer Survivor Network at its website *www.cancer.org*. Through this website cancer survivors can contact fellow survivors as well as caregivers, hook up to teleconferences, and obtain cancer information, even establishing their own confidential homepage. Among other features one can find brief inspirational profiles of others who have courageously confronted cancer.

Another online site called Malecare serves as a support group specifically for men with prostate cancer (*www.malecare.org/index.html*). Visitors, including prostate cancer patients, survivors and their families, can subscribe to a regular ezine (online newsletter) and blog (web log). They can interact with others who have gone through this disease and can find more information about their diagnosis and treatment options than their doctors may have provided.

Local in-person support groups are usually part of nationwide programs such as the American Cancer Society's Man to Man programs and men's prostate cancer groups, like those at The Wellness Community in Sarasota, Florida. It should be noted that The Wellness Community is a national organization with twenty-two local affiliates and two international affiliates in Tokyo, Japan and Tel Aviv, Israel. The Wellness Center I have frequented has four local satellite programs[4].

Us TOO International (*www.UsToo.org*) is a worldwide, multi-faceted support, educational and fundraising organization with about 325 chapters in the United States and abroad that focus exclusively on prostate cancer. It offers support groups in most of its locations. Its home page, featuring meeting chapters and support groups, has a link for viewers to "Find a Chapter Near You" and another link called "Online Communities: Prostate Pointers." This is followed by "Support for Companions and Families" and "Support for Gay Men". Each link is a virtual invitation for men with various viewpoints to delve into their own problems and figure out how best to address them. This is a self-help organization at its best.

Apart from Us TOO International and similar organizations there are numerous local prostate support services and groups abroad in various locations in English-speaking countries like Britain, Canada, and Australia, as well as other nations. For a complete and current listing of recommended prostrate cancer support organizations and other cancer resources in the United States and around the world, including details and reviews of their various offerings, see my website, *www.ConquerProstateCancer.com* or my blog *www.ConquerProstateCancernow.com.*

The primary function of support groups, whether "virtual" or in-person, is encapsulated by the central mission statement of the Wellness Community: "To help people affected by cancer enhance their health and well-being through participation in a professional program of support, education and hope." This should be the goal of all support programs that serve prostate cancer patients, survivors and those who love them.

It is immaterial whether those affected by prostate cancer elect to be supported in groups, by phone, online at sites like *www.ConquerProstateCancer. com,* or through the informal circles of family or friends. Whatever avenue they select, all who contend with prostate or other forms of cancers are entitled to find their own way toward improving their health and increasing their hope for a longer, pain-free and stress-free life.

The job of society is to make available as many resources as possible toward conquering prostate cancer. We've made good inroads, even though it feels like we're still at the starting line of this marathon race. If we keep going, the rest will follow.

14

How Do the Neighbors Cope with Pain and Stress? Profiles in Prostate Cancer, Part I

*"There are only two truths: life and death.
Everything else really doesn't matter."*
—Anonymous

You're Not Alone

If you really want to conquer prostate cancer, do yourself a favor: talk with your neighbors. Not just any neighbor, but those who have been through this disease or are currently confronting it. As I've previously noted, don't expect to handle such matters of life and death in total isolation. Instead recognize you're never in this alone.

No matter where you live, you'll find neighbors who have been in your shoes. Of course all too many men won't even acknowledge that they too have had prostate cancer. And if they do, they won't necessarily tell you the nitty-gritty about how it affected them. You wouldn't know it from my personal revelations earlier in this book, but there are many men who would rather not talk openly about their prostate cancer.

Still, don't kid yourself! Men will reveal their most private concerns if they find out your "big secret" is one they are confronting or have already faced. So don't be surprised if someone over forty or fifty will spell out what he's gone through, especially if you first tell him prostate cancer is now your lot or that of someone you love.

It's true: when I spoke with some of my neighbors about my new-found condition, they not only commiserated, but told me their tales or shared their relatives' experiences. When they open up, men, like women, tend to understand each other. Under the right circumstances we don't just talk about sports, business, or politics. We'll bare our souls if you're forthcoming too.

Perhaps this is due to some atavistic, tribal thing where one man tells another, "I'll show you mine, if you show me yours!" I'd rather think of it as basic empathy, comparable to the deep connection you see many women make all the time, even when they first meet as total strangers. We men are capable of that too, at least some of the time.

All of us need to take advantage of such opportunities to connect with our neighbors. We have a lot to learn from them—men and women alike, who have "been there and done that." The former Ma Bell phone slogan to "reach out and touch someone" can be mutually rewarding. We all benefit from sharing our personal struggles to conquer prostate cancer, either by learning something vital or solidifying what we already know. And there's always someone nearby you can talk with because prostate cancer patients and survivors live in every neighborhood across the land.

Questions to Ponder

Localized early prostate cancer is accompanied by few if any noticeable symptoms among most men at the time of diagnosis. Ask your neighbors if they felt anything before they learned they had this illness. It happens, but it's rare, since,—when first detected, this is generally an asymptomatic disease. I myself knew something was wrong before my first visit to my new urologist, but I had chalked that up to other long-term benign problems until I learned there was more to it.

Since men don't usually "feel" in advance of a diagnosis that they might have prostate cancer, it rarely causes pain or stress—not at first. However, the treatment a man chooses, whether surgery, radiation or other alternatives like hormone deprivation (before or after radiation or surgery) can be more stressful or painful than the localized disease itself.[1]

I was one of the exceptions to this rule. Even before being diagnosed with prostate cancer, I felt the constant pressure of an enlarged benign prostate and suffered a burning sensation due to prostatitis. It may also be that my small cancerous prostate growth, discovered later on, had something to do with some minor pain and stress I felt before I was diagnosed. Still, I find it remarkable that the surgery itself and its aftermath resulted in little pain or stress. I may be unique, given my background, skills and aspirations. But so is every other person. That's why I'm convinced the approaches I've described can be acquired and applied by anyone with prostate cancer or by those who care for him.

Such assurances will probably not dissuade many newly diagnosed prostate cancer patients and their families from asking pertinent questions. In my experience their most distressing concerns are: Will I ever regain control of my life? Which treatment will best serve my needs? Will the treatment option I choose increase or decrease any pain or discomfort that comes my way? How much will it affect my sex life? Will I end up peeing in my pants? These are all appropriate worries that need to be addressed; yet those who raise these vital concerns need to stand ready to resolve them, lest their worries never cease.

> *Worry is endemic in society, even when your concerns can be effectively addressed.*

Worry is endemic in society, even when your concerns can be effectively addressed. This has been noted by acclaimed psychiatrist and Adult Deficit Disorder pioneer, Edward M. Hallowell, whom I knew during my years in Boston. In his book, *Worry: Controlling It and Using It Wisely,* he provides techniques that can offset anxiety, similar to those I've offered in reference to stress reduction. He too advocates breathing techniques, prayer and meditation; appropriate medication; support from friends; reassuring statements and behaviors between spouses and life partners; sexual activity, including simple touching; and also listening or dancing to music. Even when presented with so many options to resolve their concerns, many people find it hard to stop worrying.[2] And simply singing a song or telling someone "Don't worry. Be happy!" won't "cut it" either.

Engaging in such stress-reducing behaviors can be helpful. But unless a person seeks proper guidance and develops the right mind-set, he will remain anxious, especially when initially dealing with cancer. With regard to prostate cancer many men can't help but worry if the adverse outcomes of various medical procedures will be partial or total, temporary or permanent. These are hardly minor concerns in a society that places undue emphasis on men keeping their male organs intact and fully functional. Given both external and internalized social pressures, it's not surprising that many fellow patients and survivors will get stressed at a time when cooler heads should prevail.

For these and other reasons you should put little credence in dismissive comments of well-meaning friends. Disregard those who minimize prostate cancer as an all-too-common, innocuous, or treatable disease that is not a cause for worry. I had to do that when an older acquaintance in Florida told me: "Most of us will eventually get it. It's no big deal!" Well, now that I've set aside all my initial self-denial, I'm here to tell you that it is a big deal, even though it's largely controllable. While this dismissive view is well-intended, we can't deny that some of us may develop advanced prostate cancer, with nearly 30,000 dying every year in the United States alone. This of course refers to those men whose cancer is more aggressive primarily because they didn't have it screened or detected early enough. Sometimes, though, as in the case of one man I know, a low PSA one year can be followed by a high score the next, leading to the discovery of metastatic prostate cancer. That happens too.

Even when you confirm you have localized, early-stage cancer, of the kind described in this book, don't ignore it or take it lightly, before or after you've had it treated. After all, even after a cancerous prostate has been surgically removed, prostate cancer can recur due to malignant cells that might remain undetected in the prostate bed.

I personally would not panic, though, since in the United States today there's only a one percent recurrence after five years. However it's true that patients need to know that the recurrence of cancer depends largely on how much surgical experience their doctors have before any given prostatectomy. No matter how prestigious a hospital may be, if a surgeon with less than ten hours experience performs a prostatectomy, in contrast to a doctor who has performed the same operation 250 times, the result could eventually spell the difference in cancer recurrence, namely in 17.9 percent versus 10.7 percent of the patients.[3]

After ten years it is slightly more likely that a prostate cancer survivor's cancer may recur, although nationwide the average recurrence is 93 percent after ten years and 76 percent after 15 years. One man in my support group felt he was home free ten years after a radical prostatectomy, only to learn in the thirteenth year that his cancer had returned and metastasized. While those I interviewed tended to minimize this reality, those not in denial acknowledged they felt at least a little stress in the face of the unknown.

Current or former prostate patients also ask whether their faith will help them overcome their disease. If they have little faith in a providential God, do they at least have enough faith in scientific progress, in their doctors, or in themselves? If so will they be able to say with certainty: "Eventually I'll be all right"? Then too some men wonder if their families will be supportive or evasive, dancing around the reality of their father's or brother's or son's condition. Will he be isolated or will he find suitable support to help him navigate the uncharted waters?

In short, the stresses experienced by men afflicted with prostate cancer often lead to one persistent question: will they conquer the cancer or will it conquer them?

These are just a few of the questions that plague men facing prostate cancer. Such worrisome questions are endless, yet each must be pondered and resolved in ways I've suggested in previous chapters. Otherwise patients, survivors and their families will not be able to get on with their lives.

My Survey Questionnaire

These and a host of related concerns are raised in the survey question-naire I formulated to help me write this chapter and the next two that follow. The questionnaire served as an interview schedule to gain a glimpse into the lives of sixteen other men, besides me, who had been diagnosed and treated for early, localized prostate cancer. Most of these men had conventional treatments involving radiation—whether external beam or "seeding," and surgery, whether standard or robotic. Two other men whose backgrounds I gleaned from more casual conversation (rather than using the question-naire), chose alternative treatment options, as did a third man whose case was presented by his surgeon in a printed article.

The survey I created was fairly exhaustive, as reflected in its lengthy title, "Prostate Cancer Survivor Questionnaire: How Treatment Options, Support and

Faith Helped Patients with Incontinence, Impotence/Sexual Dysfunction, Pain and Stress." The questionnaire is posted at *www.ConquerProstateCancer.com.*

Four of the patients I interviewed were prostate cancer survivors in my neighborhood, an active adult community of people ages fifty-five and older. Eight other subjects were clergymen, since one of my goals was to determine if faith was an important factor that facilitated healing in the course of prostate cancer treatments. Of these clergymen four were Christian and four were Jewish. I've already noted that three men whose profiles I'll present chose alternative approaches, including one whose published case study I condensed. A final group consisted of four laymen (non-clergy) who had robotic surgery either in Sarasota or elsewhere. For the record, with the exception of a few of my neighbors and one clergyman, I had not previously associated with or even spoke to most of those I've profiled in this and other chapters.

I felt fortunate I got a good response when I asked for survey volunteers in person, by phone or e-mail. However, since these interview subjects were self-selected, this was not a random, scientific study. These are anecdotal accounts that are to be regarded only as a preliminary report.

Those I interviewed volunteered because I assured them I would convey their cases anonymously in this book. They felt that sharing what they went through might help other prostate cancer patients. Some of the participants volunteered because they wanted to consolidate their own thoughts as they responded to my questions.

The eighteen gentlemen I spoke with shared their varied experiences with me even more candidly than I had expected. I found their openness to be astonishing. Perhaps they were willing to discuss their most intimate, personal details with me because I was a rabbi with extensive experience in keeping confidences, or because they felt I would not be judgmental. More importantly they were aware I too had been a prostate cancer patient and had "walked in their shoes." I deliberately fostered that connection by briefly comparing their experiences and mine after they responded to a few questions. In that regard I was something of a credible "participant-observer" when conversing with each of them.

The main objective of the interviews was to ascertain how positively or negatively each man responded to his cancer and its treatment. A secondary objective was to determine the role of faith, prayer and meditation in helping these patients cope. Related to this, I sought to determine whether being a clergyman, as opposed to a layperson, made a difference in helping reduce or eliminate the pain and stress of early stage prostate cancer, its various treatments and side-effects. After evaluating each case, I discovered that at times being a clergyman imbued with great faith was helpful, although sometimes it made no difference.

Because the profiles I've written are anecdotal, we should assume that other prostate cancer patients and survivors might respond differently. However, the answers I received represent a broad range of experiences. They all had important things to say about choosing a treatment; developing a trusting rapport with their doctors; and whether turning to religious faith or engaging in a religious practice helped reduce their pain and stress regarding such issues as potential impotence and incontinence. Perhaps this initial survey questionnaire will be fine-tuned at a later date and administered to a larger population. Only a broader study can validate some of the general conclusions to be drawn here.

What's Up in the Neighborhood?

As a prelude to sharing each of my four neighbors' profiles, I'd like to tell you a bit about my neighborhood in general. We live in an active 55+ active adult community. When my wife and I first moved in September 2006 from Boston's North Shore to Sarasota, we had no idea who our neighbors were. I certainly didn't think to ask how many of them were prostate cancer survivors.

Those I later identified as former prostate patients had conventional open surgery or radiation. The kinds of radiation they had included "seeding" (brachytherapy), or external beam radiation, or one of its variations, IMRT—intensive modulated radiation therapy.

What impressed me most about the neighbors I interviewed is that, had I not asked, I would never have guessed that any had been treated for cancer. All were vibrant, active individuals. Some had a prostate procedure as long as ten years ago and some more recently. Each man I interviewed was so energetic and conversational that I never suspected he went through anything remotely similar to my procedure until he told me otherwise.

At the time of the interviews these four particular men were 63 to 79. However their ages when first diagnosed and treated for prostate cancer ranged from 58 to 68. Two were Protestant and two were Jewish; but with the exception of one subject, there were few if any major differences in their overall outlook.

The names of each person I profiled, and some background details have been changed to preserve their anonymity, but all other details are precisely what each man told me. These profiles are true stories about men of various backgrounds with Gleason scores ranging from 4 to 7 ng/DL (nanograms per decileter). Their responses about their low to moderate early-stage prostate cancer are unique but have a lot in common.

The Neighbors: Four True Tales

1. Al's Story—Fitness and Faith Make for Full Recovery after Surgery

After his honorable discharge as a marine, Al worked for thirty years, four days a week, as a regional traveling sales rep for a major firm. He was first diagnosed with prostate cancer in 1996 at the age of 58. A short time later he decided to have his prostate surgically removed through radical prostatectomy. He was the first in his family to have had prostate cancer and subsequent treatment, although his brother followed him a few years later.

When he was first diagnosed, Al's PSA was 5.6. In the three previous years it had steadily gone up from 3.2 to 4.5 to 5.4. His doctor felt this progression, not to mention his moderately high PSA required a biopsy, which proved positive for cancer. It was evident that he had early stage cancer, based on a Gleason score of 6 (3+3). He did not panic over the news, since he was sure his doctor would help him get through the cancer. He stated that, "I was determined to live. I retained a rational attitude of acceptance, with the likelihood that I would be fine in the long run. Besides, I had my wife's full support."

Al's doctor informed him about the treatment options then available. The doctor, a leading professor at a major research hospital, offered the alternative treatment of experimental cryosurgery as well as radiation. However, Al quickly decided on radical prostatectomy. Al's decision to undergo this procedure came easily, especially in the absence of any statistical certainty about the effects of radiation, the leading mainstream alternative. His extreme trust in his doctor before and after the surgery made his decision that much easier.

Before the surgery Al had only one troublesome symptom: he noticed some pink coloration of his urine, ascribed to slight bleeding. He spent four days in the hospital after the surgery and was allowed to use self-administered pain medication by means of a pump. By the time he got home four days later he did not experience any pain at all from the surgery.

The only pain Al recalled was from the catheter bag. After wearing it for two weeks, it was removed and the slight pain the catheter caused ended seven days later. At no time did Al take any pain pills at home, except for Tylenol, explaining that he had a high pain threshold. Once the catheter was removed, he decided to wear an adult diaper for a month, due to excessive leaking when coughing.

For the first month after the surgery Al's penis felt numb. Despite nerve-sparing during the operation, he continued experiencing erectile dysfunction for four months, along with slight burning during urination. By the fifth month he was able to resume normal relations with his wife, without any erection device or pill. Viagra was then not available to him, anyhow.

When asked how he bounced back so quickly, Al said that he was in excellent physical shape before the surgery, due to jogging 45 miles every week! Now at age 69 he is still physically fit since he works out almost every day.

Al is a Protestant and was an active church attendee at the time of his prostate cancer diagnosis. His faith in God was very important to him. He believed in the power of healing prayers, whether recited by himself or by others in his behalf. While a bit fatalistic ("Whatever happens next, that's life!"), he felt God would take care of him. He was aware that any negative feelings about his outcome could increase his vulnerability and lower his auto-immune system. His positive outlook was the result of believing in God's healing power and trusting his own body to recuperate quickly. His wife, who has been his life companion for some forty years, continued actively supporting Al, and that made a big difference to him. Their children were equally supportive.

Al's active faith in divine Providence intensified about two years before his prostate surgery. He had taken his wife's lead in going back to church. In time he joined his church consistory and became an elder (trustee), also serving on the worship committee. After his surgery he became a prostate screening advocate at church and elsewhere, encouraging men to have their PSA tested "early and often."

2. Ben's Story: Prostatectomy and a Positive Outlook Make All the Difference

For most of his professional life, Ben worked as a supervisor at a hands-on job requiring hands-on work. At the age of 66, he was diagnosed with prostate cancer. While he did not have relatives who had prostate cancer, his dad suffered from an oversized prostate (BPH). Years later he vividly recalled how he decided on surgery and what it was like.

At the time he was diagnosed, Ben's PSA measured 6.4, up from 6 a year earlier. After a biopsy he learned he had prostate cancer, based on a Gleason score of 6. In considering his options he was not happy at the prospect of a total surgical removal of his prostate with radical prostatectomy. However, he felt encouraged to go for surgery after reading a well-known book on prostate cancer by Dr. Patrick Walsh. He also consulted with friends, including a doctor who himself had a prostatectomy a few months earlier. He talked as well with other doctors, including his son, and was spurred on by his wife, who was "a woman of action." As a result he underwent the surgery three months after he was diagnosed.

Prior to finalizing his decision on surgery, Ben felt the need to do more thorough research. He went to Johns Hopkins Hospital, where an associate of Dr. Walsh administered a diagnostic TURP test, often used to relieve the effects of an enlarged prostate. The TURP, a transurethral resection of the prostate, reconfirmed his need for further treatment. At first he gave some thought to having his prostate treated by microwave therapy, which generates a high level of heat that might have destroyed the cancerous portion of his prostate. After some deliberation and encouragement by those I've mentioned, he decided instead to have his prostate totally removed with a radical prostatectomy, to be sure no cancer would remain.

When he first learned he had prostate cancer, Ben's immediate but brief reaction was one of tremendous sadness over his plight. However, after lengthy conversations with others who had been treated for prostate cancer, he became relatively optimistic. He had extensive trust in his urologist at a Philadelphia hospital, before and after surgery. However, he was disturbed that he did not see the surgeon again during his remaining few days in the hospital.

Prior to his surgery, Ben experienced a lot of pain emanating from his prostate. After the surgery he continued to feel extreme pain, particularly in his abdomen. However he was given a self-administered morphine device, which gave him relief at the push of a button. When he went home a few days later he only needed Tylenol with codeine to get him through the first week or two of pain. Ben stated that simply knowing the pain would gradually diminish over time enabled him to bear up. He literally counted the days until the pain would disappear. His was a guarded optimism based on experiences others had shared with him.

He wore a catheter for nearly three weeks, and afterwards wore an adult diaper. For about two months he experienced stress incontinence when he laughed or lifted small objects. His incontinence lessened as he strengthened his pelvic floor muscles with Kegel exercises. Even so he continued to wear pads for another month just to make sure that his urine would no longer leak. He had experienced erectile dysfunction before his operation and this continued after his operation, causing him and his wife a degree of frustration. However they are now relatively okay with this. In other words, they have learned to live with this aspect of their lives and remain emotionally and physically very close.

Ben, a Jew, reported that his faith in God was not a large factor in his recovery, but his inherent optimism and his trust in his doctors' competence carried him through. His conviction that he would recover, coupled with his resolute will, also made a big difference. He was satisfied with his overall recovery and felt like a "poster child for prostate surgery."

3. Cecil's Story: Radioactive Seeding and a Calm Outlook Got Him Through

Cecil has had a long career as a scientist. He is a bright, spirited individual who is thin but quite vigorous. Cecil was diagnosed with prostate cancer in 1998. Five years later his brother also was diagnosed with the same illness. Prior to his diagnosis, Cecil experienced no pain at all. His PSA score was 4.5, and had ranged between 4.0 and 4.2 in the previous three years. Of the six biopsy cores, one indicated a fifteen percent presence of prostate cancer. Cecil's Gleason score of 4 (2+2) indicated his cancer was localized. He was offered the option of "wait and see", since he was assured he would more likely live many years and ultimately die of something else. However he felt he had to take some action and went to Moffitt Cancer Center in Tampa to explore his options.

After considering a wait-and-see approach, radical surgery, or seeding, he chose seeding. His son felt seeding would be best, even though the decision was Cecil's. Cecil acted on his son's recommendation, since he wanted to take some action, but preferred a non-invasive procedure. He was led to believe he would recover quickly and heal completely, although he was informed he might experience some incontinence.

The seeding caused Cecil no pain and he did not require a catheter bag afterwards. However he began experiencing some incontinence two weeks after the seeding procedure, and he continued dribbling urine for a full six months, despite practicing Kegel muscle-strengthening exercises. This caused him a great deal of stress, as did impotence, which lasted half a year as well.

When six months had passed, Cecil returned to his normal functioning. He got through his encounter with prostate cancer and its aftermath, not on the basis of his Christian faith, but because he felt confident about his doctor. The doctor, like Cecil's wife, took his temporary dysfunctions in stride, assuring him that "this too would pass." And they were correct in their assessment.

It's to Cecil's credit that, despite his six-month incontinence and erectile dysfunction, he returned to the sports activities he had always enjoyed. It helped that he was physically fit before his procedure, and that he had active sports to spur him into activity only weeks after the seeding procedure took place.

As an extra measure to assure that his prostate cancer would not recur, Cecil has made it his business to ingest a regular regimen of supplements such as fish oil, vitamins, Esta-C, calcium and saw palmetto, as well as medicine to help him with his poor cholesterol level and high blood pressure.

When asked how he's doing now, nearly ten years after his radioactive seeding, Cecil's upbeat but laconic comment is simply, "We're doing okay!"

4. Don's Story: External Radiation and "Seeding" were a Clear Preference

Don, a 63 year-old retired professional, has had more painful surgeries in his lifetime than he cares to remember. The surgeries, including a full gall bladder operation at age 26, and a botched removal of an eye cataract at age 54, convinced him that surgery was not for him. This was the main reason he decided on external radiation followed by radioactive seeding at age 62, soon after his prostate cancer was detected.

When he was first diagnosed in October 2006, he was in denial. He had been nervous about the biopsy results because he was mindful of his late father's bone cancer. Fortunately Don's doctors diagnosed his prostate cancer early. His PSA score at the time was 3.7, although a year earlier it had been just about 3. In addition he had a Gleason score of 6 and was asymptomatic when the cancer was first discovered.

As Don put it, he was initially "bummed out" by his diagnosis, but afterwards he calmed down, feeling that the doctor would help him through this latest health crisis. He made a phone call to one doctor, who recommended radiation, but Don was put off by that particular doctor's blasé tone. He met with another doctor who shared a video depicting radiation seeding. Don found this video helpful, and it enabled him to be decisive about this technique.

To assure Don the procedure would eliminate his cancer, the urologist recommended external beam radiation (IMRT) before radioactive seeding. Following both procedures, Don did not experience pain, but he was very uncomfortable. Still he maintained his trust in his doctor.

Don was given a catheter for a couple of days after the radiation seeding session. He was able to go the theater with his wife the same night the catheter was removed. However, he still found himself dripping urine in his undershorts or pajama bottoms, especially at night, and for a few weeks he found it difficult to urinate. The dripping caused him an undue amount of stress, but Don rapidly improved, much to his relief.

Don's impotence, or erectile dysfunction, lasted a month before dissipating. Due to his not being in control of his functions, his stress was so great that he ended up distancing himself from some friends. In part this was due to his feeling that they didn't know what to say to be truly supportive. As far as he was concerned all they could do was engage him in "routine chit-chat."

Don was quite relieved that he got to go home the same day of his radioactive seeding. He did not worry about being near infants, since the rest of his family was out-of-state. He was disturbed that once he got home, his best friends were not there for him. In one case, he became resentful of a former friend who had minimized the negative outcome of the radiation on his body. In fact, as Don put it, that gentleman was "grossly misinformed." However, in time Don no longer felt the intense stress that predominated both before and after his prostate procedures.

Don is Jewish, but his faith in his doctor, rather than in God, ultimately got him through his ordeal.

What's So Different about These Neighbors?

My neighbors' varied responses in the four profiles I've presented reflected their personal experiences and outlooks, and the effects of the prostate cancer treatment they chose. Once treated, most appeared to be calm and relatively pain-free, because of pain medications available to them. Before treatment, each of them seemed to have various levels of stress, at least initially, when their prostate cancers were confirmed through biopsies.

In addition each tolerated his catheter bag differently, registering either moderate or more severe discomfort. At least one felt some degree of pain afterwards. That might well have been the result of how the catheters were first placed in their bodies or the way they were removed. Then again it might have reflected how each tended to respond to his particular treatment.

In three of these four case studies of neighbors (all laymen), faith was not instrumental in helping them heal from prostate cancer. What was critical for all, however, was their trust in their doctors as well as the patient's level of physical fitness before his procedure of choice. These limited examples point to an old truism that the more fit a patient is before surgery or other medical procedures, the more likely it is that he will bounce back and return to good health, in body and soul. This is corroborated by other case studies that can be accessed at *www.ConquerProstateCancer.com*.

Finally it became clear that the emotional baggage which accompanied a patient before his prostate cancer procedure profoundly influenced which procedure he chose. This confirms the view that your recollection of past personal experiences with pain or stress will have an impact on how well you face new and potentially threatening developments.

The emotional hurdles noted here could have been reduced had these men developed coping mechanisms to offset their pain and stress, using available "tools" such as a relaxation response or guided imagery. Perhaps they would have benefited from seeing how other patients before them were able to face their diagnoses and procedures with a degree of optimism. If we would each remember that our state of mind makes a big difference, we might be better equipped to confront our worst nightmares and fears as we seek to conquer prostate cancer.

Part V:

CONQUER PROSTATE CANCER BY "HEARING" OTHER PATIENTS AND DOCTORS

15

How Do Clergymen Cope with Pain and Stress? Profiles in Prostate Cancer, Part II

"Do not weep, do not wax indignant. Understand."
—Baruch Spinoza, 17th Century rationalist philosopher

"When you pray, move your feet."
—African proverb

Seeing the Big Picture

For many of us there's a big difference between listening and hearing. All too often when you listen to people, their words go in one ear and out the other. When you truly hear them and are attentive to what they say, you're more responsive to the meaning behind the thoughts and feelings they utter. To conquer prostate cancer it's important not just to listen to the voices of experience, both doctors and patients, but to hear every nuance of those voices. To borrow from psychoanalyst Theodor Reik, you'll get a lot more out of life when you learn to "listen with a third ear."

Among various experts worth listening to are clergy who themselves had prostate cancer and contended with treatment side effects. And I don't suggest this just because I'm a rabbi. Clergymen are worth listening to because facing life and death situations have been their "bread and butter" throughout their ministry. After years of working with and for people, most clergy I know have learned to distil life events and identify what's important. By training and often by nature they are reflective, analytical, and have a tendency to place the interests of others before their own. They are public servants and servants of the Divine, who sometimes see the big picture better than the average individual.

This chapter offers readers the opportunity to "hear" how Protestant and Jewish clergy have handled their own prostate cancer diagnoses and whatever followed. The eight clergy profiles may help you see your problems more clearly, from the perspective of men of faith who were willing to share their thoughts and experiences about some of their most intimate concerns.

During November of 2007 I interviewed the four Christian clergymen and four Jewish clergymen whose profiles appear in this chapter. Initially their doctors diligently informed them that their PSA blood test scores ranged between 3.4 to 6.0, well above the newly accepted threshold of 2.5. Some had PSA scores that might have been low to start with, but quickly rose as much as half a point or more in a relatively short time. When faced with these test results, the clergy agreed to be biopsied, and discovered their prostate tumors, viewed under a microscope, registered a total Gleason score of 6 or 7, indicating they had a moderate grade of localized cancer. As with the laymen I described in the previous chapter, I've summarized the details they conveyed to me in their own words. However, their names have been changed to protect their privacy.

Protestant Ministers: Four True Tales

The ministers profiled here were in their mid-sixties to early seventies at the time of their interviews. All underwent prostate cancer procedures six months to five years earlier. When their prostate cancers emerged, they had each been active congregational leaders for a period of twenty to thirty years or more. After being diagnosed with prostate cancer, one of these men decided on radioactive seeding and the others chose to have a standard radical prostatectomy. Two of these ministers had briefly considered robotic surgery, but could not find a suitable time or physician to go that route. Here are their stories.

1. Rev. Elliot's Story: Confidence in "Seeding," but Adverse Effects

Rev. Elliott retired in 2002, after many years of serving a Boston church. A couple of years earlier, toward the end of his active ministry, he was diagnosed with asymptomatic prostate cancer. Localized cancer was found in three of his twelve biopsy cores. Together with his wife, he explored his treatment options with three oncologists. They told him that then current research literature indicated he would have an 85 percent success rate whether he chose surgery or radioactive seeding (brachytherapy). After weighing the pros and cons of each procedure he decided on seeding.

From the "get-go" Rev. Elliot exhibited very little stress, since he personally knew a number of men who had been successfully treated for prostate cancer. Besides, he was assured that his cancer was treatable. However he was a bit anxious when told he would need a biopsy. Evidently that brought home the reality that he was a cancer victim.

A broad social support system of fellow clergy and other friends helped a lot. He felt uplifted since some of the others indicated "I've been there," and still others asked, "What can I do to help?" However he did not reveal his health problem to his parishioners, since he wished to remain a "giver," not a recipient of compassion. He also felt encouraged as he spent three weeks reading extensive prostate cancer resources. Besides he was convinced he would be okay and that his doctors would cure his cancer, given the advances of medical science.

After the biopsy report Rev. Elliot was referred by one of his oncologists to an excellent urologist at Massachusetts General Hospital. He had no doubt that he was in good hands, and even some scheduling problems did not daunt him, although he had to wait five months after his diagnosis to receive the radiation seeding.

Two weeks before his procedure, a radiologist mapped out his prostate with a precise grid. Exactly thirteen days later his urologist injected 101 "seeds" into his prostate, which were subjected to radioactive beams. He felt no discomfort until the next day when his anesthesia wore off. His life-long, well-honed ability to meditate in quiet reflection helped him focus his attention elsewhere, rather than on the discomfort or pain, so he only needed a few Tylenol pills. His personal meditative practice was very helpful. Still, the routine nature of the procedure made him feel his faith was fairly unimportant as he recovered.

Eight years earlier Rev. Elliot had reduced his pain following a successful hernia surgery. His tendency to "center himself" also helped more recently, in 2006, when he underwent spinal surgery and experienced little if any pain. He also felt that his being trim, rather than obese, worked in his favor.

When asked how the radiation impacted on his church activities, Rev. Elliot said he avoided baptizing infants for two weeks and shortened his sermons! Otherwise he was able to perform all his functions within a few days of his procedure.

Rev. Elliot was "calm, cool and collected" as he recalled his radioactive seeding. However his tone grew sharper as he recalled his adverse side effects. He was quite upset when, two weeks after the seeding, his incontinence and impotence persisted. Evidently he had been assured that there would be little likelihood of side effects, but that did not turn out to be the case for him. Urinary dripping and pain from internal penile pressure plagued him in the months following his brachytherapy.

At the time of our interview in 2007 he had gained greater control over his incontinence but still wore pads as a precaution, especially when not sure if he could reach a restroom in time. Rev. Elliot tried Viagra and Cialis to offset his sexual dysfunction, but they caused his face to flush and upset his stomach, so he took Levitra instead. Because his wife remained very supportive of him, he managed to cope fairly well. However he conveyed his stress and uncharacteristic anger over some of his unanticipated developments.

For all that, he is grateful that his PSA remained between 0 and 1 since his procedure ended. His urologist has informed him that it is highly unlikely his cancer will recur, but has told him they need to keep testing him every six months just to be sure. This continued to reassure Rev. Elliot that despite its adverse side effects, radioactive seeding helped cure him of his cancer.

2. Rev. Frank's Story: Choosing Surgery with Faith in God's Grace

Rev. Frank served as a clergyman for over forty years. He was first diagnosed with prostate cancer in 2001, at the age of 73. He had already grieved over the loss of an older brother who died in 1990, following the metastasis of prostate cancer. His other younger brothers also had prostate cancer at the ages of 58 and 68, respectively. For that reason he was not surprised when the cancer was diagnosed, but he coped well physically, emotionally, and spiritually. He had known that he would most likely eventually get prostate cancer. At the same time he felt God would take care of him and not let him suffer or die.

Given his brothers' experiences he had decided that should he ever get cancer of the prostate, he would have it surgically removed right away. His close-knit family was immensely supportive of his decision. They assured him he would be okay and everything would be alright in the long run. In addition he completely trusted his doctor, who had worked with various prominent individuals who had similar problems. Rev. Frank was prepared to do whatever the doctor said was needed.

Prior to his procedure he experienced no pain at all, although he had a moderately reduced urinary stream. His pain afterwards was minimal and he was confident it would soon dissipate. He suffered from incontinence after his procedure. Reluctantly he began to wear Depends adult diapers and then pads for couple of months until the steady incontinence ended. Seven years later he still experiences stress incontinence, especially when he bends down. However, he has managed to cope, stating, "I don't like it, but I am not anxious." It was probably helpful that before the surgery Rev. Frank was physically fit, even though he had slowed down over the years.

His surgery led to sexual dysfunction (he refused to use the word "impotence"), so he has been on Viagra for the past five years. He would have liked to use a vacuum erection pump, but his doctor told him not to do so. In his case, due to his current medications, there was a danger of blood clots. His wife of several decades was supportive and understanding. For the most part they did not try to engage in sexual intercourse, yet they remain physically close, always cuddling before going to sleep.

Rev. Frank was convinced his faith helped get him through his ordeal with prostate cancer. Some of the faith principles or beliefs that helped him are reflected in statements from the Old and New Testaments: "Cast all your cares upon the Lord" (I Peter); "God is a very present help in time of trouble (Psalms); "Be strong and of good courage!" (Joshua). Rev. Frank's ability to quote Scripture by heart, in keeping with his faith tradition, gave him added strength. One biblical verse, taken from Jesus' speech at Gethsemane, was particularly helpful in his mind: "Lord, let this depart from me. Nonetheless let your word, not my word, be done."

Rev. Frank's sense of humor also helped him get through the surgery. For instance, just before he fell asleep on the operating table, he told his anesthesiologist that as a preacher, he was like the doctor, because he too puts people to sleep! The last thing he remembered before "going out" was his anesthesiologist responding with a broad grin. He also told me that once, while in the hospital, he dreamed he was preaching, and when he woke up, he was!

There was no doubt in Rev. Frank's mind that he benefited from the support of his wife and his children before and after his recovery. He was in pain, but stated other types of surgery were more painful. He told me he tends to foresee the eventual release of pain when it occurs, and says, "Physical pain rarely bothers me spiritually or emotionally."

Rev. Frank was no longer concerned about the potential danger to his life. He was quite happy that he had his prostate removed when the cancer was still localized. When asked, he indicated he felt he had conquered his prostate cancer.

3. Rev. George's Story: Facing Surgery with Meditation and Faith

Rev. George was first diagnosed with prostate cancer in the fall of 2006. As far as he knows he was the first in his family to have this disease. Previously he had at least four operations due to severe bad health, including a triple by-pass and major surgery for a torn rotator cuff, a hernia, and gall bladder. He credited his getting through each of these due to excellent medical staff and powerful medications, coupled with his long-standing practices of breathing exercises, meditation, and relaxation techniques.

The reverend gave equal credit to what he called "the beneficence of the universe." He was convinced that God was not a being he regarded as personal, but was universal. As such he stated that, "I truly believe that things will be good in the long run, even though life's struggles are hard to take until that point." He advised others to "Let go of what you can't control," much in keeping with the Serenity Prayer. In preaching about the universe's beneficence, Rev. George stated that although he did not advocate that there is a personal God who will be responsive to everyone's message, he did believe that "there's ample reason to maintain a basic trust that things will eventually work out."

For three or four years before his diagnosis he had difficulty urinating. He also had other problems associated with an enlarged prostate (BPH), although several medications had been prescribed to help control this problem.

Despite this he felt unprepared for the horrible news that he had prostate cancer. As he put it, "It was totally unexpected, and I didn't like it. It's yet another worry on top of all the other illnesses I've gone through." Later, even after selecting prostate surgery, he felt angry and frustrated. Things were no longer going to be the same for him. He also feared that the prostate cancer might have a devastating effect on his personal lifestyle.

In short, Rev. George was wary about having to put up with "more stuff" at that point in his life, as he put it. He was particularly angry largely because in his mind the prostate cancer surgery caused him more discomfort and stress than all his previous surgeries combined.

Rev. George knew about robotic surgery but was dissuaded from it by his oncologist, who stated the Reverend's rate of recovery would be no faster. The same oncologist advised him that radiation would not completely remove the cancerous prostate as effectively as a radical prostatectomy. While in retrospect Rev. George felt this advice was simplistic and partly erroneous, at the time of the consult he had full faith in his doctor.

Before the surgery Rev. George experienced no pain, but he felt moderate pain immediately after he woke up. He felt more intense pain only for a couple of days after the anesthesia wore off and while wearing a catheter for two weeks. He did not resort to any faith-related techniques but waited out the passage of pain and stress as he healed.

He experienced no incontinence before his procedure, but after surgery he felt compelled to wear adult diapers for three months, followed by using pads for three months on and off. While his urinary incontinence was stressful he was not told he could have used bio-feedback to regain his sphincter muscle strength or to strengthen his pelvic floor muscles, although he had tried practicing the Kegel method.

Due to some cancer found in the margins of his prostate, Rev. George's surgeon was able to spare only one nerve bundle. As a result he experienced difficulty getting any erection. With the use of a vacuum erection device and Viagra, he did sustain a partial erection after a couple of months, but this proved to be irrelevant due to his wife's disinterest for personal and physical reasons.

Because Rev. George is a professional counselor he had developed various methods for personal pain-reduction. For him the use of imagery had long been a way to eliminate pain, using colors (going from red to blue) or shapes (broad circles to narrow rectangles). I was delighted to hear that I was not the only one to use this technique for pain reduction.

Rev. George's faith became increasingly important to him in his long-term recovery process. For instance he practiced "meditation with the consciousness of something beyond me." However he indicated it made no sense to ask others to pray to God in his behalf, since he felt such inquiries were not effective. His words were, "You don't control God." He was convinced, though, that prayers were valuable for patients who felt comforted by others who prayed for them. He also felt there was no reason to worry about death, even though he rejected a belief in the afterlife. In his words, "Why worry about that; I won't feel anything then anyhow!" When I asked him if his outlook was typical of most ministers in his denomination, he stated he was probably an exception. For him God is good but impersonal and cannot be regulated by human beings, no matter how hard they try.

4. Rev. Henry's Story: Overcoming Surgery's Side Effects with Meditation and Reclaiming Sexual Intimacy

Rev. Henry, age 65, had a standard radical prostatectomy in the summer of 2006, three months after he was diagnosed with prostate cancer and five months before I interviewed him. His bright outlook and his candor were among the most remarkable of those who shared their prostate experiences with me.

In the course of his clerical career Rev. Henry was sequentially affiliated with various religious groups: Catholic, Protestant, and Universal Unitarian. He worked with younger and older parishioners. For many years he taught at a seminary and eventually earned his Ph.D. in Ministry.

Prior to his prostate cancer diagnosis, Rev. Henry was in excellent physical shape, exercising four times a week and weight lifting using grocery bags. About a month after his surgery he began to lift light weights again. Three months after surgery he resumed his regular weight lifting exercises at home. He felt much improved after the surgery six months before we spoke and planned to keep working actively as a chaplain for a few more years. After "retiring," he stated he hoped to spend a few more years teaching massage and methods of physical body work, combined with spiritual and emotional body work.

When I interviewed Rev. Henry, he told me he did not feel the diagnosis a few months earlier had been a death sentence. Instead he stated that, "I knew they would find a little something inside of my prostate and would use an appropriate procedure to help me." This helped him retain his optimistic outlook and take the news of his prostate cancer in stride. His wife, however, panicked when his diagnosis was first confirmed.

Following his surgery, Rev. Henry wore a pad to avoid stress incontinence when laughing or coughing. He bought an erectile vacuum device with a velcro tie for comfort (wrapped around the base of the penis to keep it erect.) He has used it when intimate with his wife, but he prefers not to use this device and just to use half a Viagra. He is concerned that his erection is not as firm as it was before surgery and that he can enter his wife only partially when they have intercourse; but he hopes things will improve with time.

Rev. Henry's wife was very supportive throughout this process. She advised him to "get rid of the cancerous prostate now" rather than accept a friend's suggestion for radioactive seeding. He also felt quite supported by his doctor who said, "If I had your condition, I would have surgery." He found he trusted his surgeon even more once the operation ended and he recuperated without incident. While he had many supporters in the community he kept this matter private. He did find a select number of his fellow clergy were helpful, especially those who had gone the route of surgery; but he did not have any people visit him at the hospital or at home, since he thought that would be more of a distraction than help him recover.

During the first hours after the anesthesia wore off, he was given a self-administered pain medication pump to apply at will. Mentally he was able to put his focus on other concerns to alleviate any pain that emerged thereafter, although he was troubled by excess gas. Once he got home three days later, he was able to eliminate all pain medication, both because he had a high pain threshold and since he could to use the power of his mind to limit any pain sensation.

He had to wear a catheter for two weeks and needed a pad for a week after that, due to incontinence. As a precaution he wore the pad a couple of additional weeks. After that he was no longer incontinent.

Of greater significance for Rev. Henry is that his erectile dysfunction led him and his wife to develop a deeper level of intimacy, spiritually and physically. Much of their physical interaction involved mutual massage. In addition she became more sexually active with him, lying nude in bed while he stood near her. They learned to take more time exploring each other's body and were quite satisfied with this new arrangement.

In that sense, impotence was not an issue for him. He felt little stress about it, and counted on getting his sexual dysfunction under control over time. He was delighted that he and his wife have had great sex although both are in their sixties. In his view their relations have become more tender and a greater source of fun than ever, in part because he has been able to rely more on his wife to reciprocate his affection for her. He also has found that the tip of his penis remained sensitive, and he maintained his penile vascular flow by masturbating in the shower. He did this to increase his ability to sustain an erection and in turn strengthen his physical bond with his wife.

Rev. Henry credited his ability to be aroused when standing near his wife because of the effect of blood draining down, which he recalled reading in a book by famed urologist Dr. Patrick Walsh. He also felt that his dry orgasm is different but not worse than before surgery. Like other patients he could produce semen before his prostate and seminal vesicles were removed, but not after his prostatectomy. In addition he and his wife have derived pleasure from his ability to ejaculate from the Cowper's gland at the tip of his penis. This gland emits a small amount of mucus-like fluid even when the penis is not erect, serving to add moisture before sexual intercourse.

Rev. Henry's faith has been important to him in the recovery process. One principle he cited was that, "You need to have faith in your body and in yourself, and not see the body and soul as mutually exclusive." He also felt it was important to consistently meditate as he does one hour a day, in order to retain a positive outlook. In his words, "Meditation needs to be a way of life." Finally he stressed the importance of educating yourself when facing a health crisis, as he did to the best of his ability. I was delighted by his unsolicited comment that the questions I raised helped him further consolidate and articulate his experiences regarding prostate cancer.

What Ministers Have in Common and What They Don't

As might be expected, the four ministers I interviewed were buoyed by their faith, some more than others. A couple of them felt seriously threatened by the news of their prostate surgery, revealing the depth of their humanity. Three dealt with their recovery from surgery or radiation with equanimity, although there were moments of anger or anxiety especially in regard to erectile dysfunction.

While a few felt they had to consign themselves to remaining where they were, sexually-speaking, at least one expected to fully overcome his moderate impotence within a year. It appears that those who were physically fit before their procedure recovered more quickly or with greater satisfaction and hope for the future.

Conservative Rabbis: More True Tales

I conducted hour-long phone interviews with four rabbis who live in different parts of the United States. Each survived prostate cancer and spoke about his experiences. Without any hesitation they told me how things were before and after their individual procedures. They described their respective prostate cancer diagnoses, which occurred between 1997 and 2006. They also told me about their recovery from their treatment options. Three indicated they had chosen radiation therapy—either external beam or seeding, if not both. Another rabbi had also been subjected to hormone therapy. Only one of the four also had standard radical prostatectomy. At the time of treatment their ages ranged from 46 to 67, although they were ages 50 to 68 when I interviewed them.

The four rabbis profiled here are affiliated with my rabbinic organization, the Rabbinical Assembly. The Rabbinical Assembly is a core part of the Conservative Movement of contemporary Judaism, which at one time had the slogan, "Tradition and Change!" These men had voluntarily responded to an e-mail I wrote asking for interviewees for my survey. Once they contacted me I used the same questionnaire I constructed earlier when contacting laymen and ministers about their experiences. Three of the four rabbis were active, full-time congregational rabbis. The fourth served as a CEO of a religious agency. Here are their stories.

1. Rabbi Isaac's Story: Standard Surgery and the Frustration
   of Erectile Dysfunction

At the time of his prostate cancer diagnosis at age 56, Rabbi Isaac had been a congregational rabbi for twenty-seven years. His father and grandfather endured prostate cancer before him. He himself had never had any other serious illness, before or after his prostate surgery ten years earlier in 1997.

At the time of his diagnosis Rabbi Isaac had no symptoms and felt he was in good shape physically and emotionally. When his prostate cancer was first confirmed, he felt unprepared for this horrible news. In his words, "I was in shock, especially since I felt I was in excellent condition." However he was quickly reassured by his physician and felt he would be okay since the doctor would help.

After consulting with both an oncologist and a urologist, he opted for a standard radical prostatectomy. He made this decision because his doctors felt its advantages outweighed radiation or other approaches. As Rabbi Isaac commented, had robotic surgery been developed or available at that time, he would have unquestionably selected that procedure instead. At any rate, he easily decided on standard surgery, believing that at the time it was in his best interest to "cancel the cancer" by eliminating the prostate altogether.

Rabbi Isaac recalled that his decision to go forward with surgery was relatively easy, since a good friend had recently had success when going through that procedure and also was "there" for him, offering emotional support and an array of reading materials. He also had a supportive GP/internist, who guided him through the decision-making process. At all times he received his wife's encouragement, and she attended each meeting with his doctors, who inspired extreme trust, both before or after the surgery.

Following his surgery Rabbi Isaac experienced moderate pain, some of it due to excess gas and constipation. This persisted until his fifth day after surgery, when he went home from the hospital. At that time he was told that, due to his excellent physical condition before surgery, he would be able to jog a mile some three weeks later, and that is exactly what occurred. Still he was only somewhat successful in eliminating his post-surgical pain. The pain medications he was given helped get him back on track, as did the feeling of uplift he got from his congregation actively praying for his quick recovery. He felt his own strong determination to get back on his feet, along with his faith in his own healing powers, were equally instrumental in his recovery. As a proactive individual he believed it was his duty to live as fully as possible and not allow himself to prolong his status as a patient.

Rabbi Isaac had to wear a catheter for nearly two weeks, and continued to "dribble" after that. This did not stop him from jogging his first mile three weeks after the surgery, but he admitted his pants "were very wet" by the time he completed his run. He felt some frustration over this but dutifully practiced the Kegel exercises to strengthen his pelvic floor muscles and prevent incontinence.

While Viagra and Levitra continued to help him sustain his erections, he conceded he has suffered emotionally from erectile dysfunction after his procedure. He felt that with time his ED lessened, but it was still difficult on him. Both he and his wife regret they had to discontinue the more rigorous sexual interchanges they enjoyed prior to his surgery. In his words, "I miss it and grieve for that which I no longer have." The pain of his loss is palpable. When asked if he and his wife get any satisfaction from intercourse after the appropriate medication, he answered, "Yes. But it is not the same as it was." This moderate impotence has not changed in the ten years since his surgery.

According to Rabbi Isaac his faith was very important in specific ways, assuring his recovery. Among the faith mantras that kept him going were the following: "God wants us to do the best we can with what we have;" "As long as God wants me on this earth, I will be here;" and "It's my determination that enables me to follow my course of action, as long as God ordains it." The last comment clearly reflected his take on how his free will related to God's will.

When asked what specific comment, from any source, he felt was most supportive in his recovery, he immediately cited his wife's words: "I'll be staying by your side no matter what." This phrase became so memorable that it has buoyed him up since the initial prostate operation.

Rabbi Isaac was asked if he thinks the prostate cancer might recur despite his radical surgery. He answered in two succinct words: "Very unlikely." He felt he was able to "conquer" the cancer for the rest of his life, along with his incontinence, pain and stress, even though he again acknowledged that he remained in mourning about the decline of his sexual potency.

He has had no major health issues since the prostate surgery. He considered himself to be in very good health—so much so that he planned on staying active as a congregational rabbi for a few more years. In his view his overall vitality remained unimpaired. In fact he had no doubt he would continue to devote his life to serving his congregation and community with the same zest as in past decades.

2. Rabbi Jonathan's Story: "On the Beam" with External Radiation—
   IMRT and Equanimity

Rabbi Jonathan heads a prominent congregation, even though he is a "second-career" rabbi, ordained a few years ago. Soon after entering his second pulpit he was diagnosed with prostate cancer at the age of 54. He did not tell his new congregation, since the diagnosis occurred just before Rosh Hashanah, the Jewish New Year. He felt he wanted his new flock to listen to him, not to commiserate over his health.

Prior to his diagnosis Rabbi Jonathan had no symptoms, although he had an enlarged benign prostate that had slowed his urinary stream. Later on, when speaking to a Man to Man support group after his treatment, he indicated that the news of his cancer did not disillusion him, although it was, "Easier on me as a patient than on my wife."

He believed God would not let him suffer or die, but said that as a person, he—like all of us—has to do his part. In reflecting further he commented, "You can't blame God for what happens. You get your life from your family, and, anyhow, God records events more than dictates what kind of year you might have. That is largely up to you."

Rabbi Jonathan decided to go for a prostate cancer procedure of external beam therapy. However he selected the more advanced IMRT—Intensity Modulated Radiation Therapy. This allowed for a huge amount of radiation aimed at the cancer, while avoiding radiation to other areas of his body. His decision came easily since he wanted to make sure his treatment would pinpoint the cancer and eliminate it, rather than allowing radioactive seeding of his entire prostate. He also wanted a procedure which would most likely not affect the other areas of his body. Surgery wasn't for him since he had a history of blood clotting. Robotic surgery was then in its infancy, and he did not want to take a chance on a brand new surgical technique, even one that might involve less blood loss.

When his prostate cancer was first confirmed, Rabbi Jonathan was not unduly upset, since he knew his cancerous tumor was at an early stage and was still small. He felt the odds were in his favor. He also was reassured as he prayed, "God, give me strength," and added, "God, thank you for the doctors whom you've endowed with knowledge and technical skills." He maintained his trust in his doctors before and after the radiation.

In the course of the external radiation treatment, Rabbi Jonathan felt some discomfort and increasing fatigue. He was still able to work at his synagogue every day, although it took some six months for his fatigue to pass. He dealt with his discomfort and fatigue by reminding himself things would get better, and they eventually did.

For the first six months after his procedure his urine kept dripping, and he needed a pad for a couple of weeks. Due to ongoing bladder pressure he remained on Flomax, although this did not help much at first. To reduce any incontinence he practiced his Kegel exercises, thus strengthening his pelvic muscles.

Rabbi Jonathan had not experienced erectile dysfunction before his procedure, but he experienced ED for the first couple of months after his radiation. He stated it was rare for him to have an orgasm, but he was able to have a full erection after two months. In part this was due to medicine injected into his penis. Meantime to make sure the cancer would not recur he had a urological checkup every six months. Rabbi Jonathan's wife has been very supportive of him throughout his cancer and treatment, even ignoring his increasing sexual dysfunction. They scaled back their intimate physical relationship, since his erections were no longer spontaneous. However his wife told him, "I don't care if you are ever firm again, as long as you are cancer-free."

Rabbi Jonathan's faith had a great impact on his recovery. He believes in the effectiveness of communal prayer. For him, "prayer is a positive force in general." His faith and the prayers of others during his recovery process helped assure him that all would go well. After telling his congregation about his prostate cancer and treatment, Rabbi Jonathan's faith community was understanding of his needs.

Asked whether he thought his cancer might return, he answered, "If it does, I'll deal with it then."

3. Rabbi Ken's Story: Prostate Cancer Times Two—
   Surgery followed by Lupron and Radiation

Rabbi Ken had been a congregational rabbi for twenty years, but for the past four years he became the CEO of a Jewish agency. In 2000, at the age of 47, he was diagnosed with prostate cancer and was treated for it. Four years later, in 2004, his prostate cancer resurfaced, and he had to be treated again.

When he was first diagnosed, Rabbi Ken's greatest fear was that his cancer might metastasize; until the bone scan indicated otherwise, he was emotionally on edge. Because he was only 47 he was shocked that he got prostate cancer. Until then, like most people, he perceived it to be an older man's illness. Expecting the worst, he initially felt he had been handed a death sentence, but his intense stress soon passed.

As a student of mindfulness meditation, Rabbi Ken regained his composure and began to practice what he preached—living in the moment. His mantra was the Hebrew word, *"Hineni"* meaning "I am here, now." He repeatedly told himself, "I don't need to look at my life for more than one year at a time." He also affirmed that "Life is full of uncertainty, so treasure every moment as it comes." These beliefs helped him release the stress that gripped him, as did the efforts of a fine therapist whose services he engaged. Coupled with his own efforts to live in the present, Rabbi Ken endorsed his therapist's reminder that "It's very important to have a strong will to live and appreciate every moment."

Rabbi Ken's religious faith also helped him reduce his anxiety over his diagnosis. At that time he recalled some of the Book of Job's closing paragraphs. That reading reminded him not to blame God for failing to immediately rectify his plight, since he is only one small part of God's large universe. He was skeptical about the efficacy of traditional prayers for his recovery, offered in his behalf by others. Still, he earnestly focused in a more positive manner on his prospects for healing (*"refuah"* in Hebrew), by praying for his own recovery as he recited similar traditional prayers.

Eager to eliminate his prostate cancer when first diagnosed in 2000, Rabbi Ken elected to have standard radical surgery (prostatectomy). He relied on the advice of one of his friends who did a lot of research, which was corroborated by an oncologist. Four years later, his PSA reading went from 0 to 0.9. At that time a biopsy indicated he had localized cancer cells in the area where the prostate had been removed. Alarmed, he agreed to receive Lupron to reduce his testosterone and prevent metastasis prior to radioactive seeding. He was stressed by the ongoing hot flashes he experienced for some eight months, and by accompanying weight gain. For all that, he managed to get through radiation seeding without incident.

Years before his first bout with prostate cancer, Rabbi Ken's father had died of a heart attack during prostate surgery. For that reason Rabbi Ken was understandably apprehensive in advance of the operation. When he woke up, he felt happy and grateful that he was still alive.

He experienced moderately high pain after the operation. The pain lasted while he was in the hospital for the next three days. He managed to get through the pain by focusing on his beliefs and principles, and by taking high-dose pain killers. Apart from this he felt that all he could do was wait it out until the pain dissipated.

He was told to wear a catheter for three weeks, which he found very annoying, and he was relieved when it was removed. After that he rarely had incontinence issues, such as leaking, and he credited his surgeon for this. Within the month he began teaching his regular adult education classes again. He began to go out and travel with family members.

Before his second bout with prostate cancer and subsequent Lupron and radiation treatments, Rabbi Ken had some erectile dysfunction. Two months after the surgery he experienced a partial return to sexual functioning. With the help of Viagra his erections became firm, but he regarded this as mechanical. As a result he felt deprived of his sexuality and saw this as a real loss. When the cancer recurred, the Lupron made getting an erection all but impossible. He was still learning to live with Lupron, "holding the effects at bay,"as he put it.

> *You have to look at the bright side, but remain a realist.*

Rabbi Ken was glad that he got through the radiation seeding without incident and that his PSA reading was near 0 again. However, because Judaism forbids tattoos, he regrets that he needed tattoo markers to guide the radiologist. He accepted the tattooing, as it was necessary for accurate radioactive seeding, but at the time he felt he was "marked for life."

During the past few years Rabbi Ken received the professional support of his son-in-law, who helped monitor his progress. He also placed his total trust in his fine doctor, knowing that as good as the physician was, there could be no guarantees his cancer wouldn't recur. He stated, "You have to look at the bright side, but remain a realist." He asked his oncologist if his prostate cancer might occur a third time. He concurred with his doctor when he replied, "Why project the worst possible outcome? Nobody knows what might happen next."

As Rabbi Ken pointed out, "Part of mindfulness meditation insists that you should not be too hard on yourself. The main thing is not to get too depressed. Rather you should enjoy the good things that surround you and recall the more fortunate elements of your life, including your personal achievements." He continued to focus on these precepts as he got back on the road to recovery.

As far as Rabbi Ken was concerned, "We are all engaged in a spiritual struggle of life against death. We will all die in the end, but meantime, we should not give up without a damn good fight."

On a final note, he conceded that his illness, and that of his father's, propelled him on his new spiritual course of engaging in community activism. He fully believes that "If you want to live, you have to act as if you want to live." He has resolved to do so in his own unique way.

4. Rabbi Leon's Story: When You Face Two Types of Radiation

Rabbi Leon, an active congregational rabbi, was diagnosed and treated for prostate cancer at the age of 67, a year before I interviewed him. He was diagnosed in February 2006 after he reported that he felt pain when urinating and saw blood in his urine. At first he was given Bactrian to stop his bleeding. Soon after that a biopsy confirmed he had prostate cancer.

When he first heard this diagnosis he felt like it was a death sentence and was very panicky. He was told that his cancer was not something to be taken lightly; however, he felt reassured when informed that he should not feel he would die from it, as it was treatable. At that point he felt he would be okay since the doctor would help. He remarked that "I knew that somehow there would be a cure, since science was so advanced."

Unfortunately Rabbi Leon's health was further compromised when he suffered from a stroke as soon as he got home from his biopsy. This combination of events caused the rabbi extreme anxiety and led to a four-hour crying spell. Fortunately his wife was with him at the time and immediately took him back to the hospital, where it was discovered that his stroke was caused by a small hole in his heart.

Despite his disbelief over these events Rabbi Leon was fortunate that he recovered fairly quickly from the stroke and was able to function normally again. At that point he had to decide on which procedure to treat his prostate cancer. Due to his stroke, surgery was not an option. After discussing the matter further with his doctors he decided on radiation beam therapy, followed by radiation seeding (brachytherapy), to make sure the cancer would be eradicated. He was told there was no great urgency to proceed, so he waited three months until he could receive radiation beam therapy daily as an outpatient for seven weeks. In July he went to the hospital part of a day for brachytherapy, or radioactive seeding treatment, a procedure which lasted the usual forty-five minutes. The day afterwards he felt so good he went to his synagogue. He did not require a catheter for either the radiation or seeding.

Rabbi Leon benefited from several sources of support. First and foremost he was able to rely on his very alert and helpful wife. His wife's father was also helpful, and his congregation was most solicitous, which made it easier for him to recuperate.

Rabbi Leon had no trouble completely trusting his urologist and radiologist, both before and after his two radiation procedures. He conceded that the mapping process before the radiation was quite uncomfortable, and indicated he was equally uncomfortable when moved around for radiation. However he was not in any real pain and felt that, "The medical staff could not have been nicer." He was impressed with the radiation waiting room's amenities, including refreshments and even diplomas for patients when they completed their radiation protocol!

Before being implanted with radioactive seeds, he was told it was not likely he would have any subsequent incontinence or pain. However he was informed it was likely he would become impotent. He was instructed not to have sex during the first ten days after the seeding, and was then later encouraged to try Viagra, which he found somewhat helpful.

While neither type of radiation caused him pain, he was alarmed when he discovered some blood from his rectum a few days after the procedure. After being assured this would pass, he proceeded to live his life as normally as possible.

Rabbi Leon did not really feel that Judaism offered direct guidance or wisdom for his new illness and recovery. However, after he was able to function normally in the restroom again, without incident, he recited the traditional Jewish prayer that praises God for giving us the ability to open our orifices from day to day.

When asked, Rabbi Leon concurred that he had "conquered" his prostate cancer and any incontinence, pain or stress associated with it, even though he still had erectile dysfunction. Overall he was happy to be alive and functioning again both at home and in his synagogue.

The Faith Factor—Comparing Clergy and Laymen

Localized prostate cancer evoked various degrees of fear in the four rabbis profiled here. Some were far more positive than others, often for good reason. For some, faith was critical for enabling equanimity and facilitating their recovery. For others faith was not as important. All, however, had developed spiritual or personal practices, including meditation or certain Jewish mantras that helped alleviate their pain and stress. Some of the rabbis eventually regarded their cancer as a thing of the past and others saw it as an actual or potential threat to their continued good health. However, all four rabbis concurred that the diagnosis and treatment of their early stage, localized cancer was a life altering event.

> *Their early stage, localized cancer was a life-altering event.*

It should be reiterated that the particular ministers and rabbis profiled in this chapter were self-selected in this survey and don't represent all American Christian and Jewish clergymen who have had prostate cancer. Still it may be concluded that the faith of some Protestant ministers and Conservative Rabbis was tangential, and the faith of others was more instrumental, as they adjusted to their new condition and treatment side effects. In most cases all eight clergymen used some aspect of their religious traditions as an emotional outlet, although this did not always alleviate their concern about longevity and mortality.

Remarkably none of the laypeople or clergy I profiled used prayer, meditation, or relaxation techniques such as guided imagery in **advance** of their particular procedures. They did not draw on their spiritual or religious backgrounds to prepare themselves beforehand for their physical ordeal. These techniques, noted earlier in this book, are not intrinsically religious but mesh with a religious outlook. These approaches can potentially reduce stress and pain prior to procedures like a biopsy, surgery or radiation.

I am convinced that doctors or their assistants should assume the responsibility of informing their patients about the value of inducing a relaxation response to optimize patients' outcomes. At the least doctors' offices should provide patient brochures, not just about treatment modalities, but resources for stress- and pain-reduction. Patients themselves should be proactive in asking their doctors specific questions. How else will you prepare yourself for whatever might happen next? For a sample of what to ask, see "Ten Vital Questions to Ask Your Doctor," at *www.ConquerProstateCancer.com*.

With some exceptions it appears that those who are spiritually and physically "fit" are more likely to cope with and conquer prostate cancer and its treatment outcome. Until a broader representative sample of the population is tested, we can tentatively assume that faith and fitness generally help people achieve greater equanimity, even though they may know that this is hardly guaranteed.

16

Real Men Make Up Their Own Minds: Profiles in Prostate Cancer, Parts III and IV

"Therefore choose life!"
—Deuteronomy 30:19

"It is now and in this world that we must live."
—Andre Gide, 20th Century writer

The Choice is Yours

When it comes to determining what medicine or procedures can enhance a patient's quality of life, doctors may know best, but their patients should have the last word. In this era of personal home computers, medical information is readily available to laymen at a keystroke. Patients can explore medical advances and treatments that address their concerns. Their doctors can help them determine what treatment best meets their particular needs, and their wives and families can offer support. However, while a doctor can advise, it's the patient who must consent. One way or the other it's up to the patient to make up his own mind.

Alternative Strokes for Different Folks— Profiles in Prostate Cancer, Part III

If the patient decides against conventional treatments like surgery or radiation, he has other options. He can choose alternative treatments such as watchful waiting, cryoablation, or high intensity focused ultrasound (HIFU). Here are brief impressions of prostate cancer patients who chose one of these alternative approaches. A thumbnail definition precedes each of three vignettes.[1]

1. Watchful Waiting

Watchful Waiting: closely monitoring a patient's condition but withholding treatment until symptoms appear or change. Also called observation, active surveillance, or expectant management.

"Watchful Waiting" was a phrase I first heard three years ago, when I developed a small hernia protruding near my groin. It didn't really hurt, although it was a bit tender to the touch. The doctor suggested we try some watchful waiting, and when I asked what he meant, he responded, "Let's just wait to see if it gets worse. We can always treat it later."

Rather than reassuring me, the doctor's comment made me anxious. With an even greater sense of urgency I said, "Doc, as long as it's small, how about we take care of it now?" He made a call to a local hernia surgeon, and scheduled me for the surgery within two weeks. Later, when I woke up from the outpatient operation, I was giddy from the anesthesia but happy it was over. It was only a couple of days later that I realized why my doctor had hesitated: the surgery hurt more than the problem it solved. Only as the pain diminished was I glad that at last it was now really behind me.

Watchful waiting in reference to prostate cancer poses the same problem but is an even bigger deal. You may recall that before I met my robotic surgeon, Dr. Carey, my first urologist told me that he had discovered the cancer at an early stage, so I didn't have to have it treated right away. He did not really recommend watchful waiting, although he stated I might wait and see whether my prostate cancer might get worse. But I reasoned to myself, if my hernia couldn't wait, why would I wait for prostate cancer treatment?

Watchful waiting did not make sense to me until I learned about its other more precise names, one older, and one new. It has also been called "observation" or "expectant management," phrases I found no more persuasive than "watchful waiting." More recently it's been renamed "active surveillance," which put a whole new slant on the value of this approach.

When a patient agrees to active surveillance, he contracts with his doctor to have his early cancerous tumor closely monitored every three to six months, to see if it gets bigger. Prostate cancer usually grows very slowly in its earliest stages. For all I know, my prostate cancer tumor might have gone undetected for several years by the time it was found. Often prostate cancer that no one ever knew was there shows up in post-mortems of older men.

There are some people who can live with a small cancer, knowing it can be treated later if the need arises. I wasn't one of them. In some cases patients are motivated to do nothing because they are at risk due to heart illness or advanced diabetes. In other cases a patient who previously had unsuccessful or painful surgery may choose to wait it out instead of taking more aggressive action. Then too, many older patients in their mid-seventies or beyond may realize they are more likely to die with prostate cancer than from it. That's particularly true if someone has a life expectancy of ten to fifteen years, or another advanced disease.

Which is more important to you— sex or your life?

When I momentarily considered watchful waiting, I was properly informed it had some advantages, since it avoided the risks of surgery. Watchful waiting by itself can help patients avoid potential incontinence, impotence, blood loss and even death. I was momentarily tempted since I was anxious about the possibility of "losing my manhood." Still, all it took to make me opt for radiation and then surgery was a single question the doctor asked me: "Which is more important to you—sex or your life?" Suddenly the decision for surgery became a lot easier.

When I realized that watchful waiting can take the form of active surveillance, I wondered, "What if the cancer metastasizes even though it is monitored?" After all, a small percentage of cancers under active surveillance, perhaps as many as three percent, can metastasize even when the patient are seen regularly by their doctors. For me that low-grade risk was greater than I could accept. I wanted the cancer out before it could do irreparable damage.

One of my prostate cancer support group members, "Ron," felt quite differently. When his cancer was first diagnosed ten years earlier, he was 59 years old. He valued his active career, his golf, and his sex life with his wife. To preserve his quality of life he avoided surgery or radiation, fearing it would harm more than help him.

As the ten years rolled by, Ron became increasingly nervous. He was the only one in our support group who had not taken firmer action with a more aggressive approach. With all the prostate cancer advances he had heard about, he felt that now it was time to do something. He realized that the decision not to take action was still a decision; but at this point he was afraid the odds of his cancer spreading were increasingly greater. Besides he realized that during the decade he had been on watchful waiting, doctors had gotten a better "handle" on prostate cancer treatment, so in many ways he felt he had been right to wait.

I asked Ron what he planned to do next. He indicated that he had begun to explore cryoablation with his urologist. That approach would treat his prostate problems directly. It would be less invasive than surgery, which he feared would ruin his active lifestyle on and off the golf course. He was a man who desperately wanted to keep things the way they were, but given the advances of science over the last decade he now stood on safer ground. Besides, as a "macho" sort of guy, he was ready to act like a "real man" and make up his mind. He felt the time to act more decisively had come.

2. Cryoablation

Cryoabaltion (KRY-oh-uh-BLAY-shun): a procedure in which tissue is frozen to destroy abnormal cells. This is usually done with a special instrument that contains liquid nitrogen or liquid carbon dioxide. Also called cryosurgery or cryotherapy.

The term cryoablation was derived from the Latin words for "removal by freezing." In part the purpose of cryoablation is to destroy only the cancerous part of the prostate, while keeping the rest intact, thereby preserving a man's erectile and urological functioning. There have been many cases where this procedure has left patients with permanent incontinence and impotence, so it is still regarded as an alternative, experimental procedure.

On occasion, in the hands of an expert cryosurgeon, these dangers can be avoided.[2] Now this procedure, when applied, has been developed in a way that avoids freezing damage to nearby organs, although the proportion of adverse side-effects remains high.

A successful application of cryoablation was reported by Dr. Winston Barzell of Sarasota, my urologist's senior colleague. Dr. Barzell wrote a paper on this procedure and offered a case study involving one of his patients.[3] After assessing Tom, his 64-year-old patient, Dr. Barzell determined the man's localized prostate cancer could be ablated. The doctor first conducted a 3-D mapping biopsy of the right side of the bladder. Then he used six probes to ablate the left side, using a "double freeze/thaw cycle." The result was that his patient's PSA reading, which had initially been 5.9, was reduced to less than 0.1 and rose only slightly to 0.7 ten months later.

In a subsequent interview Dr. Barzell stated cryoablation was useful for salvage and high grade/high stage cases. He also felt it was suitable when a patient with early cancer could have part of his gland treated and the rest preserved, as in Tom's case. Dr. Barzell indicated he did not guarantee potency, although this can occur.

The patient was very pleased with the results. He was a retired high school math teacher who also coached golf and bowling. He had six children and four grandchildren and worked part-time at a golf course. The reason he preferred cryoablation is that it would allow him to avoid the lengthy recovery required for open surgery patients. In his words, "I wanted to get back to my kids and the golf course as soon as possible."

Once he returned home he needed very little pain medication. A week later he attended a Man-to-Man meeting. The doctor actually cleared him to play golf just ten days after his treatment, and he played all eighteen holes. He recommended the treatment to others, even though it's still used sparingly because of its risks, and long term data haven't verified the value of this treatment.

3. High Intensity Focused Ultrasound

High-Intensity Focused Ultrasound (HIFU): a therapy that destroys prostate cancer tissue with intense heat-generating ultrasound.

HIFU rhymes with "haiku" but it's hardly Japanese poetry. It involves using a probe through the rectum to target prostate cancer tissue and destroy it with intense heat. The heat is instantly generated by ultrasound with a high-tech device known as the Sonablate 500. This is the opposite of the freezing therapy used in cryoablation, but is considered non-invasive and fairly consistent. According to one source, the HIFU is a treatment that is more efficacious than other prostate treatments without being more invasive. At this point, I doubt if there are any randomized empirical studies to bolster this conclusion.[4]

While HIFU is not a new prostate cancer procedure, it is now only in its third year of trials in the United States, including at three centers in Florida alone. It is expected that it will be be FDA-approved in the near future; so right now HIFU treatment in the United States is not permitted except at the research programs. This is so even though it has been available for a number of years in Canada, Argentina, Mexico, the Dominican Republic, France and other European countries, where both doctors and patients report a high degree of success. According to its website 15,000 patient have been treated with HIFU over the past fifteen years, and there are currently a total of 180 HIFU centers around the world.[5]

HIFU public relations materials maintain that twenty percent of HIFU patients experience impotence after treatment and only half a percent experience permanent incontinence. The same materials claim this compares favorably with cryotherapy, radiation, and surgery, which they state leave anywhere from 36 to 93 percent of patients impotent, and 6 to 49 percent of patients incontinent. These higher figures are in reference to radical prostatectomy and, in my mind, are not accurate in view of other reports.[6]

The HIFU website provides brief accounts of patients who were pleased with their prostate cancer treatment. They imply that the treatment was quick, painless and non-invasive. However, as noted by its administrators, HIFU patients cannot have previous prostate treatment nor can their prostate volume exceed 40 cc's, unless larger prostates first respond favorably to hormones that will shrink the size of the expanded prostate to less than 40 cc's.

At the HIFU website one patient stated that he just knew he was going to be fine, because the day he arrived, another patient who maintained a well respected prostate cancer website was there as well. I contacted this gentleman with the website and asked if he would share his HIFU treatment experience with me. Ironically he said that he was not the right person to talk with because his prostate cancer treatment did not "take." Evidently his cancer has not been successfully eliminated through HIFU. This is not surprising, as no procedure is totally risk-free, and no treatment is suitable for everyone. And I don't believe there's any treatment that can reverse metastasis or help patients completely avoid pain or stress.

Like many organizations who promote their methods, the folks at what I'll call "HIFU Central" in Canada were kind enough to suggest the name of one former patient, a man we'll call "Walter," who had volunteered to speak with anyone who inquired.

In mid-April 2008, I spoke at length with Walter about his experiences as a HIFU patient. Four months earlier he had traveled to Puerto Vallarta, Mexico, to have his cancer ablated. He told me he felt good before his asymptomatic prostate contact was detected, and he felt as good or better after he had been treated. He was happy with the results.

Before the HIFU procedure, Walter took Casodex, a prescribed drug that lowered his testosterone and reduced his prostate size from 42cc to 37cc. In turn his PSA went from 4.7 to 4.0. However, since his free PSA was 15 percent, instead of 25 percent or above, his doctor took an 8-core biopsy which was assessed with a Gleason score of 7. The same stateside doctor spent a week every month in Puerto Vallarta, Mexico, to treat his patients with HIFU, and the doctor suggested Walter go there for the non-invasive treatment.

Walter and his wife checked into their hotel room in Puerto Vallarta one evening, and the next morning went to the local hospital. They marveled at how bright and clean it appeared. Walter was ushered to a private room to put on a hospital gown and was given a sedative. During his three hour "nap," the doctor and his staff administered spinal anesthesia, which Walter didn't feel during the operation or at any point after he woke up.

Once the HIFU Sonablate 500 completed its work and the prostate was ablated, he woke up and realized that over three hours had passed by. To his delight he was totally pain-free in the hospital and also when he left the hospital later. Rather than wearing a Foley catheter, he had been given a super-pubic catheter, attached through the lower part of his abdomen directly into the bladder to avoid any penile infection.

Right after Walter had awakened, his nurses asked him if he was hungry. When he said, "Yes!", they first fed him some broth and jello, and then gave him a dinner of "tasty steak." He was discharged that same day at around

4:30 p.m. and returned to his hotel with his wife. That night he told his wife he was famished, so they ate a fairly sizable meal in the hotel's restaurant. They spent the next couple of days in their room or by the hotel pool, near a bathroom so he could empty the catheter bag as needed. The only drinks he was instructed to avoid were alcohol, since the effects of his anesthesia still lingered.

Three days after his HIFU procedure Walter and his wife flew back to the States. He visited his doctor ten days later and had the catheter removed without a hitch. After another week of dribbling urine, he said he had no signs of incontinence. By the second or third week he had resumed his normal household activities and chores and returned to work. Within a month he felt totally rejuvenated.

Three months after the procedure his PSA had dropped down to 0.2. This was evidence that the HIFU treatment had successfully "zapped" his entire prostate and that he was now cancer-free. His final piece of good news was that by the third month after returning home he was able to have full erections like he did before his cancer was diagnosed. His orgasms are dry now that he no longer has a functioning prostate, and he stated "that was different," but he enjoys sexual relations as much as before. He is a truly satisfied customer.

I imagine Walter's doctor was happy too, given the $25,000 fee Walter paid him. Since HIFU is not yet FDA-approved, Walter had to pay out-of-pocket. However he told me it was absolutely worth it, and indicated he would recommend HIFU to anyone who qualified. As a postscript to this true tale, Walter conceded that some patients have not had the same success as he has. But that is true of virtually every other prostate treatment, including robotic surgery, as you'll see next.

Robotic Patients—Profiles in Prostate Cancer, Part IV

The final set of profiles involves four prostate cancer patients who chose robotic surgery to treat their early-stage prostate cancer. For the sake of brevity I'll refer to them as "robotic patients," in place of more the accurate terminology—patients treated through "robotic-assisted, laparoscopic radical prostatectomy."

The robotic patients I interviewed lived either in Boston or Sarasota. They were between 53 to 72 years old at the time of their procedures, which had occurred from six weeks to one year before talking to me. Two happened to be Christian and two were Jewish, with varying degrees of religious conviction. As in the earlier profiles I presented, this was not a representative sample survey of robotic patients everywhere. However the subjects' anecdotal accounts typify how prostate cancer patients, besides me, have responded to robotic surgery and its aftermath.

Before their prostate cancer was discovered, each of these men had a DRE (digital rectal exam) and a PSA blood test to confirm the level of protein in their blood stream. Coincidentally the PSA of each of these four patients ranged between 3 and 4, which was relatively high compared to the 2.5 score many urologists prefer to see as normative. However each man's PSA had fluctuated by as much as 2.5 points during the year before their doctors last examined them.

Their biopsies determined that three of the four men had total Gleason scores of 6 and one registered a 7. This indicated that their tumors were relatively non-aggressive when examined microscopically by a pathologist. Their bone scans and pelvic CAT scans also confirmed the tumors were pathologically microscopic. For that reason these men were good candidates for robotic surgery.

1. Marty's Story—Recovery Despite Complications

Marty's prostate cancer was diagnosed in October 2006, after his PSA had continued to fluctuate. His father and an uncle had prostate cancer before him, so he knew he was genetically at greater risk. He also had BPH, a benign, enlarged prostate. But he never had any serious illness until his prostate cancer was diagnosed.

Given his family and medical history, Marty was not surprised about the diagnosis. Previously he had gone through a few regularly scheduled biopsies due to his doctor's concern about both his PSA level and his family history. While the previous tests indicated negative findings, his latest biopsy found he was positive for cancer, with a Gleason score of 6. He indicated he was not overly worried. However he was a bit concerned, since the new biopsy revealed he had cancer in all four quadrants of his prostate.

Before being diagnosed with prostate cancer, Marty's primary concern was that his wife had been treated for another cancer with attendant physical and emotional problems. He felt that her difficulties were far more severe than his, and this enabled him to take his own condition in stride. As he put it, "I already had a lot on my plate, and I was able to compartmentalize my new-found disease."

For these and other reasons Marty was relatively calm when he first heard about the prostate cancer. He was able to keep things in perspective because he knew it was slow-growing, he felt his doctor would help him, and he was convinced he could be cured. He also believed that God would not let him suffer or die. Given that he was only in his late forties, he simply did not feel that it was his time to go.

Marty had robotic surgery in January 2007, only three months after his diagnosis and, as it happens, the same month I was first diagnosed with prostate cancer. His decision to have robotic surgery came easily. He had quickly ruled out watchful waiting, since he did not want to worry about having the potential "ups and downs" of his condition. He had no desire to stay on his old BPH medication or be told to take some new pills. By the same token he did not want to go through periodic re-testing in the months or years ahead to see if his localized cancer might become more aggressive or not.

Marty ruled out any form of radiation. He was concerned it might eventually lead to a recurrence of his cancer. He was also informed that if he received radiation, he could not have any required prostate surgery at a later date. He did not want to take that chance either, should the cancer return.

Deciding on surgery, he chose the robotic route because of assurances of nerve-sparing, limited pain, and a quick return to his job to which he was dedicated. Some close friends, including another physician and someone who had recently gone through robotic surgery, reinforced his decision.

Unfortunately Marty's robotic surgery took six hours, rather than the usual two, because of unexpected bladder and rectal complications. The same complications resulted in a hospital stay of one week instead of the usual one day stay for most robotic-assisted patients. Given his problems, he was grateful to his doctor and retained his trust in the doctor's urological skills.

Marty took regular painkillers after the operation and felt no pain at all, although he felt a pulling sensation from some of his stitches. He was glad to get off his pain pills shortly after going home. Although he felt no pain, he suffered from extreme fatigue and found it difficult to get in and out of bed. He realized he had no choice but to wait it out until he could get going again. He made the mistake of going to work two weeks after the surgery and was so tired he barely could get through several meetings. A week later, though, he was able to return to work, restored to his customary high energy.

Incontinence was not an issue for Marty. He wore a catheter bag for about three weeks, due to his bladder complications. After the catheter was removed, he practiced his Kegel exercises to strengthen his pelvic floor muscles. While he "dribbled" only on occasion, he wore small pads in his underwear for a couple of months just as a precaution. He was able to go regularly to the bathroom without incident, since the robotic surgeon had taken such effective care not only of his prostate, but of his bladder and rectal issues.

For six months after his robotic surgery, Marty was completely impotent. Since the prostate and nearby sites were traumatized, he had no physical sensation when he attempted to engage in sexual relations with his wife. Neither a vacuum erection pump, nor Viagra and Cialis were helpful. After half a year, while continuing on Cialis, his erectile dysfunction slowly dissipated. He resolved to take things one day at a time until he could respond spontaneously without any devices or pills.

Marty credited his relatively rapid recovery not only to his robotic surgery, but to his faith in God and in himself, bolstered by his Jewish upbringing. As he put it, "As long as you keep a positive attitude, you can get better faster." Even though his post-op experience left him weak, he felt increasingly better from the first week onward.

It helped that Marty could rely on his supportive hospital caregivers before he got home. He was also appreciative of the support he got from friends and local rabbis who came by to wish him well. His family's support was immensely important. He and his wife of twenty years had always stuck by each other "for better and for worse," and both felt lucky to overcome their separate bouts with cancer.

A test six months after surgery indicated that his PSA had gone down to 1.5 and had not been completely eliminated. This was a bit disturbing, since a post-op reading is usually less than 0.2. However after another five months his PSA was down to 0.1, and he stopped worrying about any recurrence of cancer.

At the time of the interview Marty felt he had probably conquered his prostate cancer. He had no hesitation stating that he had indeed conquered his incontinence, his erectile dysfunction, his pain and his stress.

2. Ned's Story—A Positive Attitude and Unqualified Success

At the time of his diagnosis, Ned had retired from three decades as a salesman in a major department store. Ned's prostate cancer was first diagnosed in November 2006 and he went through robotic surgery in December 2007, only a month before I interviewed him. So it was little wonder that he recalled every detail of the events that preceded and followed his surgery.

When Ned's PSA was measured before his operation it seemed low, but it had previously been twice as high. Given this fluctuation he had a hunch it might indicate he had prostate cancer, and he was not totally surprised when the biopsy confirmed this.

> *Surgery did not daunt him.*

Ned did not panic because when diagnosed he was totally asymptomatic. He did not have any erectile dysfunction or incontinence before surgery, so he felt "he would be good to go" once he decided what treatment was best for him. Also, while his father had bone cancer five years earlier at the age of 89, he himself had never experienced any serious illness.

Once the biopsy confirmed the cancer, Ned was eager to totally excise it from his prostate through surgery, rather than rely on radiation, which he thought would be less conclusive. One of his relatives had both erectile dysfunction and incontinence after radiotherapy, although a neighbor who had brachytherapy (seeding) was happy with the outcome.

As a proactive individual Ned weighed his options. He managed his stress by keeping busy talking to various doctors to find out what to do. When his family physician recommended seeding, Ned countered, "If it were you who had prostate cancer, what treatment would you choose for yourself?" His doctor promptly responded, "I would go the route of surgery!" That helped, especially since Ned had concluded by then that he wanted to get rid of his whole prostate. Surgery did not daunt him, since he knew a number of people who had had surgery and survived just fine.

Ned's positive attitude was evident when he told me, "No matter what problem you have, you need to address it by getting the best professional guidance—and then make up your mind." That's exactly what he did.

He had never heard of robotic surgery until he spoke with another urologist, who was Dr. Robert Carey's colleague. In meeting Dr. Carey, Ned was impressed by his credentials and character, as well as by the features of the robotic device. He felt reassured that his nerve bundles would remain intact, and that he would probably function sexually and urologically with few limitations after the surgery. As an active golfer in good physical shape (except for some back problems), Ned felt he would readily bounce back.

Ned overcame any hesitation in choosing robotic laparoscopic radical prostatectomy when he learned of the robotic device's precision. He was intrigued that it eliminated a robotic surgeon's potential hand tremors during the operation, although he knew that would not be a problem, given Dr. Carey's reputation for having a steady hand! The decision came more easily because other physicians reinforced his choice of doctor and robotics. Plus his "significant other," a hospital volunteer, had heard only good things about Dr. Carey. It seems there is a bona fide "love fest" about the man and his skills; it's not a figment of Ned's imagination or mine.

After his friendly discussions and computer search about robotic surgery, Ned had only one dilemma: he debated whether to have the surgery in the winter or wait for summer, since he wanted to keep on playing golf with his friends before it got too hot! However some of his friends who had had prostate surgery advised him to get it done before things might get worse, and he was persuaded to go ahead sooner rather than later.

Ned experienced no pain at all before the operation, either in reference to the cancer or biopsy. He also had no pain after the robotic surgery, except when a nurse pulled out his blood drainage tube. Ned felt so good that, when he left the hospital the next day, he went home only after stopping off at Best Buy and a local supermarket.

He wore a catheter bag for only one week, and then he returned to the doctor's office to have it pulled out. Immediately afterwards he went off to eat a hearty breakfast without incident. In fact except for some occasions that induced stress incontinence it turned out that when he laughed, sneezed or coughed, he experienced no urinary dripping. He routinely used a pad for a few days, and then found he no longer had to continue doing so.

At the time of the interview, one month after surgery, Ned said he felt totally re-energized. He experienced a degree of erectile dysfunction and told me of the one a significant incident that brought him a lot of pain. He had gone to the urologist for an injection of Caverject (prostaglandin E1), which for ten to twenty percent of men can cause pain from the reaction of the medication in the penis. The doctor gave him 10 micrograms, half the usual recommended dosage. This worked well, at least to start with.

As Ned put it, "I felt myself get hard by the time I reached the elevator. My girlfriend was with me, and for her sake, as well as mine, I felt we should go home immediately and celebrate my return to virility. We did that, but then I had a real problem: I experienced the most excruciating pain of my life."

For the next five hours he found that his erection did not dissipate. He was in such pain that he called his doctor, Dr. Carey, who met him an hour and a half later in the emergency wing of the hospital. Ned received an injection of phenylephrine, which causes the blood vessels to contract and quickly resolved the matter. Later, when he was told the next dosage of Caverject could be radically reduced and still produce an erection, Ned declined the offer. Instead he decided to wait a couple of months until he could experience spontaneous erections, an outcome he fully anticipated in the near future.

Ned informed me that his girlfriend was extremely supportive of him and took everything in stride. She had accompanied him at every visit he made to the doctor and was with him before and after his surgery. As it happened, she had been previously married to a man who had ED and had used a vacuum erection pump, and that helped her keep her perspective. Ned was buoyed up by her ongoing support and caring attitude.

Ned was so confident in his recovery that he felt he had no need to pray to God. Although he was a Protestant and attended church once in awhile, he did not feel the need for God's healing presence. However he stated, "I believe that whatever comes your way, that's what God has in mind for you. He'll deal you whatever cards you can handle, and you'll do the best you can." He added that "A positive attitude is a huge part of getting through prostate cancer." In fact he reported that his doctors all said he would do fine because his attitude was so upbeat.

Ned's nearly pain-free experiences surrounding his robotic surgery (apart from his injection) was all that much more remarkable, given the daily back pains he has experienced for the past twenty years. A month after his surgery he was convinced that he was able to conquer his prostate cancer as well as any related incontinence, erectile dysfunction, pain or stress.

3. Otto's Story—Going Strong with a Sense of Humor

Otto, like Ned, had been in sales for most of his career. He was constantly on the road, driving hundreds of miles a week to cover his "territory." He was first diagnosed with cancer in October 2006, when he was 64. Throughout his life, Otto had been relatively hale and hearty, with two minor exceptions. He had asthma, which was under control. He also had BPH, a benign enlarged prostate, which was effectively treated with Detrol to relax his bladder pressure. So before his diagnosis he felt he was in good shape.

Being healthy all his life, and knowing nobody else in his family had any prostate cancer, Otto was not prepared for the dismaying news. He was disturbed that his PSA had virtually tripled in one year, and he faulted his doctor for not monitoring him sufficiently. However he believed he would be okay, once he learned that scientists had developed various treatment options that would cure him of his cancer. Besides, he believed that God would not let him suffer or die. His faith was intact and, as a Conservative Jew, he attended synagogue prayer services an average of two mornings a week and on the Sabbath. His religious outlook fortified him.

Otto's urologist assured him that his prostate cancer was probably local and slow-growing. After reviewing several treatment options, the doctor urged him to consider radiation seeding (brachytherapy). When Otto responded by indicating he wanted to get rid of his entire cancerous prostate, the doctor switched gears and recommended surgery. However the physician did not even hint that Otto might look into robotic-assisted laparoscopic radical prostatectomy.

Given his somewhat unsatisfactory experiences with his physicians thus far, Otto went with his wife to his local hospital to explore precisely what treatment was best for him. While there he talked with some friends, including a pediatric urologist who said, "See as many doctors as you can." Otto took his advice and went to a variety of medical specialists.

He began to attend a prostate cancer support group at another hospital, where various doctors offered monthly presentations. He was particularly impressed by one visiting physician, who headed up a robotics surgery team. After the lecture, Otto went up to him and asked him, "How many surgeries a year do you do?" When Otto heard that the doctor performed some three hundred operations a year, he was convinced he had found his man. Within a few days he set a February 2007 date for the daVinci robotic surgery.

Otto was particularly glad to hear the surgery would be laparoscopic and spare his nerve bundles, assuring him an eventual return to potency and continence after the surgery. He wasn't stressed that these important issues might not be resolved immediately, because he believed he would be okay in the long run. His surgeon's skill level, along with the encouragement of support group members and some long-term friends, reinforced Otto's innate optimism that everything would be fine. His wife's extremely supportive stance was reassuring as well.

Because he experienced no pain, except for excess stomach gas, Otto retained his trust in his surgeon in the days and months after the operation. He had prayed for a good outcome, although he did not ask his fellow synagogue attendees to recite a prayer for him. The reason he refrained from having a public recitation of a healing prayer was that he had previously requested that same thing for a friend, who subsequently died! Under such circumstances you can't blame Otto for being a bit superstitious.

A week after recuperating at home, Otto returned to his office. It took another week until he got over his fatigue and was able to get back on the road to resume his traveling sales job. He was grateful that the doctor had been able to remove his catheter on the sixth day after the surgery. After that, as a precaution he initially wore a Depends adult diaper, but as he put it, "I hated it." He soon switched to a small pad for three months to absorb any excess urine, especially because there were often no restrooms near his sales route. When he remembered, he strengthened his pelvic floor muscles with Kegel exercises.

Otto was still experiencing erectile dysfunction when we spoke, a year and a half after his surgery. He managed to offset this problem to some extent by using a pump, but he felt that was awkward and time-consuming. I encouraged him to try a different pump which was easier to use, and he said he would look into that. Failing that, he thought he might explore a penile implant.

Otto stated he was willing to wait a few more months to see if his spontaneous erections might return. I wished him well. After all, I had learned that not all men who have had erections prior to surgery will have an adequate erection afterwards. This is so whether they had robotic or retropubic (open surgery) nerve sparing. It may well be that having a prosthetic was appropriate for him, even though others managed either with injections, a vacuum device, penile pellets, Viagra or some other approach.

Throughout our discussion I sensed and shared Otto's frustration. He seemed to realize that this can happen to someone who has had BPH before surgery. I told him it can also happen to someone who previously had normal erections.

Otto's faith helped to carry him through his ordeal. In his words, "I feel spiritually, mentally and physically strong enough to overcome any remaining difficulties. When something goes wrong, I generally figure out the best way to resolve things, and I will now as well." His positive disposition, coupled with the support his wife and son gave him, kept him on an even keel. He was also buoyed up by the report that his prostate margins were clear and that the chances of the cancer recurring were slim.

Overall, Otto was content with his decision to utilize robotic surgery. Even though he conceded that he was still sexually impotent, he had hope for the future. The fact that he never experienced acute pain or severe incontinence was a big plus in his eyes. He truly believed he had conquered his cancer. At the end, though, he conceded he experienced occasional stress, especially since he was still "pissed off" at his original urologist. Wryly he added, "This too will pass!" While empathizing with him, I smiled inwardly as his unintended puns whizzed by.

> *He never experienced acute pain or severe incontinence.*

4. Paul's Story—Older but Eager to Keep on Going

Paul, a retired engineer and consultant, was first diagnosed with prostate cancer in September 2007. During the previous year he had begun to have difficulties urinating, and his stream had slowed down. However he had taken this in stride and continued his day-to-day functions without any problems. But when he learned of the prostate cancer, the news initially numbed him. He felt unprepared for this development and acutely sensed his mortality. Still, after speaking to several doctors, he felt things would turn out alright with the proper treatment, and as a believing Christian he had faith in God's providence.

The doctors he saw gave him a book and a pamphlet, apart from talking with him. They felt he was not a candidate for "watchful waiting," given his vigor and family longevity. This was to his credit, since he was already in his early seventies.

He ended up thinking that he would have surgery, but he was terrified by the prospect of impotence and incontinence. After researching robotic-assisted surgery and speaking with the surgeon who would take care of him, it took him only fifteen minutes to "sign on," confident now that his fears were exaggerated. His hesitation dissipated when his surgeon told him he did 150 robotic surgeries a year. At that point Paul set aside any thoughts about trying hormone treatment or radiation instead.

After his surgery in January 2008, Paul retained his confidence in his surgeon. Even an hour of extreme post-op pain did not faze him in the long run, since he felt fine after that. He was convinced he successfully eliminated any pain or discomfort. This was the case even though he took only two pain tablets in the hospital before going home the next day.

Paul's wife had initially been scared of the robotic device. She worried about what would happen if there were suddenly an electrical failure. Once reassured that standard surgery was always a back-up alternative, she confirmed Paul's feeling that he had taken the right course of action.

As a devout Catholic, Paul's strong faith led him to sense that he was in contact with God, and that "Someone was watching over me." He stated he was able to stay in touch with God in body and in spirit, and this helped reduce his pain and stress, even though he felt a bit strained by all he went through.

He conceded that he found his catheter to be annoying and stressful, and was glad when it was removed a week later. He had begun doing Kegel exercises before the surgery and resumed as soon as he could ten days later. That and meditation, along with wearing adult diapers for a couple of days due to mild urinary dribbling, kept him calm and confident that his incontinence would pass.

Paul felt that his experience was not intense, compared to some major surgery his wife had recently gone through. His erectile dysfunction was not of any consequence, since his wife was incapable of intercourse at that time. However, he used a vacuum erection pump as his surgeon instructed, to avoid any penile vein atrophy.

Paul did not use any guided imagery to control his fears or stress, but his conscious beliefs and positive thought processes were helpful. His wife's support, despite her condition, added to his optimism, as did the support of various friends.

Paul was so determined to get back on his feet that he walked five miles a day even before his catheter bag was removed. In part he was motivated to regain his strength because he had lost twenty pounds in the previous two months. His doctors suspected he might have colon cancer, although he did not feel any related symptoms. He planned to be in as good a shape as possible for his colonoscopy, two weeks after our interview.

Paul's prostate surgery made him feel his mortality, even though he came through it with flying colors. At the end of the interview he told me that he truly believed he had conquered prostate cancer, along with his incontinence, pain or stress. As he put it, "the jury was still out" regarding his erectile dysfunction, which he hoped he would overcome in time.

My Robotic Postscript

The four patients who chose robotic-assisted surgery did so only after carefully considering their other options. They all chose this form of surgery with the assumption that this procedure, in the hands of expert surgeons, would be the most beneficial in the long run. All were happy with their decision and its outcomes. In every case incontinence was not a problem, although each in his own way still struggled with erectile dysfunction.

What is most striking, though, is that ED was seen as a short-term problem, which could be resolved through appropriate methods. For each of these men, like myself, devices or pills generally remedied their erectile dysfunction, and with one exception, impotence was no longer a major problem. At the very least these men felt that ED, while a source of discomfort or stress, could be managed without questioning their virility. This was in contrast to some of the men described earlier, who chose other treatment options.

No matter what the treatment, confidence in one's doctor and support by family and friends were crucial. These elements helped reduce the stress of prostate cancer and its outcomes or side effects. Faith in one's capacity to recuperate was also important. For those who were so-minded, faith in God added an extra layer of hope and meaning.

Virtually none of these patients cursed the moment that prostate cancer struck. All seemed to look on their illness more as a chronic disease than as a death blow. This could well be because these robotic-assisted patients, like the others described in this book, were diagnosed with early, localized cancer.

In retrospect, I cannot assert that any of the nineteen men I have profiled erred in choosing one option over the other. All were treated by competent doctors whose skills and attitudes did much to help their patients. With few exceptions, these patients, even when burdened with sadness at a major life change, were able to get back into their daily routines in relatively short order. This applies as well to other patients described at *www.ConquerProstateCancer.com*.

To choose or not to choose—that is the question. As noted earlier, even watchful waiting—the decision not to choose—is a choice.

Of course it's true that our choices are often dictated by the resources available to us. Had I not been referred to my urologist, Dr. Carey, and had he not performed many robotic surgeries before I came along, perhaps my decision would have been different. At the very least I would have felt compelled to find an experienced robotic surgeon by going to Tampa or Miami or out-of-state, if I still felt robotic-assisted surgery was in my best interest. On the other hand, had the opportunity for robotic surgery not been available locally, I'm not sure I would have chosen to go to a robotic center in a far-off location, since that would have added to my family's stress. Fortunately I never had to ponder such a course of action.

> *To choose or not to choose— that is the question.*

Even a year and a half later, on the occasion of our 36th wedding anniversary on September 3, 2008, my wife and I remained relatively content. New health concerns, unrelated to the cancer, cooled our ardor, but we remain each other's lover and best friend.

I will always wonder to what I should attribute my good fortune in meeting with my talented and dedicated robotic surgeon—a mere twenty minutes from my Sarasota home. Was it just lucky timing, good fortune, fate, or the hand of God that led me to this particular surgeon and this outcome? After my surgery, Yvonne reflected about the nature of coincidence.

With the help of doctors, family and friends, Ed chose surgery. In the end, though, his decision was the result of a series of coincidences, although I think God was very much around and within us in helping us make a decision. It turned out that Sarasota Memorial Hospital had recently acquired the newest surgical robot. At the same time, a local

Together for 36 years—September 3, 2008. Seventeen months after robotic surgery to eliminate prostate cancer.
Photo credit: Herb Paynter

urology practice managed to convince one of the top robotic surgeons in Miami to join the surgical staff here on Florida's west coast. How lucky we were that Dr. Carey moved from Miami to Sarasota just two months before we settled here.

—Yvonne

Personal decisiveness ... close family and friends ... coincidence ... and the presence of God combined to make this the best option for my prostate problems and that of a number of other individuals. Sometimes it seems as if the decision has already been made by the time you stumble across it.

17

Robotic-Assisted Surgery— The Debate Goes On between Critics and Proponents

"For every opinion, there is an equal and opposite opinion."
—Anonymous

"Sooner or later, our technology is going to catch up with us."
—Anonymous

Is Robotics the Way to Go?

Prostate cancer patients exploring treatment options would do well to consider robotic-assisted surgery, since in many cases it's the best way to go. However, as with open surgery, it can only be utilized for patients whose cancer is localized in the prostate. Equally important it applies only to patients whose doctors have expertise in robotic surgery. In addition patients need to confirm with their doctors that this is the best treatment available to cure their cancer and help restore their quality of life. This approach served my needs and has worked well for thousands of men. It might be right for you and your family.

Robotic surgery offers slight advantages over open surgery. It allows most patients to be discharged from the hospital after one night, rather than two or three nights; it typically enables the patient to stop pain medication several days before most open surgery patients; and because it involves a minimally invasive laparoscopic approach, there is significantly less blood loss.

Robotic surgery also enables patients to return to their daily activities a few days or weeks earlier than open surgery patients. Its enhanced magnification, more than twice that of standard surgery, does not necessarily assure greater success in eradicating prostate cancer or avoiding impotence and incontinence. But knowing your surgeon can see everything so clearly "from the inside out" is reassuring. It makes a difference to patients that the surgeon is confident he can spare nerves that preserve potency and continence. (This is true of experienced traditional surgeons who can also accomplish this with standard surgical glasses that have 4x magnification.) No less important is robotic surgery's built-in assurance of tremor-free surgical movements while automatically scaling down the surgeon's slightest hand motions at the console, transforming inches to millimeters.

While robotic surgery offers these and other important enhancements compared to standard surgery, it's important to reiterate that present scientific literature does not reveal any definitive difference between most treatment options, in terms of cure rates and patient longevity. Few studies have attempted to scientifically validate which approach is best suited to meet patients' needs in general.

In 2005 researcher Diane Robertson co-authored a summary of various evidence-based studies comparing the benefits of different prostate cancer surgeries. In her view, these do not demonstrate that robotic surgery leads to a better cure rate compared to standard surgery. While most doctors measure cure rate by observing actual survival, she posits that a cure rate can be measured by the number of cancer cells on the removed prostate and by each patient's PSA level after surgery. Her findings applied to robotic, laparoscopic or standard surgery. However, her report at that time revealed that removing a cancerous prostate through robotic surgery led to less blood loss compared to open surgery,[1] which was remarkable for the newer technology.

Robertson's report refers to another study which shows that hospital stays of robotic surgery patients were half that of prostate cancer patients who had open surgery: about one versus two days. For many this is hardly a major difference. She also notes an old study that after robotic surgery most patients need a catheter for up to a week, whereas open surgery patients require a catheter for an average of two weeks. A 2007 report by the Mayo Clinic, though, indicates that open surgery patients, after a one- to three-day hospital stay, will likewise need a catheter for either one or two weeks until their urinary tracts heal.[2]

My having a catheter bag for eighteen days made me an exception that proves the rule: I needed the catheter for more than two weeks, not because I had robotic surgery but because Dr. Carey elected to perform a bladder neck reconstruction. As he told me the day after the operation, I had an enormous median lobe of prostate tissue that until surgery had distorted my bladder neck. During the operation, he felt that my chance at good long-term continence would best be served by performing a bladder neck reconstruction and tubularization prior to reconnecting the bladder neck with the urethra. Dr. Carey added that the future of robotic surgery lies in training surgeons to be able to perform operations for cases as difficult as mine.

Robertson's report notes that only five percent of robotic surgery patients had complications. Ten percent had complications if they used laparoscopic surgery without robotic assistance, and fifteen percent of open surgery patients had complications. These findings can still be contested now, three years after her report, but seemed significant to a number of people at the time.

An additional advantage of robotic surgery is that due to the quarter-inch key-hole incisions, as opposed to a 4"–7" abdominal cut in open surgery, patients have little if any scarring and tend not to bleed internally. In addition they can anticipate going back to normal activity within ten days as opposed to six weeks following open surgery.[3]

In my experience these features make patients less anxious about potential pain. As noted previously, this is also due to the perception that increased magnification in robotic surgery makes for greater accuracy, while the robotic device's capacity to "scale down" the surgeon's hand movements helps avoid an untoward effect on the patient if the surgeon's hand begins to tremble.

These issues inspire patient confidence. However they are not themselves sufficient justification for saying robotic surgery is superior to open surgery. Ultimately what counts most is that both robotics and open surgery may well offer the same cancer cure rate for the long haul and provide equal results regarding quality of life outcomes like potency and continence.[4]

The biggest downside of robotic surgery is probably the expense. It costs close to 2 million dollars to purchase the machine and about $120,000 a year to maintain it. This translates into a per-patient cost of about $1,000 more for robotic prostate surgery than standard surgery. However, some doctors maintain that the cost-saving inherent in a one-night hospital stay versus two or three, counter-balances the extra per-patient expense. The likelihood of robotics "getting it right" the first time makes it even more cost-effective.

Whether you choose robotic or retropubic open surgery to eliminate prostate cancer is a highly subjective decision. In describing my satisfaction with robotics I, like others, have offered mostly anecdotal evidence. That will have to suffice until evidence-based medical research can validate or reinforce what we believe.

Can Anyone Be Completely Pain-Free and Stress-Free?

As a gerontologist I knew long before my robotic surgery that we're bound to have multiple health problems as we get older. Partial loss of hearing, smell and sight and a shortened vertebra due to gravity and increasing spinal compression, are just a few of the many different potential developments that can affect even the most active person age fifty and over. I have learned this not just from my doctoral studies but from my own personal experience. Each of these particular concerns had an impact on me before I reached my current age of 64, although I've done my best not to let such concerns get me down.

Beyond this, illnesses like my diabetes or neuropathy, can "do a number" on folks as they age. They sure have on me! Of course if you're subject to these health issues, there are always new medications or diet plans that can lighten your load.

Everyone faces the aging process and pain or loss differently. One person might experience a conglomeration of illnesses, while others are relatively healthy. Besides, the effects of aging are not all negative, and aging itself is largely subjective. Many individuals describe getting older or having a health concern as painful or difficult, but others will take these matters in stride. Clearly aging, like beauty, is often in the eyes of the beholder.

With increasing age and accumulated life experiences we're repeatedly exposed to emotional and physical pain. Pains and stresses we accumulate can gain a life of their own. People's pain is often out of control, even when analgesics are available. Some experts assert that, "Chronic pain is one of the most pervasive and intractable medical conditions in the U.S., with one in five Americans afflicted." An American doctor from the Cleveland Clinic noted that, "There is no cure for chronic pain, period!"

However medical science has developed an arsenal of new, creative ways to battle both chronic and short-term pain.[5] Physicians tell us that even chronic pain can be treated after an initial trauma. For instance it's possible to use a nerve block, like that administered to a soldier injured in battle or an athlete on the playing field, or someone suffering from a very painful illness somewhere on the "home front." As an example, my wife, Yvonne, like six million other Americans, has contended with disabling fibromyalgia and chronic fatigue for years. But for limited durations, she has benefited from various medicines to keep her alert and relatively pain-free.

Pain due to prostate difficulties can also be reduced through medical treatment and with alternative approaches, including relaxation techniques explored earlier. We can look forward to health technology improving to meet our needs. Meantime it's important to acknowledge that pain, like age, is relative.

As for stress—if you're alive, you can count on it!

As for stress—if you're alive, you can count on it! Stress is inevitable as our life circumstances change. Some stress is good—it keeps us on our feet and motivates us to accomplish our objectives. Stress can get worried adults to seek medical attention when injured. Stress can get parents to "shlep" their children from one activity to another, to make sure they get ahead in life. Stress can get you to spend time and effort giving back to the community, while demonstrating you really care.

Stress can also be life-saving. Without it you'd never jump back to the curb in time as a car rushes by, endangering your existence. Nor would a lifeguard, like my daughter, manage to jump into the water to save someone's life, if her adrenalin didn't kick in. Stress can help us make it through the day. Actually, stress can simply help us make it altogether!

However, other forms of stress are not desirable. In those cases stress can agitate us, overwhelm us and weigh us down. Stress can prevent us from making rational decisions to find out if we have prostate cancer, and stress can prevent us from doing something about it once it's been confirmed.

Stress, like pain, is inevitable. Our lives cannot be totally pain-free or stress-free. Whether you adapt a-fight-or-flight approach to life's problems, the stresses that bombard you are either useful or detrimental. Much of the time, though, they help you make life-and-death choices that can keep you out of trouble! Even stress and pain which bring you to a stand-still can be beneficial. Such pain and stress may compel you to consult with those who can provide medical help, money, or love, before you consider what steps to take.

From time immemorial, pain and stress have accompanied us through our lives. With proper medical treatment and medication, supplemented by "centering" ourselves, we can reduce the duration and intensity of our pain or stress, and we can master ever more effective coping skills. This is so even though pain and stress are here to stay.

Medical Technophobia

We live in the personal computer era. Most of us have benefited enormously from ever-expanding medical technology that we can access through the "windows" of our home office monitors. This is true in many countries, both in the West and East. For instance, very large personal computer monitors keyed into a particular patient's vital signs, can be found in numerous hospital corridors, signaling healthcare providers outside patient rooms when a patient's life is at risk. My sister in Israel, a former post-cardiac care nurse, told me this made quite a difference, not just to her patients but to the way she practiced medicine.

We live in a time when robotic machines are increasingly part of our culture. Some of the most advanced robots in 2008 are those developed by Honda Motor Corporation. Honda personnel recently displayed two humanoid robots programmed to work together serving drinks and hors d'oervres on social occasions. These machines have been programmed to move around people, through sensors that predict human movement. The robots go off to a recharging station when their batteries fall below a certain level.[6]

In the health industry, the daVinci robotic device my urologist used to eradicate my cancerous prostate is also the wave of the future. I imagine that in time medical robots may well be programmed to operate independently during surgery with a minimum of human supervision and intervention. Within a decade it may be possible for an experienced robotics surgeon, sitting at his hi-def 3-D console monitor, to apply his skills across the globe, assisted by local doctors.

In view of these developments there's ample reason to disagree with professionals and pundits who look askance at robotic medical devices. You might wonder how anyone could object to such beneficial technological developments, but it does happen. Take, for example, Dr. Dale Magee, in his 2007 inaugural address as the new President of the Massachusetts Medical Society. Dr. Magee wrote a helpful newsletter column titled, "Steps to Being a Smarter Patient." In that column he told people not to be sucked in by "the latest and greatest" in medical technology, be it lasers, robotics, or genetics. From his point of view these are new methods and more time is needed to judge how successful they really are.[7]

Dr. Magee might be right hypothetically. However he would not be correct if he were referring to robotic machines like the da Vinci system. These machines do have a track record indicating they are safe for patients, even though that record has been established only over the past eight years.

In fact, while the robotic device utilized in my surgery in April 2007 was relatively new, it was already a second-generation product! It had been improved a year earlier with the addition of a fourth robotic arm. It also introduced a new camera that provided higher definition and magnification, allowing for a three dimensional view of my internal organs. This, and the scaled-down movements of a trained surgeon's hands, continues to make for a relatively safe, reliable operation.

While many individuals may be alternately impressed or intimidated by robotic machines, these devices are hardly a passing fad. This invention is just one of many robotic developments we have yet to witness. Clearly its use in the hands of capable surgeons compares favorably with more traditional surgery.

It seems to me that doctors should encourage patients to explore every available technique at their disposal, and avoid pre-judging a program adversely because it's new. If we always adapted such a wary outlook, life in this fast-paced world would be filled with far more missed opportunities.

In the few years it has been used, the robotic machine has acquired new applications. It has been adapted for use in hysterectomies, kidney surgery, stomach bypass, and cardio-thoracic surgeries. In mitral heart valve replacements, patients no longer have their breast bone broken to repair the heart. This application is so practical that in December 2007, Sarasota Memorial Hospital announced it accepted the donation of a second robotic machine used exclusively for heart procedures.

Incidentally the same machine can now reverse a prior vasectomy—for those who are fortunate enough to have such a need! This is an expensive way to do this procedure, but it is safe, reliable technology at its best. Additional uses will unfold in the future.

Dr. Magee's comments about implicitly trusting our doctors as the best source of information are also questionable. I agree that a patient's trust in his doctor is essential, but it should not be absolute and must be earned. I have come to this conclusion because I trusted my first urologist, Dr. Jones, more than I should have. I give him kudos for accurately diagnosing me with prostate cancer. But in retrospect I gave him too much credit when I let him convince me that standard surgery or radiation would be my best two options. In addition, had I not trusted him so completely, I might have avoided the testosterone deprivation medication he prescribed, leading to chemical castration followed by extended sexual dysfunction for nearly a year. Had I questioned his judgment then, I would have enjoyed intimate relations with my wife much sooner.

My experience and that of others should encourage prostate cancer patients to get a second or even a third opinion. It's very important to corroborate any treatment that will be used to alter your body. Read the opinions of others and ask questions of your own urologist to make sure you get the best course of treatment possible. Once you make an informed decision about the best medical care available, then you are indeed best off trusting your physician while putting your faith in God!

I would not want to end this segment without reinforcing some of Dr. Magee's more persuasive, positive comments. For instance he urges patients to "learn with caution," "keep your medical information current," "think twice about tests," and "ask questions about treatments." Exercising caution before you decide if robotics or other modalities are right for you makes a lot of sense. If you reflect before taking a medical leap, you will make a more informed decision. You may in fact find out that the latest technology might not be best for you. This is true especially if your prostate cancer has metastasized or if surgery is counter-indicated due to heart disease. Ultimately patient self-care is your privilege and responsibility. Your doctor should guide you to make an informed decision without your becoming overwhelmed. However no one can, or should, try to make up your mind. You, not your doctor, have the final say in what's right or wrong for you. After all it's your life.

Should You Reject Surgery, No Matter What?

To help their patients select an appropriate treatment option, most urologists map out a range of choices their patients could make. Then it's up to the patient to figure out which option is best for him. However, it's a truism that if you ask a urologist enough times what treatment option he recommends most, he will eventually underscore the advantages of his own specialty, be it surgery, radiation, or some other approach. This is to be expected since (a) his professional experiences back up his point of view, and (b) his family's "bread and butter," that is, his income, depends on persuading you he's right!

If you want to conquer your prostate cancer, you need to consider all your options. Don't listen unless the doctor bases his conclusions on a complete assessment of your condition and on a full awareness of all the treatment methods.

To conquer your prostate cancer, consider all your options.

For instance sometimes watchful waiting may be the best approach, especially if a person is older than 75. One study, based on examining 13,537 men, points out that there is always a danger of over-treatment, especially if it can be determined that a man's slow-growing tumor could never cause a health problem or result in death. According to research scientists, watchful waiting, a.k.a. active surveillance, may be the wisest course of action from a clinical and public health perspective.[8]

This may be particularly true of men in their eighties through nineties, given their more limited life expectancy. However, one could take issue with the arbitrary cut-off age of seventy-five, given that many individuals may live another twenty to thirty years. If my prostate cancer had been discovered not at age 62 but 72, I'm not convinced I would have wanted to embark on the path of active surveillance. Being told that it's likely my prostate cancer will not get more aggressive for the next ten or fifteen years might not do. After all, as I've noted, as of June 2008, my mother is still alive at 94, and my father's mother lived until 96.

But it's vital to recall that no surgery should be taken lightly, given the attendant risks. It may be that active surveillance in special cases is less damaging than more active procedures. This is particularly true if an older man is diagnosed with a very early prostate cancer accompanied by a low PSA score. As long as a patient is properly monitored at regular intervals, every three months, with PSA readings and biopsies, active surveillance might make sense.[9]

Questioning whether a patient should do anything more than active surveillance is one thing. Denouncing a treatment option as totally off-limits is another. Yet that's precisely how all prostate surgery has been billed in various circles. While I'm an educator, not a physician, such a conclusion rankles me.

Take for example a column on nutrition and eating by health advocate Amanda Ross. In an e-mail called "Health e-Tips," she wrote an article to her subscribers with the following subject line: "When your doctor says 'SURGERY', turn to the one who says 'Never!'"[10]

Ms. Ross' objections to surgery are based on her assumption that ninety percent of certain surgeries are totally unnecessary. She not only lambastes surgery but also prescribed drugs, with rare exceptions. Evidently this is because she favors more natural alternatives.

For corroboration she draws on the work of "Country Doctor," Alan Inglis, M.D., who proclaims in the headline of an article that "Up to 90% of certain surgeries performed in the U.S. are completely unnecessary." He denounces most surgeries, including prostatectomies, but touts the benefits of cod liver oil, turkey stuffing and onions! It appears, then, that Ms. Ross' anti-surgery stance may be because of her interest in giving people home-based, alternative medical information, apparently in conjunction with Dr. Inglis, rather than promoting mainstream procedures or prescribed drugs.

On one hand Dr. Inglis rightly suggests that everyone who considers surgery should be sure they know the attendant risks. This is an important observation, which has been picked up by the popular press for all kinds of surgery. On the other hand, as paraphrased by Ms. Ross, Dr. Inglis feels radical prostatectomy should not be a routine patient choice given its adverse treatment outcomes, not to mention because "1 percent of patients" can die after this surgery, as compared to "only 3 percent", who die of prostate cancer even when they don't go under the knife.[11] Ironically, as revealed elsewhere in his writings, one surgery he advocates under certain circumstances, as do other caring doctors, is bariatric surgery for obese patients, if they can't lose weight any other way. In such cases, he has indicated that surgery is indicated in order to avoid diabetic or cardiac incidents.

Ms. Ross is not the only person to take the anti-surgery stance. A physician, Dr. Bradley Hennenfent, M.D., co-founder of the Prostatitis Foundation in Smithshire, Illinois, wrote a book called *Surviving Prostate Cancer without Surgery*, which he published in January 2005. Dr. Hennenfent gets right to the point when he states that, "I believe most prostate cancer surgery has been a sham." He even cites a dramatic incident in 1994, when a patient who had been rendered incontinent and impotent by his prostate surgery, shot his urologist in the groin, so his doctor could experience a similar outcome. While the doctor survived, his functions were reportedly impaired.

Dr. Hennenfent goes on to state that surgeons make their living through surgery and patients need to be aware of this as they become better informed about the alternatives.

To bolster his case, Dr. Hennenfent cites two longitudinal studies in Scandinavia, comparing the outcomes of watchful waiting and surgery. The studies concluded that watchful waiting and other treatment modes were as effective as surgery or more effective.[12] This was in contrast to surgery that left men weakened, often incontinent, sexually dysfunctional, depressed and emasculated—in other words, physically and emotionally traumatized. Given all this, Dr. Hennenfent wonders how it is that thousands of prostate operations go on every year. He would rather have patients avoid surgical side effects by utilizing less invasive treatments.

Dr. Hennenfent concludes that radical prostatectomy "is a sacrifice, not a cure." To this he adds that "controlled scientific evidence shows that radical prostatectomy is a failure." His views are endorsed by Dr. Gary Onik, whose comments are featured on the back cover of Dr. Hennenfent's book. Dr. Onik found his colleague's comments so persuasive that he wrote, "I expect that within five years we will see the death of radical prostatectomy as a treatment for prostate cancer." Dr. Onik is the Director of Surgical Imaging at the Celebration Health Hospital in Celebration, Florida. He is no fly-by-night observer of the surgical scene.

While not denying Dr. Hennenfent's observations that prostate surgery can potentially wreak havoc in a man's life, I am living proof that the opposite can occur: When I had an enlarged prostate and prostatitis before my surgery, I was extremely uncomfortable and frequently in pain. Now, after the diagnosis of cancer and my decision to have a robotic prostatectomy, I feel great! Although I still have a degree of erectile dysfunction, nerve sparing during surgery has allowed me to have a resurgence of sexual intimacy with my wife, which is mutually satisfying, even though our disabilities have led to reduced frequency. On top of that, my initial post-op incontinence was accompanied only by mild discomfort and stress and became a thing of the past in less than three weeks. So I ask you, can surgery be all that bad?

To repudiate surgery as an acceptable and often preferred method for curing prostate cancer is problematic, to say the least. No less an authority than Dr. Patrick Walsh of Johns Hopkins Hospital in Maryland has pointed out that surgery is the gold standard, since the prostate is totally removed with whatever cancerous cells were present.[13]

Even though surgery is often the best approach for many patients, some proponents of radiation treatment regard surgery as generally less effective or too invasive and risky to consider. Those who prefer radiation are correct in concluding radiation patients tend not to experience pain in the prostate area because of treatment. However after treatment radiation therapy can result in a painful burning sensation of the urethra or rectum.

Radiation can also result in impotence for at least half of men treated, unless a more advanced mapped-out radiation is planned. In that regard many radiation patients may have as poor an outcome as some surgical patients, if not worse. On the other hand surgical patients may experience both positive and adverse results. These are not just my views but those of prominent leading Johns Hopkins researchers like Drs. Walsh, DeWeese and Eisenberger, according to a recent article in the *New England Journal of Medicine.*[14]

My contributing author, Dr. Carey, feels strongly that urologists who limit their practice to one or two treatment modalities do a disservice to their patients. Yet it's a fact that some practices are supported by a particular industry which underwrites a given doctor's practice. In such situations, or when a urologist with limited training is able to offer only one or two tools of the trade, patients are sometimes wrongly persuaded to pick a treatment that might not be best for them.

While still deciding what to do, every patient should be told the pros and cons of various treatments, depending on that patient's personal history. Since there are relatively few, small randomized studies, it's impossible to conclude that one approach is invariably superior—or inferior—to others for all patients. To sum up, all treatments should be presented in an equally balanced fashion in the spirit of a multi-disciplinary cancer center.[15]

Robotics and Other Prostate Procedures—What's Next?

This book's emphasis on robotic surgery was inspired by the virtually painless and stress-free robotic surgical procedure I experienced in April 2007. That option was suitable for me for many reasons, including that I had localized, not metastatic prostate cancer. Had that not been the case, I would have probably needed to go through chemotherapy.

Looking back, I really have no reason to bemoan my cancer. Instead I can only thank God that it had not spread to my pelvic area or beyond.

Throughout this book I've openly expressed a bias for robotic surgery since I feel it really saved my life. However I've consistently asserted that it is not the only way to deal with localized prostate cancer, since various treatment options are currently available.

What about the future? Four or eight or twelve years from now I'm convinced that new, even less invasive approaches using robotic technology will be employed, due to advances in nano-technology. In time pre-programmed robotic humanoids may well go beyond their current capacity to perform more complex tasks. Perhaps robots might even be "taught" how to work independently at a doctor's voice command in local operating theaters or across the globe by remote control.

Other approaches will also be developed to ease the plight of prostate cancer patients and their families. Recent advances in prostate cancer research imply we might eventually eradicate all forms of prostate cancer with drugs and vaccines, given recent progress in chemotherapy and drug protocols now under review.[16]

Current research indicates that approaches for prostate cancer prevention are not as far off as we may think. Scientists may be able to use vaccines to ward off cancer as early as five years from now. The work of the Cancer Prevention Center headed by another anti-establishment visionary, Dr. Samuel Epstein, may have a hand in this by helping people limit or eliminate toxic causes of this disease. So too will recent research findings at the Kimmel Cancer Center in Philadelphia, where experiments with mice in February

2008 have discovered that a key to metastatic progression of prostate cancer may be found in a protein called Stat3.[17]

Until prostate cancer is prevented, one promising approach for a cure that would eradicate the disease is proton therapy. According to one report, "About 65 percent of all prostate cancer patients can be treated with high-dose proton therapy, which spares the rectum and bladder and leaves both urological and sexual functions intact." This occurs because proton rays, while fifteen percent more powerful than X-rays, do not harm surrounding

American Cancer Society's "Relay for Life," April 18, 2008. Celebrating survival exactly one year (and 6 days) after robotic surgery to eliminate prostate cancer.
Photo credit: Herb Paynter

tissue and they stop after hitting the cancerous sections of the organ they are aimed at. The result is that after-effects, so far, appear to be far less than other types of radiation treatment.[18]

Another promising method, now under investigation, makes use of lasers. According to that report a new drug called "Tookad" (Hebrew for "kindled" or "warmth of light"), has been developed jointly by some Israeli scientists and a Dutch company. In limited trials, patients who had recurring prostate cancer, long after radiotherapy, volunteered to have plant chlorophyll and then tiny fiber-optic cables injected into their system through needles. These illuminated and then eliminated the diseased prostate as heat was administered in increasingly higher doses without affecting the surrounding organs.[19]

This approach can be repeated several times to eliminate the cancer while preserving bladder control and sexual functioning. Evidently it's much less invasive than current surgical and radiation treatments and can be applied to outpatients. As a result scientists look forward with great anticipation to further testing results. New advances in the future will be tracked at *www.ConquerProstateCancer.com*.

Could it be that robotic surgery and alternative treatments will be replaced by laser treatment or even preventative vaccinations? Perhaps eventually. In the meantime all current options remain viable under certain circumstances. If we've learned anything from history, it's that as long as a disease is widespread, there will be a proliferation of approaches to find the best remedies.

Somewhere, somehow a magic bullet remains "out there," which we have yet to discover. The field of medical research to eliminate all forms of cancer, making it possible for more ill people to survive and thrive, is rife with activity. Whether the total conquest of prostate cancer or any other form of cancer will take place in our lifetime remains to be seen.

The Last Word:
What Counts Most

"Remember the three R's: Respect for self,
Respect for others, and Responsibility for all your actions."
—Anonymous

It seemed like deja vu all over again. On May 7, 2008, right after reviewing some of my editor's book manuscript revisions, I drove with my wife, Yvonne, to Sarasota Memorial Hospital for laparoscopic surgery. Nearly thirteen months had passed since my previous laparoscopic operation, when my prostate was robotically removed. This time I was hospitalized as an outpatient, slated to stay overnight following a hernia repair on my stomach.

Apart from the fact that both surgeries were laparoscopic, there was a direct connection between them. Evidently the hernia had developed over the largest entry point made during the previous operation. It was centered precisely where the robot's 3-D camera had first been inserted and later pulled out a year earlier, and it was also where my prostate had been extracted. Evidently the hernia developed because my stomach muscles got weaker after the radical prostatectomy. This was not unusual, at least not according to a Baylor University medical school report.[1]

Two weeks before scheduling this new operation, I recall asking my hernia surgeon if there was anything I should know in advance. His terse response was, "Yes! After the surgery, your stomach will hurt like hell for a solid week!" Regrettably he kept his promise. But at that point I already knew that this operation would not be substantially harder than the last one, even if it might be more painful afterwards.

By now I had developed a whole arsenal of meditation and relaxation techniques which you've read about in the preceding chapters, and I was prepared to apply them as I did before, to reduce my pain and stress. Another technique I had developed since my original surgery was to ask my doctor hard questions, such as, "How much will it hurt? Why? And what can I do about the pain?" You too would do well to question your medical caregivers until you feel you have a handle on what they are about to do for you and to you. By directly confronting your doctor with these issues you can also be more prepared for what lies ahead. And if they don't have all the answers, you can look them up for yourself as I did, or ask others who've already gone through your type of ordeal.

My last minute decision to consent to the hernia operation left me little time to prepare myself physically, emotionally and spiritually. I began by meditating for a few days before I went under the knife. Just as I had done a year earlier, I visualized embracing the surgery, confident that once the problem was removed, it would no longer trouble me. In my mind I vividly imagined myself entering the operating room, not with anxiety but with a heightened expectation that the surgical team would do their part. I knew this would help me overcome all my fears once the day of surgery arrived. In fact this approach allowed me to see my surgeon, not as some opponent who, in my subconscious mind, was about to "knife" me, but as my ally who would help me get rid of physical limitations that were more than skin-deep. I then foresaw leaving the hospital relatively pain-free a day after lying on the operating table. And when "crunch time" came, that is exactly what happened 23 hours later.

At first the stomach hernia surgery really knocked me out. After the ninety minute operation ended it took a few hours before I fully woke up from the heavy anesthesia. Finally I had the strength to stand up and slowly hobble around my room with my rolling catheter bag pole in hand. Later that night, when I was flat on my back in my hospital bed, the nurse dropped by unannounced and hurriedly said, "It's coming out!" I didn't know what she meant until she directed me to take in a short breath and then breathe out hard. Puzzled, I did as she asked, and immediately comprehended, when she unceremoniously lifted my "Johnnie" and gave my catheter cord a mercifully brief yank.

I was content to be continent again. But by the time I spoke up to ask how she knew I'd be okay without the catheter bag, she had already left the room.

Efficient?: Absolutely! Communicative?: Hardly! I could only guess that I had passed some unknown test demonstrating I could "hold it in" again. I was confused but relieved, knowing that from here on I was permitted to wander about free of the catheter pole to which I had been tethered. Still, that night I slept fitfully because, as in most hospitals, the nurse and her assistant made their nightly rounds, repeatedly checking patients' vital signs. It's almost as if they purposely woke us up to see how well we were sleeping.

When the surgeon showed up the next afternoon to see me, my capable and much more personable day nurse proudly told him I was good to go. In fact I had slowly paced the hospital corridor for hours to regain my strength and get back into the swing of things. What the nurse didn't tell the doctor was that I also had developed a habit of walking with both my hands on either side of my swollen stomach to keep it from shaking. I looked like a pregnant woman holding on to her midsection with her baby kicking inside. Every step hurt, but I was determined to keep on moving.

Like Dr. Carey a year before, my hernia surgeon was at first hesitant to release me from the hospital, and he offered to have me stay another night; but I said "No thanks!" I realized that leaving the day after the serious operation I went through was hardly in keeping with the usual four- to five-day hospital stay after an abdominal hernia repair, at least according the Baylor University report I mentioned earlier.[2] It was even less than the two to three night stay my surgeon told me was typical for his patients. But I was ready to go home and nothing could stop me.

I knew then that I was really onto something which others could apply with equal success. The only problem was that for awhile I continued to experience pain and stress with every step I took, in contrast to events after the prostatectomy. As a result I stayed on Percocet and Ibuprofen for four solid days. That's when I did it again: I stopped all my meds and went back to my desk at home, spending hours daily reviewing my book, as I prepared it for publication. I worked as intensely on the book manuscript at the end of the long writing process as I had a year earlier when I first started a week after my robotic surgery.

Given all my mind-body preparations, I was mildly upset about the minor aches I experienced during the next three additional weeks. My doctor had told me I'd feel a lot of pain because the stomach, unlike the pelvic area, is filled with nerve endings. And he had added, "Your stomach constantly moves as you breathe in and out and is bound to hurt whenever you have to turn around."

Remarkably, after the first seven days at home my stomach stopped hurting even when I walked. It only pained me to get in and out of bed. Once I became still, the pain completely dissipated. It also helped that I managed to breathe fairly shallow breaths and suppress any coughing. You might say that the fear of sheer agony motivated me. In the final analysis my capacity to stay calm for the sake of self-preservation again illustrated the power of mind over matter.

Two weeks after the operation, most of the post-surgical stomach swelling was gone. I felt fairly normal again, except for some limited aching here and there. I felt really good that I was able to defy the hernia surgeon's warning that it might take up to three months before I would feel okay.

I'm convinced that healing quickly is not just something you're born with. It's an art and skill that's self-taught. Nor is there a linear learning curve that assures you that doing well in one surgery means you'll get through the next with flying colors. That depends on how you feel before each surgery, and whether you try to apply lessons learned from past events to new conditions. In short, whether ill or healthy, you're always evolving in your efforts to master your life. On top of that you have to rely on your doctor's experience and skill, as well as his humanity, to get you through.

A few years ago I made a pastoral visit to a congregant in the hospital. He had always exhibited a rather gruff exterior, but was a decent man. While we were talking, he mentioned that he needed urological care and was about to get fitted with a catheter without sedation. After pausing for a moment, he told me that he did not care if his doctor had good bedside manners, as long as he was technically proficient. I respectfully disagreed, saying, "If I can't have a urologist who is both technically proficient and has good bedside manners, get me another doc!"

I have always felt that a doctor's genuine concern is as needed as is his skill, if a patient is to conquer a disease like prostate cancer and recover quickly. That Dr. Carey was both skilled and caring certainly helped in my case. And while my hernia surgeon lacked what I would consider an all-essential bedside manner, he too was proficient and relatively upbeat and caring.

The science and art of medicine, when linked with an innate humanitarianism, is one of the most powerful combinations imaginable. How odd then that the human race has been dubbed *"Homo Sapiens,"* a Latin phrase meaning "people [men] endowed with intelligence." In my view there are other dominant characteristics we share besides intelligence.

Some have described the human race differently, such as sociologist and kinesiologist, Professor Elliot Avedon. During my doctoral program studies with him at Columbia University Teachers College in the early 1970's, I recall his use of the phrase, *"Homo Ludens,"* Latin words that describes humans as "playful creatures."

I would contend that we might also dub ourselves as *"Homo Credo"* and *"Homo Caritas"*—humans imbued with life-affirming beliefs coupled with love and empathy. In the context of this book, we need to care for individuals who face cancer and other illnesses. At the same time we and they have to believe they can "make it" with our help and by virtue of their own determination. In part a patient's resolve can be buttressed by his faith and his ability to apply pain- and stress-reduction techniques like biofeedback, affirmations, and calming visualization. Fusing self-care with humanitarian concern and advanced technology can benefit us and those whose health is at risk.

Above all we need to strive for what Tony Robbins calls "CANI" (pronounced "Can I"),—the process of "Constant And Never-ending Improvement."[3] In medical settings this applies to caregivers and patients alike, as they seek better ways to enhance patients' lives. It also applies to researchers who seek better methods for treating and curing prostate and other cancers. Only the quest for self-improvement, that is, for honing one's personal and professional skills, will help us conquer prostate cancer. This belief is at the core of this book and its corresponding online site *www.ConquerProstateCancer.com*.

Nobody wants cancer, nor would we wish it on others. Still, this dread disease can have a silver lining. A person's battle with cancer can become a learning experience. It can motivate better self-care while enhancing a closer connection to healthcare providers or to those who also have cancer. In the past year or so I've increasingly grown to view things this way, as Yvonne reflected a year after my prostate cancer surgery:

> *Our family's experience with cancer and robotic surgery had such an emotional, physical and spiritual impact on all of us, but mostly on my husband, the patient and now the Cancer Survivor. Still, it's with trepidation that each coming year, we will require twice-annual PSA testing to*

check for prostate cancer cells which might have escaped undetected into other parts of his body.

At the same time we have become more attuned to other prominent illnesses, such as breast, lung, or colon cancer. Now that we live in Florida, my husband is particularly aware of the need to avoid melanoma and other skin cancers.

Ed's concern about skin cancer was largely due to his caring for a forty-year-old congregant with melanoma and his family for two years before the man died, when we still lived in the Boston area. In addition Ed's concern about melanoma was due to his lack of "locks" on his head, since he's mostly bald! But he's right on top of that—no pun intended!

—Yvonne

An elderly and wise member of my former congregation was a chaplain's assistant in World War Two. In time he evolved into an astute businessman, a philanthropist and a community leader, who gained a lifetime of wisdom in the course of his eighty-five years. He often reminded me that we are not just human beings, we are human "becomings."

In the struggle to cope more effectively with prostate cancer, let's hope we don't take two steps backward for every step forward, individually or collectively. Instead let's do whatever we can to make steady progress by remaining informed, so we can safeguard everyone's well-being including our own. Only then will we all be able to live, laugh and love without end.

Each of us must evolve to the point where our self-understanding and our shared, mutual concern will enhance the human condition and benefit ourselves and others. When that happens, we human "becomings" will have truly arrived.

Rabbi Ed Weinsberg, Ed.D., D.D.
July 2008

LIVE life passionately
LAUGH until your belly hurts
LOVE unconditionally
—Anonymous

GRAND FINALE:

CONQUER PROSTATE CANCER

Bonuses and Updates
for Our Readers

As a prostate cancer survivor, rabbi and gerontologist I've presented my views in this book on ways to conquer prostate cancer and related pain or stress. I've done so by accentuating the importance of robotics and other treatment options, relaxation techniques, faith, supportive friendships, and bonding through sexual intimacy. These and related issues are also addressed at our new blog and website, *www.ConquerProstateCancerNow.com* and *www. ConquerProstateCancer.com.* I invite you to check these out after reading this book and later again, both for free bonuses and to view material that supplements and updates what you've read here.

You can also check out the helpful information and products we offer, many of them at no charge. This includes a link to videos of others who benefitted from Intuitive Surgical's da Vinci prostate cancer robotic surgery, or to access da Vinci robotic surgery medical centers around the world. There's another link for viewing a video that shows an actual robotic surgery, for those with a strong constitution! Our website will help you find other prostate cancer blogs and websites. We also offer tips on detecting and treating prostate cancer through various treatment options, coping with treatment side effects, and a list of questions to ask your doctor.

If you visit us at the new blog or website, please share your thoughts about this book, and tell us your personal story as a prostate cancer patient or survivor. We hope you'll also share your stories or concerns about others with prostate cancer (patients or survivors), or describe the experiences of wives and other family members.

I will also answer your personal questions related from a patient's point of view. For more technical questions, I will defer to the website's doctors-in-residence, Dr. Carey and Dr. Kauder, the urologists whose depth of experience and wealth of insights added so much to this book. Please note that, like this volume, both the blog and website aim to provide educational information and resources. While you're welcomed to ask whatever relevant questions you have on your mind, we advise you to consult your own doctor before you make any medical decisions.

Like me a number of prostate cancer patients and survivors would like to "give back" by actively helping new prostate cancer patients and their families. This kind of personalized patient education can't be beat for the satisfaction it will give you. Our blog and website will provide you with some training "tools" you can use as you reach out to others, the way I've reached out to you through this book. See *www.ConquerProstateCancerNow.com* or *www.ConquerProstateCancer.com* for details.

Others would like to contribute directly to prostate cancer support and education organizations like those that benefit from the sale of this book. Toward that end, you can make donations to these organizations by following the links on our site, or you might encourage your acquaintances to buy a copy of this book.

We invite you to make your suggestions for specific topics or areas of discussion you think our blog or website should address. You're welcomed to visit us at any time, day or night. We'll be there for you 24/7.

End Notes

Introduction: What You Can Do When the Going Gets Tough

1a. The National Cancer Institute's "Cancer Stat Fact Sheet" states that 91% of new prostate cancer cases are localized or at a regional stage—spread to the lymphnodes (*www.seer.cancer.gov/statfacts*). I also spoke with Milton Eisner, a demographer at the National Cancer Institute, Cancer Statistics Branch, Surveillance Research Program, who works with SEER surveys (Surveillance, Epidemiology, and End Results). He sent me a data sheet indicating that 80.6% (N=78,265) of the prostate cancer population at the time of diagnosis, had localized cancer; and 10.5% (N=10,186) on diagnosis were found to have metastases spread to the pelvic area adjacent to the prostate. This was based on SEER data collected between 1985 and 1986. This is my reason for stating that three-fourths or more of newly diagnosed American patients were found to have localized prostate cancer. See also SEER Stat Vers 6.4.4.

1b. *The Charlie Rose Show,* PBS, March 31, 2008. Available from the National Prostate Cancer Foundation.

2. Dr. David Kauder, personal communication March 2008.

3. Prostate Cancer Foundation letter, April 2008.

4. "What Are the Key Statistics about Prostate Cancer?" *Cancer.org,* American Cancer Society (June 2007): Cancer Reference Information *http://www.cancer.org/docroot/CRI/content/CRI_2_4_1X_What_are_the_key_statistics_for_prostate_cancer_36.asp*

5. Dr. David Kauder, personal communication, March 2008.

6. Dr. Robert A Batler, "Robotic Radical Prostatectomy; The New Gold Standard?" *Dr. Batler's Blog* (Sept. 29, 2007) *http://drbatlersblog.blogspot.com/2007/09/laparscopic-robotic-radical.html.*

7. "Researchers Develop Successful Test Vaccine that Prevents Development of Prostate Cancer," *PR-USA.net,* March 3, 2008. Originally reported in *Cancer Research,* February 1, 2008.

8. Nick Miller, "New Treatment Hope in Prostate Cancer Fight," (April 16, 2008). Article on two new drug treatments for prostate cancer. *www.theage.com.au/news/national/new-treatment-hope-in-prostate-cancer-fight/2008/04/15/1208025189634.html.*

9. "Prostate Cancer Related Statistics," Prostate Cancer Foundation of Australia (2007): *www.prostate.org.au/prostate-cancer-related-statistics.php*

10. "Treatment for Localized Prostate Cancer," Uro Today (May 11, 2008): *http://www.urotoday.com/browse_categories/treatment_for_localized/1025/*

11. *Uro Today*

12. Jeri Maier, "Questions about Boomers and Related Issues" (Oct. 2007), *Boomers International http://www.boomersint.com/quesans.htm.* The U.S. census of 2000 projected a total of 178 million men of all ages in the U.S.A. by the year 2030. One third of that number would be 58 million men over the age of 65, so there are some discrepancies in these projections. In 2000 the total US population was approximately 286 million, including 148 million men. *http://www.census.gov/population/projections/SummaryTabA2.pdf.*

13. Apart from references noted previously, statistics cited in the first two parts of the Introduction are based on reports from the following sources: the International Agency for Research on Cancer, Cancer Mondial website, *www-dep.iarc.fr,* 2002; the *ACS Facts for 2008;* the "Prostate Cancer Coalition Fact Sheet, 2007"; the U.S. Census Bureau, 2000; *Cancer Research UK:* "CancerStats Key Facts on Prostate Cancer," reported online at *http://www.info.cancerresearchuk.org/cancerstats/types/prostate/;* the *Surveillance Epidemiology and End Results (SEER) Project,* 2003 statistics, based on age, as confirmed though e-mail correspondence with Dr. Milt Eisner, Health Statistician, Cancer Statistics Branch, National Cancer Institute, Bethesda, Maryland at *eisnem@mail.nih.gov; www.hifu-planet.com/2_English/4_Patient-s-stories/208_Roland-Muntz_-Chair-of-the-Association-ANAMACAP.html.* See also "The Baby Boom Grows Old," extracted from "Sick to death and Not Going to Take It Any More," *www.mywhatever.com/cifwriter/library/sicktodeath/sick104.html.* The author points out that in 2000, 12 percent of the population—35

million, were 65+ years old; by 2030 (when Baby Boomers will be ages 65–85), 22 percent of Americans—80 million, will be 65+.

14. Gerald Secor Couzens, "Detection Comes Earlier, and So Do Tough Questions," *New York Times* April 8, 2008.

15. Secor Couzens.

16. Patrick Walsh and Janet Farrar Worthington, *Dr. Patrick Walsh's Guide to Surviving Prostate Cancer*, New York: Warner Books, 2001 and 2007: 34.

17. This understanding of cancer and its treatment, including non-traditional alternative approaches, is based on the thoughts of Dr. Laurence Magne, "Curing Cancer Today," Issue 14, *www.cancer-free-for-life.com*.

18. *http://www.davincisurgery.com/about_prostate.aspx*.

19. Jeremy Maddock, *http://www.immunewellness.com* and *www.immune wellness.com/selenium.htm*.

20. *Prostate Cancer Information Blog, http://www.cancer-data.com/blog/178/ prevent-prostate-cancer-with-diet/*. Also "Top 5 Antioxidant Foods." *www. naturalhealthblog.savvy-cafe.com/top-5-antioxidant-foods-2008-04-05*.

21. Prostate Cancer Information (July 2007), *http://www.cancer-data.com/blog/ 246/how-to-lower-risk-of-advanced-prostate-cancer*.

22. Alex Fir and Isobel Nut. 14470. *http://ww.cancer-data.com/blog*.

23. *www.preventcancer.com*

24. *NCI Cancer Bulletin*, vol. 4/no. 3 (Jan. 16, 2007), *http://www.cancer.gov/ cancertopics/prostate/weightgain0307*

25. First reported in the Oct. 31, 2007 online edition of *Genome Research*. Also: Reinberg, Steven, "Gene Variant Doubles Risk of Prostate Cancer in Black Men" Nov. 2, 2007: *HealthDay Reporter. http://www.washington post.com/wp-dyn/content/article/2007/11/02/AR2007110201717.html*

26. National Cancer Institute (Dec. 12, 2007). *http://www.cancer.gov/ cancertopics/pdq/genetics/prostate/HealthProfessional/page2*.

27. National Cancer Institute (Dec. 12, 2007). *http://www.cancer.gov/ cancertopics/pdq/genetics/prostate/HealthProfessional/page2*. Based on a statistical assessment in 2003.

28. Dr. David Lee, Chief of the Division of Urology at Penn Presbyterian Medical, cited in *Science Daily*.

29. *The Charlie Rose Show*, PBS, March 31, 2008.

30. Dr. David Kauder, personal communication March 2008.

31. Based on personal communication with Dr. Robert Carey, January 2008, and on material from Intuitive Surgical, manufacturer of the da Vinci surgical robot.

Chapter 1: How to Confront the "Big C" Calmly

1. Dr. David Kauder, personal communication: less than 30 percent of cancers actually show up as an abnormality on the ultrasound. The bulk of them are invisible. The biopsies explore the common areas of the prostate where cancer is found. That is why it is considered random. Both Dr. Kauder and Dr. Carey told me that Dr. Jones' decision to use an ultrasound two weeks before my biopsy was not in keeping with the standard of care. An ultrasound is to be administered immediately before a biopsy.

2. Kim Y, et al., "Quality of Life of Couples Dealing with Cancer: Dyadic and Individual Adjustment among Breast and Prostate Cancer Survivors and Their Spousal Caregivers," *Annals of Behavioral Medicine* 35(2) (2008). Cited in "Treating Wife's Stress May Be Indirect Care for Men with Prostate Cancer" by Taunya English, *www.SeniorJournal.com* (March 24, 2008).

3. "Prostate Cancer Diagnosis," *Everyday Health*, Harvard Health Publication series. *http://www.everydayhealth.com/publicsite/index.aspx?puid=855F5078-E74F-489C-A1BC-F04933DA6B77&ContentID=210802&ContentTypeID=57&contentPage=3&searchTerm=.* Dr. Donald Gleason was a pathologist who in 1966 worked out a way to grade the severity of prostate cancer based on the appearance of the cancer cells under a microscope.

4. Peter Scardino and Judith Kelman, *Dr. Peter Scardino's Prostate Book: The Complete Guide to Overcoming Prostate Cancer, Prostatitis, and BPH*, 2006. Also Strum, Stephen and Donna Pogliano, *A Primer on Prostate Cancer: The Empowered Patient's Guide*, 2005. Also Lange, Paul, *Prostate Cancer for Dummies*, 2003.

5. "2007 Prostate Cancer Symposium Highlights," *Coping with Cancer Magazine* (May/June 2007): 45.

6. *http://neurosurgery.mgh.harvard.edu/ProtonBeam/ProtonRadiosurgery Brochure.pdf. http://neurosurgery.mgh.harvard.edu/ProtonBeam. http://neurosurgery.mgh.harvard.edu/ProtonBeam/http://neurosurgery.mgh.harvard.edu/ProtonBeam/*

7. Dr. David Kauder, personal communication. Details about HIFU in Canada, including patient success stories, and comments about United States protocol testing as of April 2008, can be found at *www.hifu.com.*

Chapter 2: Cancer of Not, Where Sex Really Starts

1. Lupron depot is a gonadotropin releasing hormone analog which is an agonist. It would decrease the amount of testosterone, the male hormone produced by a man's testes or gonads. *www.lupron.com.*
2. *Sarasota Herald-Tribune,* (April 22, 2007). Details about the Massachusetts *Male Aging Study on Impotence,* cited in the next paragraph, can be found on-line at *http://www.junkscience.com/jun99/feldman.htm*
3. The full title of Jed Diamond's book is *The Irritable Male Syndrome: Understanding and Managing the Four Key Causes of Depression and Aggression,* published by Rodale, Inc., Pennsylvania, September 2004. Two of his earlier books were *Male Menopause* and *Surviving Male Menopause: A Guide for Women and Men,* published respectively in 1998 and 2000 by Sourcebooks, Naperville, Illinois.
4. The association of hormone therapy and heart disease for patients on hormone therapy for a long time, like five years, is underscored by radiation oncologist, Dr. Henry Tsai, M.D. of Harvard University in "2007 Prostate Cancer Symposium Highlights" in *Coping with Cancer Magazine* (May/ June 2007): 45.
5. "Hot Flashes in Men—Mayo Clinic Researchers Describe a Treatment," Science Daily (October 19, 2004). *http://www.sciencedaily.com/releas es/2004/10/041019085808.htm.* Also "Prostate Cancer Treatment Cuts Hot Flashes," *www.Moldova.org* (June 4, 2007); Article based on a report presented at the 2007 annual meeting of the American Society of Clinical Oncology. *http://it.moldova.org/stiri/eng/51012.*
6. Dr. Robert Carey, personal phone conversation, June 25, 2007.
7. Ruth Westheimer, *Dr. Ruth's Sex After 50: Revving Up the Romance, Passion and Excitement,* 128–129.
8. *www.drlauraberman.com* (April 26, 2007).
9. Ralph and Barbara Alterowitz, *Intimacy with Impotence: The Couple's Guide to Better Sex after Prostate Disease,* originally published in 1999 as *The Lovin' Ain't Over.*

10. Irwin Kula, "Sacred Sex", *Simple Wisdom Series,* Jewish Television Network, 2003, *www.simple-wisdom.com.*

Chapter 3: When Burning Your Bridges Makes Sense

1. One of the early references to Suetonius' report is found in *The Ancient World, Vol. V* by Victory Duruy, noted at *www.EyeWitnesstoHistory.com.*
2. Conversation with Nora DeStefano, Development Specialist, Intuitive Surgical.
3. "Robotic Surgeon Makes the Cut on Challenging Prostatectomies," *The New America—Investor's Business Daily,* May 3, 2007: A5. For hysterectomy and other robotic applications like mitral heart valve surgery repairs see *www.davincisurgery.com/procedures.*
4. Paul Lange, *Prostate Cancer for Dummies,* Wiley Publishing Co., 2003: 317–321.
5. Lange: 131.
6. *www.intutivesurgical.com.*
7. Theodor Reik, *Listening with the Third Ear: The Inner Experience of a Psychoanalyst,* New York, Farar, Strauss and Giraux, 1948 and 1975.

Chapter 4: How to Diminish your Pain and Retain Less Stress

1. Some of the suggestions can be found on internet sites like *Mental Health America (www.mentalhealthamerica.net/go/information/get-info/ stress/coping-with-stress-checklist)*; Harvard University's *Healthy Living Center* columns at *Everyday Day Health (www.everydayhealth.com/print view.aspx)*; "Healthy Aging" (*www.healthyaging@everydayhealth.com*); "Healing Cancer Naturally *(www.healingcancernaturally.com/laughter-is-medicine.html)*; and "Learning Strategies" (*www.LearningStrategies. com/Qigong/Study1.html*).

   A few notions I cover in this chapter can also be found in books like Dr. Herbert Benson's most recent Harvard publication, *Stress Management: Techniques for Preventing and Easing Stress—A Special Health Report* (2007); Richard Patt and Susan Land, *The Complete Guide to Relieving Cancer Pain and Suffering* (1994); John Sarno's *Healing Back Pain: The Mind-Body Connection* (1991); and Martha Davis, et al, *The Relaxation and Stress Workbook* (2000, 4th edition). See also

Dr. Amit Sood, "Mayo Clinic's Top 10 Complementary Therapies," *BottomLineSecrets@BottomLineSecrets.com,* May 11, 2008. Among non-conventional approaches Dr. Sood recommends are guided imagery, hypnosis, meditation and spiritual practices like prayer.

2. A few of these suggestions and many others can be found in the "Top 10 Real-Life Ways to Take Charge of Your Stress," published online by the *Healthy Living Center* at *www.everydayhealth.com.*

3. Harold H. Benjamin, Ph.D., offers other "stress-busters," including additional humorous anecdotes at *www.healingcancernaturally.com/laughter-is-medicine.html.*

4. Reinhold Niebuhr, *The Essential Reinhold Niebuhr: Selected Essays and Addresses,* Yale University Press, 1987.

5. "Great Quotes On Line," *Bartleby.com,* Quote 1472.

6. *www.healthyaging@everydayhealth.com.*

7. Rob Stein and Shankar Vedantam, "Patients Take Many Paths in life with Cancer," *Washington Post,* cited in *Sarasota Herald-Tribune,* March 30, 2007: 2A.

8. Other approaches, including progressive relaxation techniques, can be found at *Healthyaging@everydayhealth.com.*

9. *www.LearningStrategies.com/Qigong/Study1.html.*

10. *www.mentalhealthamerica.net/go/information/get-info/stress/coping-with-stress-checklist.*

11. The Healthy Living Center, *www.everydayhealth.com.*

Chapter 5: What Self-Help Guru, Tony Robbins, Taught Me About the Mind-Body Connection

1. Anthony Robbins, *Awaken the Giant Within: How to Take Immediate Control of Your Mental, Emotional, Physical and Financial Destiny!* Simon and Schuster, 1992, and *Unlimited Power: The New Science of Personal Achievement,* Simon and Schuster, 1997.

2. For an article offering other ways to reduce dental stress, see "Overcoming Dental Anxiety" at *www.Healthyaging@everydayhealth.com.* Many of that article's suggestions are similar to my thoughts regarding prostate cancer patients' stress reduction.

Chapter 6: How to Visualize and Relax Before Surgery

1. A.D. Domar, J.M. Noe, and H. Benson, "The Pre-operative Use of the Relaxation Response with Ambulatory Surgery Patients," *Human Stress, 13(3)* (Fall 1987): 1010–7. Also see J. Loesderman, E.M. Stuart, M.E. Mamish, and H. Benson, "The Efficacy of the Relaxation Response in Preparing for Cardiac Surgery," *Behavioral Medicine 15(3)* (Fall 1989): 111–7.

2. Peggy Huddleston, *Prepare for Surgery, Heal Faster: A Guide of Mind-Body Techniques*, Angel River Press, 2nd Edition 2006. Readers can order the book and Relaxation CD at *www.HealFaster.com* or call (800) 726-4173. Both the book and CD will be mailed the same day you order them.

3. This includes Brigham and Women's Hospital (a Harvard Medical School teaching hospital), the New England Baptist Hospital in Boston, New York University Medical Center in New York City, and Kaiser Permanente Sara Clara Medical Center in Santa Clara, California.

4. Huddleston, 250–261.

5. Huddleston, 32.

6. Huddleston, 228.

Chapter 7: Going Under the Knife Doesn't Have to Be Scary— Robotic-Assisted Surgery Revealed

1. "Close-up View of Robotic Surgery for Prostate Cancer." Video posted by Thomas Jefferson University Hospital. Jan. 2006. *www.leechvideo. com/video/view1880380.html.*

Chapter 8: Home, Sweet Home—Recovering from Post-Surgical Stress

1. Dr. Kegel, a California gynecologist, originally developed the Kegel method in 1948 to help women reduce incontinence after childbirth through pelvic contractions. Later on women and men were directed to exercise their pelvic muscles to stem incontinence whenever necessary. Dr. Kegel felt that biofeedback was an important element to maximize the effectiveness of this exercise. Kegel exercises also can help strengthen a sexual response during intercourse. See "Do the Kegel —the Pelvic Squeeze" at *http://www.dothekegel.com/arnie/index.html;* see also "All

About Kegels: What Your Doctor Isn't Telling You," at *http://www. kegelmaster2000.com/kegels.htm.*

Chapter 9: Sex Again, When You're Up For It, Part I

1. Marc B. Garnick, M.D., "A Patient's Story: Why One Man Chose Robotic-Assisted Laparoscopic Prostatectomy," in *Perspectives on Prostate Disease,* Vol. 1, No. 1, Harvard Health Publications, Cambridge, MA, Jan. 2007.

2. Dr. Ruth Westheimer, *Sex After 50: Revving Up Your Romance, Passion and Excitement!* Sanger, CA, Quill Driver Books/ Word Dancer Press, Inc., 2005.

3. Other books by prostate cancer survivors dealing explicitly with sexual experiences were mentioned earlier as I commented on my sex therapy sessions. Another helpful text is *Coping with Erectile Dysfunction: How to Regain Confidence and Enjoy Great Sex,* by Michael Metz and Barry McCarthy (2004). A book that will provide further perspective is *Fast Facts: Erectile Dysfunction* by Culley Carson, et al., (2007).

   The American Cancer Society also offers important sexual guidance for prostate cancer patients who have problems. This is a comprehensive, yet concise overview called "Detailed Guide: Prostate Cancer—Surgery," available at *www.cancer.org/docroot/CRI/content/CRI_2_4_4X_Surgery_ 36.asp?sitearea=.* That document includes a section called "Sexuality and Cancer: For the Man Who Has Cancer and His Partner." Among the main points are that impotence can last up to two years and that as many as seventy percent of patients can experience impotence, defined as "You cannot get an erection sufficient for sexual penetration." Specific recommendations include exploring ways with your urologist or therapist to enhance sexual responses. Other effective guidelines include helpful hints about positions for enhancing sexual intercourse. Also see "Ways of Dealing with Sexual Problems," at *http://www.cancer.org/ docroot/MIT/content/MIT_7_2X_Ways_of_Dealing_With_Sexual_ Problems.asp?sitearea=MIT.*

Chapter 10: Sex Again, When You Can Get It Up, Part II

1. Paul H. Lange, "Resolving Erectile Problems," *Prostate Cancer for Dummies,* 241–246.

2. Dr. David Kauder, personal communication, March 2007. See, webcast transcript in an interview conducted by Dr. David Marks, "Penile Pump

Implants: A Long-Term Solution?" available at *www.californiaoncology. healthology.com/urologic-health/video3071.htm*. The Mentor Corporation's initial prostate implant production is referred to online at *www.answers. com/Mentor+Corp.?cat=biz-fin*, in their company report, p.6.

3. Lange.

4. *www.passionprescription.com*, Jan 1, 2008.

5. Bob Berkowitz and Susan Yager-Berkowitz, *He's Just Not Up for It Anymore: Why Men Stop Having Sex, and What You Can Do about It*, HarperCollins Publishers, 2008, 13.

6. *www.timm.com*.

7. For a listing of several vacuum erection devices, see the appendix of Ralph and Barbara Alterowitz' book *Intimacy with Impotence*, page 150.

8. Elliott Dorff, personal communication, April 2008. Dr. Dorff reviews traditional Jewish rationales for avoiding masturbation in "Preventing Pregnancy," Chapter 5 of his book, *Matters of Life and Death: A Jewish Approach to Modern Medical Ethics*, pages 116–120.

9. Dr. Paul Lange points out that the male body has a mechanism for orgasm independent of achieving an erection. *Prostate Cancer for Dummies*, Chapter 19, "Resolving Erectile Problems," 234.

10. I've written a longer narrative of this encounter in my "Love Journal," which appears at my website, *www.ConquerProstateCancer.com*.

11. This view is shared by Virginia and Keith Laken in *Making Love Again*, page 165, and by Michele Weiner-Davis, *The Sex-Starved Wife: What to Do When He's Lost Desire*, Simon and Schuster, 2008.

12. Rabbi Irwin Kula, "Sacred Sex," *Simple Wisdom Series*, Jewish Television Network, 2003. *www.simple-wisdom.com*.

13. Michele Weiner Davis, *The Sex Starved Wife: What to Do When He's Lost Desire*, Simon and Schuster, 2008.

14. *New England Journal of Medicine*, August 23, 2007. This study was part of the National Social Life, Health and Aging Project (NSHAP).

Chapter 11: Where Medicine and Faith Meet

1. David Kraemer, "Why Your Son (or Daughter), the Doctor, Really is God," *Conservative Judaism, Vol. 59, No. 1* (Fall 2006): 72–79. This outlook is concretized on page x of Dr. Jacob Teitelbaum's Acknowledgments, in his

2006 book, *Pain Free 1–2–3: A Proven Program for Eliminating Chronic Pain Now,* where he states, "I would like to thank God … for using me lovingly as an instrument for healing." Similarly some Protestant traditions indicate God works through us. See Rev. Dutch Sheets, "The Necessity of Prayer," in *Intercessory Prayer: How God Can Use Your Prayers to Move Heaven and Earth,* Regal Books (1996): 21–34.

2. Dale A. Mathews, *The Faith Factor,* Penguin Press, 1998: 19–20.

3. Reported in *The American Heart Journal* (April 4, 2006), cited in the *Harvard University Gazette* (April 7, 2006) *www.hno.harvard.edu/ gazette/2006/04.06/05-prayer.html;* and in Gregory Lamb, "Study Highlights Difficulty of Isolating Effect of Prayer on Patients," *Christian Science Monitor* (April 3, 2006). This last article noted that nearly half of Americans in 2004 recited prayers for their own health, and about one-quarter of Americans recited prayers for the healing of others. See "Allow Prayer and Meditation to Comfort You," in *Living with Cancer One Day at a Time,* Life Lights, Jewish Lights Publishing (A division of Long Hill Partners), Woodstock, VT (2000): 5.

4. Emotional and Mental Health Center, "Strategies for De-stressing," *Every-day Health* (Undated). *www.everydayhealth.com/publicsite/index. aspx?puid=896ea383-5547-4e9b-b33b-5485f6757489.*

5. Dutch Sheets, *Intercessory Prayer: How God Can Use Your Prayers to Move Heaven and Earth,* Ventura, CA, Regal Books, A Division of Gospel Light, 1996: 28–29. A website dedicated to intercessory prayer can be found at *www.prayerworksbecause.com/useful.php.*

6. Joseph Telushkin, *Words that Hurt; Words that Heal: How to Choose Words Wisely and Well,* NY, William Morrow and Company, 1996.

7. Peggy Huddleston, *Prepare for Surgery, Heal Faster: a Guide of Mind-Body Techniques,* Cambridge MA: Angel River Press (2006): 135–197.

Chapter 12: Why Family and Friends Make All the Difference

1. Harvard Health Publications Special Health Report, "Stress Control: Techniques for Preventing and Easing Stress: 2002." Cited in *www.everyday health.com,* Oct. 14, 2007.

2. *AARP Bulletin,* October 2007: 26.

3. Interdependence is described in Martin Buber's book *I and Thou*. This book is about the I-Thou relationship in which people treat each other as subjects to be respected, not as objects to be mistreated or ignored.

4. Loral Langemeier, *The Millionaire Maker's Guide to Creating a Cash Machine for Life,* New York: McGraw Hill, 2007.

5. *www.chickensoup.com/cs.asp?cid=about.*

6. Robert D. Putnam, *Bowling Alone: The Collapse and Revival of American Community,* Simon and Schuster, 2000; and Robert D. Putnam and Lewis Feldstein, *Better Together: The Book,* Simon and Schuster, 2003.

7. *http:/www.everydayhealth.com/cs/forums/default.aspx?GroupID=24.* Also American Cancer Survivor's Network, *http://www.acscsn.org/ Forum/Discussion/summary.html.*

8. Dr. Sheldon Cohen's work was reported by University of Chicago researchers in the August issue of *Current Directions in Psychological Science* and was also summarized in *AARP Bulletin* Oct. 2007: 16. The work of Schimmel and Fox can be found on "Cancer Talk: Voices of Hope and Endurance from The Group Room, the World's Largest Cancer Support Group," *www.vitaloptions.org/resources cancertalk.htm.*

9. The rabbinic Hebrew concept of *"bikkur holim"*—"visiting the ill," with its intrinsic guidelines, depends on this form of friendly visitation and care of those who would otherwise be neglected.

Chapter 13: Support Groups Near and Far

1. Comments broadcast before Marc Victor Hansen's MegaSpeakerEmpire Conference Preview Presentation, Oct. 14, 2007, presented online at *www.megaspeakingempire.com/preview_schedule/askthanks.php.*

2. *www.vitaloptions.org/resources_cancertalk.htm.*

3. Selma Schimmel and Barry Fox, *Cancer Talk: Voices of Hope and Endurance from the Group Room, the World's Largest Cancer Support Group,* Broadway Books, a division of Random House, 1999. For computer access to all Cancer Talk archived radio programs see *www. vitaloptions.org.*

4. *www.wellness-swfl.org.*

Chapter 14: How Do the Neighbors Cope with Pain and Stress? Profiles in Prostate Cancer, Part I

1. Cited from Feb. 13, 2007 report linked at *www.UsTOO.org*.

2. Dr. Edward Hallowell, M.D., *Worry: Controlling It and Using It Wisely*, New York, Random House, 1997: 164–165.

3. These precise statistics were derived from a study of 72 surgeons who operated on 7,765 men between 1987–2003, and may no longer apply, given advances in surgical techniques and training. See "The Surgical Learning Curve for Prostate Cancer Control After Radical Prostatectomy," *Journal of the National Cancer Institute Vol. 99, No. 15* (Aug. 1, 2007): 1171–1177, cited in "Experience Counts for Prostate Surgery," *American Cancer Society News Center On-Line*, August 3, 2007, *http://www.cancer. org/docroot/NWS/content/NWS_1_1x_Experience_Counts_for_Prostate_ Surgery_Success.asp*.

Chapter 15: How Do Clergymen Cope with Pain and Stress? Profiles in Prostate Cancer, Part II

Chapter 16: Real Men Make Up Their Own Minds: Profiles in Prostate Cancer, Parts III and IV

1. The first two definitions that follow were provided by the National Cancer Institute. The third definition is mine, based on available literature at the Prostate Cancer Foundation website.

2. Paul H. Lange, M.D., *Prostate Cancer for Dummies*, Wiley Publishing Co., 2003: 179–180.

3. Winston Barzell, "Focal Cryoablation: Patient Selection and Case Study," Monograph Reprint, International Society of Cryosurgery, *Prostate and Renal Cryoablation Case Study Review Briefing Series*, Number 1, Publication 1004, 2006. Cited with permission of the author.

4. Ron Israeli, M.D., and John Rewcastle, PhD, "HIFU for PCa: Technical Considerations and Clinical Outcomes," *Contemporary Urology, Vol. 19, No. 9* (Oct. 2007): 26–36.

5. *www.HIFU.com*.

6. HIFU Administration, *A Patient's Guide to Prostate Cancer and Sonablate HIFU*, Toronto: *High Intensity Focused Ultrasound Patient Information*, 2006: 8. The report appears to be based in part on outdated journal

articles. At any rate the data cited is contradicted elsewhere by various specialists, including open surgery specialist and medical researcher, Dr. Patrick Walsh.

Chapter 17: Robotic-Assisted Surgery—The Debate Goes On between Critics and Proponents

1. Diane Robertson, co-author, "Minimally Invasive Prostate Removal Aided by a Robot Has Possible Benefits, High Cost," *Medical Procedure News,* Aug. 29, 2005, *www.news-medical.net/?id=12745.*

2. Mayo Clinic Staff, "Surgery: Radical Prostatectomy" (May 14, 2008), *http:///www.mayoclinic.com/health/prostatecomy/PC00016.*

3 Cleveland Clinic Glickman Urological and Kidney Institute, chaired by Dr. Inderbir Gill. *http://my.clevelandclinic.org/urology/default.aspx?WT. mc_id=1327.*

4. Urologists at the Cleveland Clinic claimed that 85% of their robotic patients return to potency. Dr. Walsh, on The Charlie Rose Show (March 2008), claimed that open surgery can produce a 98% potency rate in otherwise healthy men 60 and under.

5. Mary Carmichael, "The Changing Science of Pain", *Newsweek,* June 4, 2007: 40–47.

6. "Robots are Getting Smarter and They are Working Together," *Sarasota Herald-Tribune* (Dec. 12, 2007): A8.

7. B. Dale Magee, M.D., "Steps to Being a Smarter Patient," *Living 50+,* Feb. 29, 2007: 14.

8. *Journal of the National Cancer Institute* (2006) 98:1134–1141, reprinted in *www.ivanhoe.com/FirstToKnow.*

9. For a view favoring active surveillance and delayed treatment, see Laurence Klotz, "Low-Risk Prostate Cancer Can and Should Often be Managed with Active Surveillance and Selective Delayed Intervention," Nature Clinical Practice Urology Vol. 5, No.1 (Jan. 2008): 2–3. Also see *www.nature.com/clinicalpractice/uro.* These are very special cases with low PSAs and low Gleason scores with few positive cores and a low percentage of the core that may have been positive showing cancer.

10. Amanda Ross, *Nutrition and Healing* (July 27, 2007). Received as an e-mailed newsletter from *healthtips@heathiernews.com*. Original report at *http://www.testcompany.com/archive/July2007-29/0176.html*. Also see Dr. Ranit Mishori, "Do You Need This Surgery, *Parade Magazine* (May 25, 2008): 4–5.

11. Amanda Ross, *Nutrition and Healing.*

12. Survey findings noted in the *New England Journal of Medicine,* Sept. 2002.

13. Patrick Walsh and Janet Farrar Worthington, *Guide to Surviving Prostate Cancer,* Warner Books (2001): 289.

14. Patrick C. Walsh, Theodore L DeWeese, and Mario A. Eisenberger, *New England Journal of Medicine 2007,* 357: 2696–2705.

15. Patrick C. Walsh, Theodore L DeWeese, and Mario A. Eisenberger, *New England Journal of Medicine 2007,* 357: 2696–2705.

16. See Paul Zatz' summary of proceedings of the National Conference on Prostate Cancer in September 2007. Paul is president of Man to Man in Sarasota, Florida, and his account appears in that organization's December 2007 meeting notice.

17. Samuel Epstein, "Information from the 'Safe Shopper's' Bible," *Hidden Toxins in the Home Blog,* July 20, 2007, *http://ecosense123.blogspot.com/2007/07/information-from-safe-shoppers-bible-by.html*. See also "Blocking Prostate Cancer," an eLab article at *Scientist Live,* June 4, 2008, *www.scientistlive.com/lab?/Biotechnology/2008/06/02/20504/Blocking_prostate_cance/ist* Live.

18. This is noted in the July 2007 issue of *Oncolog,* online magazine published by M.D. Anderson Medical Center in Texas, which updates physicians on the latest progress in medical research. See *http://www2.mdanderson.org/depts/oncolog/articles/pf/07/7-8-julaug/7-8-07-1–pf.html*.

19. As reported in Britain's *Sunday Times,* this experimental approach is currently undergoing trials at University College London (UCL) and in Canada, in conjunction with an Israeli company. The British news report was reproduced in a newsletter edition (June 13, 2007) of "MaleCare: Men Fighting Cancer Together," *www.malecare.com/prostate-cancer-news_11.htm*.

The Last Word: What Counts Most

1. "Hernia Repair Abdominal", Michael E. DeBakey Department of Surgery Website, Baylor College of Medicine, *http://www.debakeydepartment ofsurgery.org/home/content.cfm?proc_name=hernia+repair+ abdominal&content_id=274.*
2. "Hernia Repair Abdominal."
3. Anthony Robbins, "On Track Resources for Creating an Extraordinary Life," *http://www.tonyrobbinsaudiobooks.com/self_improvement_ resources.html.*

References

I. PRINTED RESOURCES

Books

Alterowitz, Ralph and Barbara. *Intimacy with Impotence: The Couple's Guide to Better Sex after Prostate Disease.* Cambridge, MA: Da Capo Lifelong Books (Perseus Books Group), 2004. Originally published as *The Lovin' Ain't Over.* Cambridge, MA: De Capo Lifelong Books, 1999.

Bard, Robert. Prostate Cancer Demystified. Bloomington, IN: AuthorHouse, 2007.

Benson, Herbert. *Stress Management: Techniques for Preventing and Easing Stress: A Special Health Report.* Cambridge, MA: Harvard Publications, 2007.

Berkowitz, Bob, and Susan Yager-Berkowitz. *He's Just Not Up for It Anymore: Why Men Stop Having Sex, and What You Can Do About It.* New York: Harper Collins Publishers, 2008.

Buber, Martin. *I And Thou.* New York: Simon and Schuster (a Touchstone edition), 1996. (Originally published by Charles Scribers Sons, 1970.)

Butler, Robert, and Myrna Lewis. *The New Love and Sex After 60.* New York: Ballantine Publishing Group (Random House, revised edition),1993. Originally published by Harper and Row, 1976.

Canfield, Jack, et al. *Chicken Soup for the Surviving Soul: 101 Stories about Those Who Have Survived Cancer.* Deerfield Beach, FL: Health Communications, 1996.

Dahm, Nancy. *Mind, Body, and Soul: A Guide to Living with Cancer.* Garden City, New York: Taylor Hill Publishing, 2000.

Davis, Martha, et al. *The Relaxation and Stress Workbook.* Oakland, CA: New Harbinger Publications (4th edition), 2000.

Diamond, Jed. *Male Menopause.* Naperville, IL: Sourcebooks, 1998.

Diamond, Jed. *Surviving Male Menopause: A Guide for Women and Men.* Naperville, IL: Sourcebooks, 2000.

Diamond Jed. *The Irritable Male Syndrome: Understanding and Managing the Four Key Causes of Depression and Aggression.* Emmaus, PA: Rodale, Inc., 2004.

Dinkin, Roxane. *Living with Cancer One Day at a Time.* Woodstock, VT: Jewish Lights Publishing, a division of LongHill Partners, 2000.

Dossey, Larry. *Healing Words: The Power of Prayer and the Practice of Medicine.* New York: HarperCollins (Harper Paperbacks), 1993.

Dorff, Elliott. *Matters of Life and Death: A Jewish Approach to Modern Medical Ethics.* Philadelphia: Jewish Publication Society, 1998.

Ellsworth, Pamela, et al. *100 Questions and Answers About Prostate Cancer.* Sudbury, MA: Jones and Bartlett Publishers, 2003.

Gray, John. *Men are from Mars, Women Are from Venus: The Classic Guide to Understanding the Opposite Sex.* New York: HarperCollins, 1994.

Hallowell, Edward. *Worry: Controlling It and Using It Wisely.* New York: Random House (Pantheon Books), 1997.

Hansen, Mark Victor and Art Linkletter. *How to Make the Rest of Your Life the Best of Your Life.* Nashville, TN: Nelson Books, Thomas Nelson Publishers, 2006.

HIFU Administration. *A Patient's Guide to Prostate Cancer and Sonablate HIFU.* Toronto, Canada: High Intensity Focused Ultrasound Patient Information, 2006.

Howe, Desiree Lyon. *His Prostate and Me.* Houston, TX: Winedale Publishing, 2002.

Huddleston, Peggy. *Prepare for Surgery, Heal Faster: A Guide for Mind-Body Techniques, 2nd edition.* Cambridge, MA: Angel River Press, 2006.

Kabat-Zinnn, Jon. *Full Catastrophe Living: Using the Wisdom of Your Body and Mind to Face Stress, Pain, and Illness.* New York: Bantam Doubleday Dell (Delta Trade Paperback), 1990.

Kirby, Roger, Simon Holmes, and Culley Carson. *Erectile Dysfunction, 2nd edition.* Oxford, England: Health Press, 1998.

Laken, Virginia and Keith. *Making Love Again.* East Sandwich, MA: Ant Hill Press (North Star Publications), 2002.

Lange, Paul. *Prostate Cancer for Dummies.* New York: Wiley Publishing Company, 2003.

Langemeier, Loral. *The Millionaire Maker's Guide to Creating a Cash Machine for Life.* New York: McGraw Hill, 2007.

Marks, Sheldon. *Prostate and Cancer: A Family Guide to Diagnosis, Treatment & Survival.* Tucson, Arizona: Fisher Books, 1995 (revised 1999).

Matthews, Dale. *The Faith Factor: Proof of the Healing Power of Prayer.* New York: Penguin Group (Putnam), 1998.

Metz, Michael, and Barry McCarthy. *Coping with Erectile Dysfunction: How to Regain Confidence and Enjoy Great Sex.* Oakland, CA: New Harbinger Publications, 2004.

Neurnberger, Phil. *Freedom from Stress.* Honesdale, PA: Himalayan International Institute, 1981.

Niebuhr, Reinhold. *The Essential Reinhold Niebuhr: Selected Essays and Addresses.* New Haven, CT: Yale University Press, 1987.

Patt, Richard and Susan Land. *The Complete Guide to Relieving Cancer Pain and Suffering.* New York: Oxford University Press, 2004.

Putnam, Robert and Lewis Feldstein. *Better Together: The Book.* New York: Simon and Schuster, 2003.

Putnam, Robert D. *Bowling Alone: The Collapse and Revival of the American Community.* New York: Simon and Schuster, 2000.

Reik, Theodor. *Listening with the Third Ear: The Inner Experience of a Psychoanalyst.* New York: Farrar, Straus and Giroux, 1948 and 1975 (2nd edition).

Robbins, Anthony. *Awaken the Giant Within: How to Take Immediate Control of Your Mental, Emotional, Physical and Financial Destiny.* New York: Simon and Schuster (a Fireside Book), 1992.

Robbins, Anthony. *Unlimited Power: The New Science of Personal Achievement.* New York: Simon and Schuster (a Fireside Book), 1997.

Rossman, Martin. *Fighting Cancer from Within: How to Use the Power of Your Mind for Healing.* New York: Henry Holt Company (an Owl Book), 2003.

Sarno, John. *John Sarno's Healing Back Pain: The Mind-Body Connection.* New York: Warner Books, 1991.

Sarno, John. *The Mindbody Prescription: Healing the Body, Healing the Pain.* New York: Warner Books, 1998.

Scardino, Peter and Judith Kelman. *Dr. Peter Scardino's Prostate Book: The Complete Guide to Overcoming Prostate Cancer, Prostatitis, and BPH.* New York: Penguin Group, 2006.

Schimmel, Selma and Barry Fox. *Cancer Talk: Voices of Hope and Endurance from The Group Room, the World's Largest Cancer Support Group.* New York: Broadway Books (Random House), 1999. (See also *www.vitaloptions.org/resources/cancertalk.htm*)

Sheets, Dutch. *Intercessory Prayer: How God Can Use Your Prayers to Move Heaven and Earth.* Ventura, CA: Regal Books, A Division of Gospel Light. 1996.

Smith, Howard, and Bruce, Debra. *The Women's Guide to Ending Pain: An 8-Step Program.* Hoboken, NJ: John Wiley & Sons, 2003.

Strum, Stephen and Donna Pogliano. *A Primer on Prostate Cancer: the Empowered Patient's Guide.* Hollywood, FL: The Life Extension Foundation, 2005.

Teitelbaum, Jacob. *Pain Free 1–2–3: A Proven Program for Eliminating Chronic Pain.* New York: McGraw Hill, 2006.

Telushkin, Joseph. *Words that Hurt; Words that Heal: How to Choose Words Wisely and Well.* New York: William Morrow and Company, 1996.

Vine, David. *Living with Cancer: A Practical Guide.* New Brunswick, NJ and London: Rutgers University Press, 2006.

W, Bill. *The A.A. Way of Life—A Reader: Selected Writings from A.A's Co-Founder.* New York: Alcoholics Anonymous World Service, 1967.

Walsh, Patrick and Janet Farrar Worthington. *Dr. Patrick Walsh's Guide to Surviving Prostate Cancer.* New York: Warner Books, 2001 and 2007 (1st and 2nd editions).

Walsh, Patrick, and Janet Farrar Worthington. *The Prostate: A Guide for Men and the Women Who Love Them.* New York: Warner Books, 1995.

Weiner-Davis, Michele. *The Sex-Starved Wife: What to Do When He's Lost Desire.* New York: Simon and Schuster, 2008.

Westheimer, Ruth. *Dr. Ruth's Sex After 50: Revving Up the Romance, Passion & Excitement!* Sanger, CA: Quill Driver Books/Word Dancer Press, 2005.

Wilkinson, Greg. *Understanding Stress.* New York: Family Doctor Publications, Dorchester Publishing, 2006.

Magazine and Journal Articles

Associated Press Release. "Robots are Getting Smarter and They are Working Together." *Sarasota Herald-Tribune* December 12, 2007: A8.

Benson, Herbert, et al. "Study of the Therapeutic Effects of Intercessory Prayer (STEP) in Cardiac Bypass patients A Multi-Center Randomized Trial of Uncertainty and Certainty of Receiving Intercessory Prayer." *The American Heart Journal, Vol. 151, Issue 4* (April 2006): 934–942. Cited in Cromie, William, "Prayers Don't Help Heart Surgery Patients," *Harvard University Gazette* (April 7, 2006). *www.hno.harvard.edu/gazette/2006/04.06/05-prayer.html.*

Carmichael, Mary. "The Changing Science of Pain." *Newsweek* (June 4, 2007): 40–47.

Cohen, Sheldon and other researchers at the University of Chicago. "Current Directions in Psychological Science." August 2007. Summarized in *AARP Bulletin* (Oct. 2007): 16.

Domar, A.D, J.M. Noe, and H. Benson, "The Pre-operative Use of the Relaxation Response with Ambulatory Surgery Patients," *Human Stress, 13(3)* (Fall 1987): 1010–7.

Garnick, Marc. "A Patient's Story: Why One Man Chose Robotic-Assisted Laparoscopic Prostatectomy." *Perspectives on Prostate Disease* Vol. 1. No. 1, Harvard Health Publications, Cambridge, MA, January 1, 2007.

Israeli, Ron, and John Rewcastle, PhD, "HIFU for PCa: Technical Considerations and Clinical Outcomes." *Contemporary Urology, Vol. 19, No. 9* (Oct. 2007): 36.

Kelly, Brad. "Robotic Surgeon Makes the Cut on Challenging Prostatectomies." *The New America—Investor's Business Daily* (May 3, 2007): A5.

Kim, Y, et al. "Quality of Life of Couples Dealing with Cancer: Dyadic and Individual Adjustment among Breast and Prostate Cancer Survivors and Their Spousal Caregivers." *Annals of Behavioral Medicine 35(2)* (2008). Cited in "Treating Wife's Stress May Be Indirect Care for Men with Prostate Cancer" by Taunya English. *www.SeniorJournal.com* (March 24, 2008).

Klotz, Laurence. "Active Surveillance versus Radical Treatment for Favorable-Risk Localized Prostate Cancer." *Oncology, Vol. 7, No. 5* (2006): 355–362.

Klotz, Laurence. "Low-Risk Prostate Cancer Can and Should Often Be Managed with Active Surveillance and Selective Delayed Intervention." *Nature Clinical Practical Uroogy,* Vol. 5, No. 1 (2008): 2–3.

Kraemer, David. "Why Your Son (or Daughter), the Doctor, Really is God." *Conservative Judaism, Vol. 59, No. 1* (Fall 2006): 72–79.

Lamb, Gregory. "Study Highlights Difficulty of Isolating Effect of Prayer on Patients." *Christian Science Monitor* (April 3, 2006).

Litwin, M.S. and D.C. Miller. "The Surgical Learning Curve for Prostate Cancer Control After Radical Prostatectomy." *Journal of the National Cancer Institute Vol. 99: No. 15* (August 1, 2007): 1171–1177. Cited in "Experience Counts for Prostate Surgery," *American Cancer Society News Center On-Line* (August 3, 2007). (*http://www.cancer.org/docroot/NWS/content/NWAS_1_1x_Experience_Counts_for_Prostate_Surgery_Success.asp*)

Loeb, Stacy and William Catalona. "Low-Risk Cancer patients Face Over-treatment." *Journal of the National Cancer Institute,* 2006; 98:1134–1141; also published as "Counterpoint: The Case for Immediate Active Treatment". *The Journal of Natural Comprehensive Cancer Network, 2–7, 5(7): 699–702;* reprinted in *www.ivanhoe.com/FirstToKnow.*

Loesdermanm, J., E.M. Stuart, M.E. Mamish, and H. Benson. "The Efficacy of the Relaxation Response in Preparing for Cardiac Surgery." *Behavioral Medicine 15(3)* (Fall 1989): 111–7.

Magee, B. Dale. "Steps to Being a Smarter Patient." *Living 50+* (Feb. 29, 2007): 14.

Marshall, Lisa. "Hormones Got You Down? It's Not Just a Female Thing." *Sarasota Herald-Tribune* (April 22, 2007).

Mishori, Ranit. "Do You Need This Surgery?" *Parade Magazine* (May 25, 2008): 4–5

Reinberg, Steven. "Gene Variant Doubles Risk of Prostate Cancer in Black Men." *HealthDay Reporter* (Nov. 2, 2007). *http://www.washingtonpost.com/wp-dyn/content/article/2007/11/02/AR2007110201717.html.*

Secor Couzens, Gerald. "Detection Comes Earlier, and So Do Tough Questions." *New York Times* (April 8, 2008).

Stein, Rob, and Shankar Vedantam. "Patients Take Many Paths in life with Cancer." *Washington Post,* cited in *Sarasota Herald-Tribune* (March 30, 2007): 2A.

Tsai, Henry. "2007 Prostate Cancer Symposium Highlights, presentation on hormone therapy." *Cancer Magazine* (May/June 2007): 45.

Walsh, Patrick C., Theodore L DeWeese, and Mario A. Eisenberger. *New England Journal of Medicine 2007; 357:* 2696–2705.

Urology, Vol. 5, No.1, (January 2008): 2–3 See also: *www.nature.com/clinical practice/uro.*

Zatz, Paul. "Untitled summary of proceedings of the National Conference on Prostate Cancer, September 2007." *Man to Man Newsletter* (Dec. 2007).

Journals

AARP Bulletin (October 2007). Article on page 26 of this issue refers to Leslie Bennett's book, *The Feminist Mistake.*

Caring4Cancer. *www.Caring4Cancer.com.* Offers advice on practical and emotional issues for men and women who have various cancers and side effects.

Cure Magazine. www.curetoday.com. Cancer updates, research and education.

Heal: Living Well after Cancer. www.healtoday.com.

New England Journal of Medicine (Sept. 2002 and Aug. 23, 2007). Important articles on prostate cancer.

WebMD Magazine. www.WebMD.com.

II. INTERNET RESOURCES

Website Articles, Pamphlets and Books
Listed by Author or Organization

American Cancer Society. "Detailed Guide: Prostate Cancer—Surgery." *www. cancer.org/docroot/CRI/content/CRI_2_4_4X_Surgery_36.asp?sitearea=*

American Cancer Society. "Sexuality and Cancer: For the Man Who Has Cancer and His Partner" in "Ways of Dealing with Sexual Problems." A concise overview that offers sexual guidance for prostate cancer patients and survivors and their partners. *www.cancer.org/docroot/MIT/ content/MIT_7_2X_Ways_of_Dealing_With_Sexual_Problems. asp?sitearea=MIT.*

American Cancer Society. "What Are the Key Statistics about Prostate Cancer?" June 2007, in Cancer Reference Information. *http://www.cancer.org/docroot/ CRI/content/CRI_2_4_1X_What_are_the_key_statistics_for_prostate_ cancer_36.asp.*

Batler, Robert. "Robotic Radical Prostatectomy; The New Gold Standard?" *Dr. Batler's blog* (September 29, 2007). *http://drbatlersblog.blogspot.com/2007/ 09/laparscopic-robotic-radical.html.*

Benjamin, Harold. "Laughter is the Best Medicine." *Healing Cancer Naturally.* List of suggested "stress busters." *www.healingcancernaturally.com/laughter-is-medicine.html.*

Berman, Laura. Dr. Berman, a noted sex therapist, advises women how to respond when their partners have erectile dysfunction. *www.passion prescription.com.* (Jan 1, 2008)

Cohen, Leah (Editor). *Living with Prostate Cancer Blog: A Wife's Passion. www.prostatecancerblog.net.*

DeAngelis, Barbara. Comments during a MegaSpeakerEmpire Conference Preview Presentation (Oct. 14, 2007). *www.megaspeakingempire.com/preview_schedule/askthanks.php.*

Duruy, Victor. *The Ancient World, Volume V. www.EyeWitnesstoHistory.com.*

Epstein, Samuel. "Information from the 'Safe Shopper's' Bible." *Hidden Toxins in the Home blog* (July 20, 2007). *http://ecosense123.blogspot.com/2007/07/information-from-safe-shoppers-bible-by.htm/.*

The International Agency for Research on Cancer. Cancer Mondial Website (2002). *www-dep.iarc.fr.*

Magne, Laurence. "Curing Cancer Today," Issue 14. *www.cancer-free-for-life.com.*

Marks, David, M.D. "Penile Pump Implants: A Long-Term Solution?" Webcast transcript of an interview available at *www.californiaoncology. healthology.com/urologic-healtah/video3071.htm.*

Mayo Clinic Staff. "Surgery: Radical Prostatectomy." (May 14, 2008). *http://www.mayoclinic.com/health/prostatecomy/PCooo16/.*

Mentor Corporation Report. Reference to prostate implant production is to be found on-line at *www.answers.com/Mentor+Corp.?cat=biz-fin,* p.6.

Miller, Nick. "New Treatment Hope in Prostate Cancer Fight." (April 16, 2008). Article on two new drug treatments for prostate cancer. *www.theage.com. au/news/national/new-treatment-hope-in-prostate-cancer-fight/2008/04/15/1208025189634.html.*

National Cancer Institute. (Dec. 12, 2007). Re: statistical likelihood of prostate cancer according to age cohort. *http://www.cancer.gov/cancertopics/pdq/genetics/prostate/HealthProfessional/page2.*

National Cancer Institute (2008). "Cancer Stat Fact Sheet." *www.seer.cancer. gov/statfacts.*

Perisho, Jerry. Author of *I Barf, Therefore I Am: A Sensitive Comedy Writer's Relationship with Cancer.* A comedy writer diagnosed with prostate cancer tells his story with humor and optimism. *www.JerryPerisho.com.*

"Prostate Cancer Statistics in Australia." *www.prostate.org.au/prostate-cancer-related-statistics.php.*

Robbins, Tony. "On Track Resources for Creating an Extraordinary Life." *www.tonyrobbinsaudiobooks.com/self_improvement_resources.html.*

Robertson, Diane, et al. "Minimally Invasive Prostate Removal Aided by a Robot Has Possible Benefits, High Cost." Medical Procedure News (Aug. 29, 2005). *www.news-medical.net/?id=12745.*

Ross, Amanda. *Nutrition and Healing.* (July 27, 2007).Received as an e-mailed newsletter from *healthtips@heathiernews.com.* Original report at *http://www.testcompany.com/archive/July2007-29/0176.html.*

Website Articles, Pamphlets and Books Listed by Title

"All About Kegels: What Your Doctor Isn't Telling You." *http://www.kegel master2000.com/kegels.htm.*

"The Baby Boom Grows Old." Extracted from *Sick to Death and Not Going to Take It Any More. www.mywhatever.com/cifwriter/library/sicktodeath/sick104.html.*

"Cancer Facts and Figures 2008." American Cancer Society. *www.cancer.org/downloads/STT/2008CAFFfinalsecured.pdf.*

"CancerStats Key Facts on Prostate Cancer." Cancer research in the United Kingdom. *www.info.cancerresearchuk.org/cancerstats/types/prostate/.*

"Coping with Stress Checklist." Mental Health America. *www.nmha.org/go/information/get-info/stress/coping-with-stress-checklist/.*

"Do the Kegel—the Pelvic Squeeze." *www.dothekegel.com/arnie/index.html.*

Emotional and Mental Health Center. "Strategies for De-stressing." *Everyday Health.* (Undated). *www.everydayhealth.com/publicsite/index.aspx?puid=896ea383-5547-4e9b-b33b-5485f6757489.*

"Genetics of Prostate Cancer." National Cancer Institute on-line issue (December 12, 2007). *http://www.cancer.gov/cancertopics/pdq/genetics/prostate/HealthProfessional/page2.*

"Hernia Repair Abdominal." Michael E. DeBakey Department of Surgery Website, Baylor College of Medicine. *http://www.debakeydepartmentofsurgery.org/home/content.cfm?proc_name=hernia+repair+abdominal&content_id=274.*

"Hot Flashes in Men—Mayo Clinic Researchers Describe a Treatment." Science Daily (October 19, 2004). *http://www.sciencedaily.com/releases/2004/10/041019085808.htm*

"Obesity and Weight Gain Linked to Cancer Mortality." NCI (National Cancer Institute) Cancer Bulletin, vol. 4/no. 3 (Jan. 16, 2007). *http://www.cancer.gov/cancertopics/prostate/weightgain0307*

"Overcoming Dental Anxiety." Dental Health Center. Everyday Health. *http://www.everydayhealth.com/publicsite/index.aspx?puid=986fc30f-4b15-4a47-8120-5acb5c85769e.*

"Prostate Cancer Diagnosis." *Everyday Health,* Harvard Health Publication series. *http://www.everydayhealth.com/publicsite/index.aspx?puid=855F5078-E74F-489C-A1BC-F04933DA6B77&ContentID=210802&ContentTypeID=57&contentPage=3&searchTerm="Prostate Cancer Fact Sheet."* (2007). *www.nationalprostatecancerfoundation.org*

"Prostate Cancer Treatment Cuts or Flashes." *Moldova.org.* (June 4, 2007). Article based on a report presented at the 2007 annual meeting of the American Society of Clinical Oncology. *http://it.moldova.org/stiri/eng/51012. http://it.moldova.org/stiri/eng/51012.*

Quote 1472 (origins of the "Serenity Prayer"). *Great Quotes On-Line. www. Bartleby.com.*

"Stress Control: Techniques for Preventing and Easing Stress: 2002." *Harvard Publications Special Health Report.* (Oct. 14, 2007). *www.everydayhealth.com.*

"Top 5 Antioxidant Foods." *www.naturalhealthblog.savvy-cafe.com/top-5-antioxidant-foods-2008-04-05*

"Top 10 Real-Life Ways to Take Charge of Your Stress." *The Healthy Living Center. www.everydayhealth.com.*

"Treatment for Localized Prostate Cancer." *Uro Today.* (May 11, 2008). *http://www.urotoday.com/browse_categories/treatment_for_localized/1025/*

Website Articles and Issues Listed by Topic

"Boomers. Demographic projection for the year 2030, predicted during the U.S. census of 2000." *www.boomersint.com/quesans.htm.*

High Intensity Focused Ultrasound. *Resources on High Intensity Focused Ultrasound.*

www.hifu-planet.com/2_English/4_Patient-s-stories/208_Roland-Muntz_-Chair-of-the-Association-ANAMACAP.html.

Prayer, Intercessory. *www.prayerworksbecause.com/useful.php.*

Surveillance Epidemiology and End Results (SEER) Project 2003 Statistics. National Cancer Institute. *www.cancer.gov.*

III. ADDITIONAL INTERNET RESOURCES

Websites That Provide Prostate Cancer Support and Education

American Cancer Society. Services include nationwide Man-to-Man prostate cancer support group funding and related fiscal and informational resources. *www.AmericanCancerSociety.org.*

. American Cancer Survivor's Network. *http://www.acscsn.org/Forum/ Discussion/summary.html*

Cleveland Clinic Glickman Urological and Kidney Institute, chaired by Dr. Inderbir Gill. *http://my.clevelandclinic.org/urology/default.aspx?WT. mc_id=1327*

Conquer Prostate Cancer website and blog. Updates to this book, by the author and publisher, Health Success Media. *www.ConquerProstateCancer. com,* and *www.ConquerProstateCancerNow.com.*

Intuitive Surgical. Manufacturer of the da Vinci robotic devices. Robotic-assisted prostate cancer treatment and information, including patient profiles. *www.davincisurgery.com/about_prostate.aspx.*

Malecare. International support and education for prostate patients, survivors and their families. *www.malecare.com.*

National Cancer Institute. Research and information center in Bethesda, Maryland, that provides information on all forms of cancer, including prostate cancer. *www.nci.nih.gov.* Also see Cancer Information Service (CIS). *http://cis.nci.nih.gov.* This website is a valuable resource for researchers who wish to contact NCI's Cancer Statistics Branch demographers, including Milton Eisner, cited in this book.

National Prostate Cancer Coalition. *www.FightProstateCancer.org.*

Prostate Cancer Foundation. *www.ProstateCancerFoundation.org.*

Us TOO! International. Support and education for prostate patients, survivors and their families, with 350 chapters around the world. *www.ustoo.org.*

The Wellness Community. Cancer organization, including prostate support groups, with over twenty chapters in the United States and abroad. *www.thewellnesscommunity.org.*

Note: Other websites are posted at *www.ConquerProstateCancernow.com.*

Websites on Cancer or Related Subjects

Cancer Match. Blogs and chat room for cancer patients suffering from various cancers, including prostate cancer. *www.cancermatch.com.*

Cancer Prevention Coalition, directed by Dr. Samuel Epstein in Chicago, Illinois. This organization strives to expose environmental causes of cancer, which may be overlooked by other established governmental and voluntary cancer organizations. *www.preventcancer.com.*

Chicken Soup for the Soul book series and website. How the more than 100 volumes in this series of books evolved, including many stories about cancer. *www.chickensoup.com/cs.asp?cid=about.*

Genome Research. (Oct. 31, 2007). *www.genomeresearch.com.*

Healing Cancer Naturally: Laughter is Medicine. www.healingcancernaturally.com/laughter-is-medicine.html.

Healthy Living Center columns from Harvard University.

"Everyday Day Health." *www.everydayhealth.com/printview.aspx.*

"Hernias and Other Health Issues." Baylor University Debakey Department of Surgery. *www.debakeydepartmentofsurgery.org/home/content.cfm?proc_name=hernia+repair+abdominal&content_id-274.*

"Learning Strategies." *www.LearningStrategies.com/Qigong/Study1.html.*

Lupron. Prostate cancer hormone website. *www.lupron.com.*

Oncolog, M.D. Anderson Medical Center (Texas) On-Line Magazine. Updates physicians on the latest progress in medical research. For example see *http://www2.mdanderson.org/depts/oncolog/articles/pf/07/7-8-julaug/7-8-07-1–pf.html* (July 2007).

Proton Beam Therapy. *http://www.neurosurgery.mgh.harvard.edu/ProtonBeam.*

Support Groups. Support groups for various health disorders and related health issues. *http://www.everydayhealth.com/cs/forums/default.aspx? GroupID http://www.everydayhealth.com/cs/forums/landing.aspx.*

Vacuum Erect Device. *www.timm.com.*

Vitamins, Minerals and Supplements. Informative commercial site.

www.immunewellness.com and *www.immunewellness.com/selenium.htm.*

IV. VIDEOS

The Charlie Rose Show. PBS. March 31, 2008. Available at the Prostate Cancer Foundation website. *www.ProstateCancerFoundatio.org.*

"Sacred Sex." *Simple Wisdom Series with Rabbi Irwin Kula.* Jewish Television Network. 2003. *www.simple-wisdom.com.*

"Close-up View of Robotic Surgery for Prostate Cancer." Video posted by Thomas Jefferson University Hospital. Jan. 2006. *www.leechvideo.com/ video/view1880380.html.*

Index

CONQUER PROSTATE CANCER

A Post-Op Primer

Prostate Prescriptions

A POST-OP PRIMER
What to Expect from Your Robotic Surgery
—by Dr. Robert Carey, M.D., Ph.D.

Your surgeon. Before an operation no surgeon can promise any patient a perfect outcome devoid of all complications. But a surgeon can inform his patients of the likelihood of a very positive medical outcome based on previous records specific to that surgeon. The patient should feel free to ask his doctor how many robotic prostatectomies he or she has performed and what the rates of continence and potency are specific to the surgeon's practice. Patients are also entitled to ask if the surgeon has had fellowship training and how long he trained for robotic surgery. Well qualified surgeons dedicated to performing robotic prostatectomies are generally quite comfortable telling you their specific professional history.

The operation and post-operative phase. Robotic surgery usually takes 1.5 to 2 hours from the induction of anesthesia to the closing of the skin. If your surgery requires additional procedures, either to assure your return to continence or because you are a high-risk case, the operation may last longer than two hours. 95% of patients are discharged home the next day and will have their catheter removed in one week. The catheter may be kept in the bladder longer if bladder neck reconstruction is required or if you have diabetes or other medical conditions that can slow wound healing. You and your surgeon need to develop a high degree of trust and you should sense a high measure of concern for your well-being before you allow the surgeon to operate on you. Following your successful surgery you should also have a strong sense that you can also rely on the surgeon's advice regarding your recuperation, in terms of the activities and methods of self-care before and after you leave the hospital

Activity. You will be up and walking a few hours after surgery. It would be best if you would gradually increase your physical activity by walking daily, so that by day 7 you will be able to walk at least one mile. I discourage heavy lifting and strenuous or dangerous activity for 3 weeks, but walking on a flat surface or a treadmill stimulates recovery and will not hinder the healing process. The use of light arm weights and mild stretching while walking will help you return to your preoperative function level more quickly. In the first three weeks, avoid activity that puts you at risk for unexpected exertion or trauma such as boating alone, climbing a ladder, or doing yard work. The more active you are, the faster you will recover.

Bowel activity. Your first bowel movement should come within 72 hours of the surgery. If bowel activity returns more slowly, use Milk of Magnesia or prune juice to stimulate initial activity. Walking and sitting up, as opposed to lying down, will stimulate a return to bowel activity. Do not give yourself suppositories or enemas. If you have not had a bowel movement within 4 days of surgery, you should inform your surgeon.

Incision care during and after surgery. At the end of your operation, your robotic incision sites will be closed beneath the skin with an absorbable suture and surgical glue will be placed on the surface of the incision. This glue will slowly come off over a period of 2 to 3 weeks. You will not have to remove staples or stitches. As your surgery ends, a small drain will be placed at one incision site. This drain will remove any residual air or fluid that remains in your abdomen after the surgery. With rare exception, this drain will be removed within 12 to 18 hours after surgery. You may shower within 24 hours of having their drain removed. Clean the incision sites with soap and water and lightly pat it dry. Do not scrub the glue off. It will come off on its own.

Diet. Although you can have anything to eat that you are hungry for, I encourage post-operative patients to emphasize drinking fluids first to maintain excellent hydration. You should produce about 2 – 3 liters of urine per day. The principal fluid for consumption should be water, but other drinks such as coffee, tea, sodas, electrolyte drinks, and milk shakes are fine in reasonable amounts. Solid food should be introduced starting on post-operative day 1 in amounts you find comfortable. Should you develop mild nausea, take in less solid food and emphasize more fluid consumption.

Medications. When patients go home they are given a prescription for an antibiotic and a stool softener twice daily, as well as a generic narcotic pain medicine to be taken as needed. Every patient's perception of pain is different, and I want each patient to be comfortable. It is appropriate that you may experience some abdominal discomfort after the surgery, but most patients report that their peri-operative pain is much less than they expected. Some patients find their post-operative pain does not require any medication at all, while others may need to stay on medication for a couple of days or more. If you require medication you can use Tylenol alone or the prescribed narcotic for pain relief. For those who were on a regimen of aspirin, Plavix or Coumadin before the prostate operation, ask your surgeon how soon afterwards you should start taking such medications again.

Risks. The risk of a major visceral injury (bladder, bowel, ureter, vascular, rectum) is less than 1%. If this happens your surgeon will repair it and work with you to make sure you have a good long-term outcome, but your recovery will be slower. The rate of intra-operative transfusion in my hands is zero percent. The chance of a patient needing a peri-operative blood transfusion is less than 1%.

Continence. 95% of patients are continent (using no pads) within 3 months. 67% are completely continent within 1 month. In my experience no patient has ever required an artificial urinary sphincter due to incontinence, nor has anyone required a bladder neck contracture requiring dilation. I encourage men to learn Kegel exercises in the weeks prior to the operation so they will be prepared for the immediate post-operative period. I also provide my patients with personal instructions and direct them to numerous websites dedicated to post-prostatectomy Kegel exercise training.

Sexual and penile rehabilitation. Before your operation discuss your prospects for a nerve sparing procedure with you surgeon. Not everyone is a candidate, particularly those with high grade disease or if we suspect you have an extraprostatic extension of the prostate cancer into the neurovascular bundles. For those who are candidates, your surgeon should describe an *athermal approach to dissection*. Specifically, endovascular staplers and thermal gadgetry such as a harmonic scalpel should not be used at the prostatic pedicles or neurovascular bundles. An athermal technique refers to the surgeon's refraining from cauterization. This is critical to a nerve sparing procedure, to make sure there is no heat-related injury to the nerves during dissection.

The vast majority of men who have bilateral nerve sparing, and who have spouses or partners interested in continuing sexual intercourse, will return to erections sufficient for penetration within one to two years after surgery. Although some may return to spontaneous erections immediately, others may require penile rehabilitation with a vacuum erection device, intracavernosal injection therapy and/or the use of phosphodiesterase V inhibitors (sildenafil, vardenafil, and tadalafil, a.k.a., Viagra, Levitra and Cialis). It's up to each patient, in consultation with his surgeon, to decide which therapy is most comfortable and best for him.

For those who elect penile rehabilitation therapy with alprostadil alone or with Trimix, I recommend a regimen with regular scheduled injections every two or three days. Patients begin with a low dose and advance slowly to avoid the complication of priapism (painful erections that do not go down spontaneously after orgasm). The injections themselves do not cause pain, but overdosage can lead to painful erections, after which patient compliance is understandably compromised. The goal is to achieve blood flow and erections starting within a month of surgery for those who have not resumed spontaneous erectile activity. Alprostadil is the exact natural substance that is released during normal erections. Injection therapy simply gives direct infusion of this natural substance into the penile corpora to generate erections. A return to spontaneous erectile activity is faster and more reliable for patients who tolerate and comply with rehabilitation than those who simply await a return of function.

PSA follow-up after surgery. One of the advantages of surgery is that your entire prostate will be removed. Unlike other forms of prostate cancer treatment that leave residual prostate tissue, the PSA after surgery should be undetectable. I require a PSA test for most patients every three months for the first year and taper the frequency in most cases after that. With an undetectable PSA, there is no need to have computed tomography (CT) scans, positron emission tomography (PET) scans, magnetic resonance imaging exams (MRI), or expensive arrays of laboratory tests. With an undetectable PSA, the chances of any of these tests being positive for prostate cancer are practically zero. Your surgeon will follow you and be responsible for your prostate cancer recovery and any complications or questions that arise.

PROSTATE PRESCRIPTIONS—Part I
—by Dr. Robert Carey, M.D., Ph.D.

Androgen Deprivation

Androgen deprivation, or medical castration therapy, is used for advanced or high risk prostate cancer. This therapy prevents the synthesis of testosterone in the testicles and replaces the surgical removal of the testicles (surgical castration). Medical castration is reversible with time. Androgen deprivation is carried out through injections every three months or through the placement of an implant that will last for one year. Either of these may be administered in your surgeon's office.

The active medicine in the implant or the injection is the same, a leutinizing hormone releasing hormone agonist that acts at the level of the patient's brain to prevent the testicles from producing testosterone. Upon the initial administration there is a flare or rise in the testosterone levels that rapidly reduces to castrate levels within days. The reason your urologist will prescribe Casodex (see below) at the time of your beginning androgen deprivation therapy is to block the testosterone receptors during the transient rise in testosterone. A normal testosterone level in a male is between 250 ng/mL to 900 ng/mL. Castrate levels are between 20 ng/mL to 40 ng/mL.

There are of course side effects to reducing the testosterone levels in a man from normal to castrate. The most common complaint in my practice is that there is a lack of energy immediately and development of hot flashes comparable to what women experience in menopause. There is also loss of libido, loss of erections, shrinkage of testicular size, loss of muscle mass and bone mineral density, and with time an increase in the risk of adverse cardiovascular events. Therefore, although androgen deprivation is an essential component to management of advanced metastatic prostate cancer, its use must be administered judiciously and all risks, benefits, and potential side effects explained to the patient in detail. Historical misuse of androgen deprivation by the previous generation of urologists for low risk, low stage disease has appropriately led to bad popular press. If you have been offered androgen deprivation and the justification for its use in your case or the potential side effects have not been described, a second opinion is warranted. In my practice, I have found that if patients are counseled thoroughly and the side effect profile is described ahead of time, the tolerance to and appreciation for androgen deprivation is greatly enhanced

Non-steroidal anti-androgens

Bicalutamide (Casodex), the most commonly used non-steroidal anti-androgen, blocks the action of androgens by blocking the androgen (testosterone) receptor. Its mechanism of action differs from that of LHRH agonists, which prevent the synthesis of testosterone by the testicles. Casodex may be used as monotherapy or with an LHRH agonist, which is referred to as combined androgen blockade. The use of Casodex will shrink the prostate and it will result in a large reduction of the baseline PSA. Casodex is a true anti-cancer drug in that it increases progression free survival in men with advanced prostate cancer. Its advantage to castration alone is that it blocks the androgen receptors that would otherwise be targets for testosterone produced by the adrenal glands of otherwise castrated men. A common secondary usage is that Casodex may be administered to devascularize and shrink the prostate while the patient is awaiting radiation therapy or suffering hemorrhagic or obstructive complications secondary to radiation.

Most patients tolerate Casodex monotherapy better than combined androgen deprivation, and for that reason monotherapy with Casodex is seeing increased usage for older and sicker patients as first line therapy. Nevertheless, patients should be warned regarding the potential for breast tenderness, decreased energy, libido, and potency, and increased risk of adverse cardiovascular events with chronic use of Casodex even as monotherapy.

Alpha blockers

For men with obstructive symptoms associated with their prostates, alpha blocker therapy has been a mainstay of urologic treatment. As the prostate becomes larger or more obstructive to the bladder outlet, men will sense that their urinary stream is weaker and that they have difficulty starting their stream. In the worst case scenario, men may go into complete urinary retention, unable to void their urine at all and requiring an immediate trip to their urologist or to the emergency room.

Alpha blockers help by relaxing the smooth muscle in the prostatic urethra and bladder outlet, allowing for a more reliable, stronger stream of urine. It is important to understand that alpha blockers do not shrink your prostate, but rather promote better urine flow by relaxation of the smooth muscle tissue. Several alpha blockers, **terazosin** and **doxazosin**, are off patent and can be obtained at very low cost (usually the $4.00 per month plans that are marketed by some pharmacies). These two drugs, however, are non-selective for the prostatic urethral receptors and in some patients can cause a dangerous drop in blood pressure leading to a condition called orthostatic hypotension (dizziness due to rapid blood pressure drop when a man rises to standing position from a sitting position). There are selective alpha blockers available, such as **tamsulosin** (Flomax) and **alfuzosin** (Uroxatral), that are much less likely to have the side effects of orthostatic hypotension. Your urologist can help you determine your individual risk and help you make the decision regarding which medication is best for you. Most prescription medication plans have favorable co-pays for Flomax or Uroxatral, making the difference in cost from the generic medication very small, particularly if the patient is at risk for fall or syncope.

If you elect to have a radical prostatectomy, where your entire prostate is removed, you will not need the use of an alpha blocker after your surgery, even if you were on one before. Your prostate has been removed, and you no longer have an obstruction. On the other hand, if you elect to have radiation therapy, alpha blocker therapy is often an essential part of your initial and long term treatment. The prostate and bladder outlet may swell and become more obstructive after placement of radioactive seeds or initiation of radiation therapy. Chronically, you may have better urinary symptoms with daily use of an alpha blocker. Each case varies and your urologist will help you select the drug that best suits your situation.

5-alpha reductase inhibitors. Finasteride is a selective of inhibitor of Type II 5α-reductase, an intracellular enzyme that converts the androgen testosterone into 5α-dihydrotestosterone (DHT), which contributes to the development and enlargement of the prostate gland. **Dutasteride (Avodart)** is an inhibitor of both Type I and Type II isoforms. *These 5-alpha reductase inhibitors, unlike alpha blockers, do actively shrink the prostate. A 20 to 40% shrinkage can be expected over a three to six month period of continuous usage.* Also, these drugs devascuarlize parts of the prostate, making hemorrhagic complications during radiation or ablation therapy less likely. Although the noted effects are not immediate, improved urinary symptoms can be expected after six months for benign prostatic overgrowth. It is important to note that neither finasteride nor Avodart are approved as anti-cancer drugs alone. They are used as an adjunct to radiation or ablation therapy when there is a need to shrink the prostate prior to treatment, just as these drugs are commonly used in benign prostate disease to shrink the prostate. These drugs also modulate PSA, roughly cutting the true PSA in half with chronic usage. Thus, a PSA of 5 for a patient on a 5-alpha reductase inhibitor is equivalent to a true PSA of roughly 10.

Finasteride has been popularized through its use in the prostate cancer prevention trial (http://www.cancer.gov/pcpt). Although complex and controversial, this trial is cited by the National Cancer Institute to have demonstrated a clear reduction in the incidence of prostate cancer in those men taking finasteride rather than placebo. A similar trial (REDUCE, Reduction with Dutasteride of Prostate Cancer Events) is underway with Avodart. Common side effects which occur in some but not all patients taking 5 alpha reductase inhibitors include decreased sex drive, decreased ejaculate volume, enlarged breasts and tenderness in males, loss of or decrease in erectile function. Also, these drugs should not be taken or handled by children or women who are, or may become pregnant.

PROSTATE PRESCRIPTIONS—Part II

—by Dr. Robert Carey, M.D., Ph.D

This partial, alphabetical listing of many drugs used to treat the prostate also indicates the names of pharmaceutical companies and distributors.

Bisphoshonates for prevention of bone mineral density loss

Zometa – zoledronic acid administered as an intravenous infusion (3.0 – 4.0 mg depending on the patient's renal function). Distributed and marketed by **Novartis Pharma, AG**. http://www.us.zometa.com.

LHRH (GnRH) agonist therapy for medical castration

Eligard – leuprolide acetate available as one- and three-month depo injection. Distributed and marketed by **Sanofi-Aventis**. http://www.eligard.com.

Lupron – leuprolide acetate, one-, three-, and four-month depo injections therapy. Distributed and marketed by **Abbott Laboratories**, Abbott Park, Illinois. http://rx.lupron.com/homepage.

Trelstar – triptorelin pamoate, available as one- and three-month depo injection therapy. Distributed and marketed by **Watson Pharmaceuticals**. http://www.trelstar.com.

Vantas implant - histrelin, available as a one year implant. Distributed and marketed by **Indevus Pharmaceuticals**. http://www.vantasimplant.com.

Viadur implant – leuprolide acetate available as a one year implant. Distributed and marketed by **Bayer Healthcare Pharmaceuticals**. http://www.viadur.com.

Zolodex – goserelin acetate, available as one- and three-month depo injection. Distributed and marketed by **AstraZeneca Pharmaceuticals, LP**. http://www.zoladex.com.

Nonsteroidal anti-androgen therapy

Casodex – bicalutamide. It blocks the body's receptors for androgens (testosterone). Distributed and marketed by **AstraZeneca Pharmaceuticals, LP.** http://www.casodex.com.

Phosphodiesterase V inhibitors for offsetting erectile dysfunction

Cialis – tadalafil. Available in dosages 5 mg daily or 10 mg to 20 mg prior to sexual activity. Distributed and marketed by **Eli Lilly and Company.** http://www.cialis.com.

Levitra – vardenafil. Available in dosages 2.5 mg to 20 mg. The usual recommended starting dose is 10 mg, not to be taken more than once daily. Distributed and marketed by **Bayer Healthcare Pharmaceuticals, GlaxoSmithKline,** and **Schering-Plough.** https://www.levitra.com

Viagra – sildenafil. Available in dosages 25 mg to 100 mg. Distributed and marketed by **Pfizer.** http://www.viagra.com.

Vasodilation therapy for erectile dysfunction

Alprostadil – Prostaglandin E1 is a vasodilator available for direct injection into the corpora of the penis. Many **compounding pharmacies** will mix this in a formulation specific for the patient's needs. Availability is limited to local compounding pharmacies or to those that provide mail order. As a generic, it is much less expensive than the pre-packaged injectables. Since it is premixed (and must be kept refrigerated), one only loads the syringe with the quantity needed. Often this leads to excellent economy as there is no wastage of the drug. In my practice I use **The Family Pharmacy of Sarasota,** 3644 Webber Street, Sarasota, FL 34232, 941-921-6645, Toll Free 888-245-0070. http://www.familypharmacy.org/aboutus.htm.

Caverject – alprostadil formulated for direct injection to the corpora in the penis. Distributed and marketed by **Pfizer.** http://www.caverjectimpulse.com.

MUSE – intraurethral suppository of alprostadil. Distributed and marketed by **Vivus Inc**. http://www.muserx.net.

Trimix or Bimix – mixtures of alprostadil with papaverine and phentolamine to provide optimal erections and minimize side effects. A sample mix might be paparavine 30 mg, phentolamine 2 mg, & alprostadil 20 mcg. This is available only through **compounding pharmacies** as noted above.

Alpha blockers

Flomax – tamsulosin. Usual dosage 0.4 mg daily. Distributed and marketed by **Boehringer Ingleheim** and **Astellas**. http://www.4flomax.com.

Cardura XL – doxazosin extended release tablets. Usual dosage 4 mg daily. Distributed and marketed by **Pfizer**. http://www.carduraxl.com.

Terazosin and **Doxazosin** are generic alpha blockers available at most pharmacies.

Uroxatral – alfuzosin. Usual dosage 10 mg daily. Distributed and marketed by **Sanofi-Aventis**. http://www.uroxatral.com.

CONQUER PROSTATE CANCER

Robotic Machines, Doctors and Patients (Photo Series)

Demonstrating the da Vinci Robotic Device

The Doctor Gets Set for Robotic Surgery

A Patient Returns to His Active Lifestyle
A Week after Robotic Surgery

The Author's Reunion with His Robotics
Surgeon And Medical Team

DEMONSTRATING THE DA VINCI ROBOTIC DEVICE

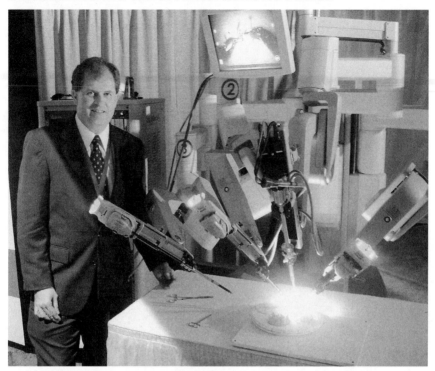

Dr. Carey demonstrates the da Vinci robotic system to other urologists at the World Congress of Endourology in Cleveland, Ohio, 2006. This symposium was held shortly after the introduction of Intuitive Surgical's newest robot, the da Vinci S model featured here. This robot has four arms with effective lengths extended, compared to previous designs with just three robotic arms. The newer da Vinci also features high definition screens and improved instrument coupling devices for the surgeon's assistants as well as improved dissection instruments.

Photo credit: Intuitive Surgical

THE DOCTOR GETS SET FOR ROBOTIC SURGERY

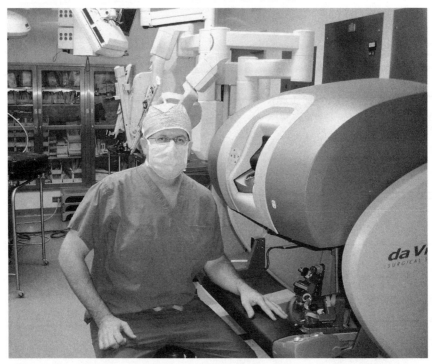

Dr. Carey in his surgical scrubs sits next to the da Vinci console just before a robotic prostatectomy,—the surgical removal of his patient's prostate. The da Vinci console's 3-D high definition monitor, with ten times magnification, gives the doctor the clearest possible "inside view" of his patient. Dr. Carey will control the da Vinci machine's arms from the console after the patient is positioned next to the robotic device (in background), about 10 feet from the console. A robotic operation is major surgery, but most patients are discharged home the next day.

Photo credit: Tariq Hakky

A PATIENT RETURNS TO HIS ACTIVE LIFESTYLE
A WEEK AFTER ROBOTIC SURGERY

It doesn't take long for a man to get back to his daily routine soon after getting home from robotic surgery. A patient is usually discharged from the hospital one day after his surgery and recuperates quickly. This vigorous 77 year old man returned to his gym workout and to teaching speed bag techniques a week after Dr. Carey operated on him.

Pictured: Ernest Oriente, an internationally acclaimed speed bag instructor.

Photo credit: Dr. Donna Carey

THE AUTHOR'S REUNION WITH HIS
ROBOTICS SURGEON AND MEDICAL TEAM

Reunion of the author, prostate cancer survivor Rabbi Ed Weinsberg (back row, right), with contributing author and surgeon, Dr. Robert Carey (front row, right) and his medical team in Sarasota Memorial Hospital's operating room a year and a half after robotic surgery. At the back of the room the da Vinci robotic device hovers over the entire group.

Photo credit: David Dessauer

CONQUER PROSTATE CANCER

The Authors and Medical Advisor

MEDICAL ADVISOR

Dr. David Kauder, M.D.

David Kauder, M.D., of Marblehead, Massachusetts, graduated from the State University of New York Downstate Medical Center in Brooklyn with a Medical Doctor degree in 1971. He is a Board Certified urologist who did his urology training at the University of Minnesota in Minneapolis after two years of general surgery at the University of Vermont.

Dr. Kauder, now semi-retired, was in active clinical practice of urology for 30 years and was the managing partner for one of the largest urology practices in Massachusetts. He is a past president of the Massachusetts Association of Practicing Urologists and a former member of the American Urological Association's Health Policy Council.

Dr. Kauder has served as a volunteer visiting urologist in poverty-stricken countries. He is also a voluntary medical consultant at *www.ConquerProstate Cancer.com.*

CONTRIBUTING AUTHOR

Dr. Robert Carey, M.D., Ph.D.
Photo credit: Dr. Donna Carey

Robert Carey, M.D., Ph.D., of Sarasota, Florida, is a robotic surgeon at the Urology Treatment Center of Sarasota, Florida State University College of Medicine. A consulting editor for the *Journal of Robotic Surgery,* Dr. Carey trains other surgeons nationwide in the use of the da Vinci robotic surgical system. A frequent lecturer on urologic oncology, Dr. Carey received first prize at the World Congress of Endourology in 2006 for his essay describing the direct, real-time temperature monitoring for radiofrequency ablation of renal tumors.

Dr. Carey received his M.D. degree at the Medical College of Georgia. His residency training in surgery and urology, and a fellowship in robotic surgery, laparoscopy, and endourology, were completed at the University of Miami.

He earned his Ph.D. in Chemistry from the Massachusetts Institute of Technology. Previously he received a B.S. in chemistry and B.A. in foreign languages at Wofford College in Spartanburg, South Carolina.

Dr. Carey was awarded a National Institutes of Health Fellowship in the Department of Chemistry at Harvard University. He served as an assistant professor at the Institute of Organic Chemistry at the University of Lausanne, Switzerland, and at the University of Georgia.

Dr. Carey holds multiple patents for the automation of peptide and protein synthesis using robotic systems. Through his pharmaceutical company, Max C Pharm, Dr. Carey has patented a drug delivery system for treatment of urothelial cancer of the kidneys and ureter.

Apart from his full-time surgical practice, Dr. Carey is a voluntary medical consultant at *www.ConquerProstateCancerNow.com.*

AUTHOR

Rabbi Edgar Weinsberg, Ed.D., D.D. ("Rabbi Ed")
Photo credit: Roger Surprenant

Ed Weinsberg of Sarasota, Florida, is an ordained rabbi, gerontologist, prostate cancer survivor and patient healthcare educator. After his successful robotic surgery for prostate cancer at Sarasota Memorial Hospital in April, 2007, he was moved to share his and others' experiences by writing this book.

His views on prostate cancer and related concerns have been featured in the U.S. and abroad on *The Group Room Cancer Talk Show*, a weekly broadcast from Los Angeles, accessible at *www.VitalOptions.org*. His comments on coping with prostate cancer have appeared on prominent newspaper blogs and websites, such as the *Chicago Sun-Times*, the *New York Times*, the *LA Daily News*, the *London Times Online*, *USA Today*, and *U.S. News and World Report*. His comments can also be viewed on sites like *Erectile Dysfunction Connection*, *Living with Prostate Cancer*, and *The "New" Prostate Cancer Info-Link*.

Rabbi Ed is the primary author and voluntary moderator of *Conquer ProstateCancerNow.com,* the companion blog to this book under the aegis of Health Success Media, LLC. Apart from his frequent blog posts, he published "The Patient as Healer—How to Alleviate Your Pain and Stress,"—adapted from this book. This article is posted on the web page of Us TOO International, the world's largest prostate cancer education and support organization, with its main office in Illinois. It is also featured in Us TOO's printed **Hotsheet,** posted in November 2008.

Rabbi Ed earned his Master of Hebrew Literature (M.H.L.) in 1970 and his rabbinic title at New York City's Jewish Theological Seminary in 1972. He earned his Ed.D. degree in gerontology at Columbia University Teachers College in 1974. Earlier he received a B.A. at UCLA, after completing his studies in Hebrew literature as well as German, English, history and psychology.

His career included serving 30 years as the rabbi of three congregations; a year as an adjunct professor at SUNY, Utica; and three years at Beit Berl Teachers College in Kfar Sava, Israel, as a Lecturer in Jewish Studies and Coordinator of Educational Gerontology. He also co-founded Hospice Care of Utica, New York, and throughout his career served as a part-time psychiatric center, nursing home and police chaplain and consultant. Currently he serves on the Executive Board of the Sarasota chapter of Man to Man, which provides educational and supportive services under the aegis of the American Cancer Society.

While serving a Boston congregation for 21 years (1985–2006), Rabbi Ed appeared frequently on public access radio and television. He also published book reviews and newspaper and journal articles, addressing religious and interfaith concerns and topics like volunteerism and Holocaust education.

He was awarded an honorary Doctor of Divinity degree from the Jewish Theological Seminary in 1998. His efforts on behalf of others were acknowledged when he received the Samuel Stahl Award for Community Service, in memory of media personality Lesley Stahl's uncle; and the Leonard Zakim Humanitarian Award for Furthering Interfaith Understanding, in memory of the Boston Anti-Defamation League's dynamic executive director. In 2001 he was listed in *Who's Who in America.* In August 2006 he became Rabbi Emeritus of his former synagogue, Congregation Shirat Hayam of the North Shore (Boston).

Rabbi Ed and his wife Yvonne moved from the Boston area to Sarasota in September 2006 to live near their family.